Mastering MariaDB

Debug, secure, and back up your data for optimum
server performance with MariaDB

Federico Razzoli

BIRMINGHAM - MUMBAI

Mastering MariaDB

First published: September 2014

Production reference: 1170914

Published by Packt Publishing Ltd.
Livery Place
35 Livery Street
Birmingham B3 2PB, UK.

ISBN 978-1-78398-154-0

www.packtpub.com

Cover image by Karl Moore (karl@karlmoore.co.uk)

Credits

Author
Federico Razzoli

Reviewers
Josh King

Daniel Parnell

Giacomo Picchiarelli

Philipp Wollermann

Commissioning Editor
Kunal Parikh

Acquisition Editor
Reshma Raman

Content Development Editor
Akshay Nair

Technical Editor
Mrunmayee Patil

Copy Editors
Sarang Chari

Mradula Hegde

Adithi Shetty

Project Coordinator
Swati Kumari

Proofreaders
Stephen Copestake

Paul Hindle

Joanna McMahon

Indexer
Hemangini Bari

Graphics
Abhinash Sahu

Production Coordinator
Shantanu N. Zagade

Cover Work
Shantanu N. Zagade

About the Author

Federico Razzoli is a software developer, database consultant, and free software supporter. He has been working on websites and database applications since 2000, and has used MySQL extensively throughout this period. He is now an active member of the MariaDB community.

About the Reviewers

Josh King works as the Senior Systems Software Engineer for Kualo Web Hosting and has been using and administering databases for well over a decade. He is also an active developer specializing in system performance and the Linux kernel. He has been a contributor to the numerous Linux and open source projects as well as a member of several organizations, such as the League of Professional System Administrators (LOPSA) and the Free Software Foundation.

He works with cloud and high-availability solutions, as well as Windows and BSD platforms. He is a recipient of the LOPSA Professional Recognition award for excellence and professionalism in Information Technology, and has written papers on numerous subjects dealing with the performance and optimization of the Linux operating system.

He currently resides in Texas with his wife and children.

Daniel Parnell has been messing around with computers since a very early age. He started working with an AIM-65, through a Commodore VIC-20, Commodore 64, Apple IIe, Commodore Amiga, an ICL Concurrent CP/M86 machine, and Apple Mac Plus to various PCs and Macs today.

Of late, Daniel has been working on web applications for the health care industry using Ruby on Rails, and building a rich web application using a JavaScript frontend and an Erlang backend.

When Daniel is not coding or tinkering with electronic gadgets around the house, he is spending time with his family. His son died late last year at the age of 6 of an untreatable neurodegenerative disorder called Battens disease.

Giacomo Picchiarelli is a test and software engineer with 6 years of experience in designing data-driven applications and MySQL administration. He has a strong background in Linux systems and test-driven development.

Philipp Wollermann is a Software Engineer currently working for Google in Germany. His experience with MariaDB comes from having run his own Linux-based web hosting business for over 5 years, and from working for CyberAgent, Inc. in Tokyo, where he helped optimize web applications and database performance.

www.PacktPub.com

Support files, eBooks, discount offers, and more

For support files and downloads related to your book, please visit www.PacktPub.com.

Did you know that Packt offers eBook versions of every book published, with PDF and ePub files available? You can upgrade to the eBook version at www.PacktPub.com and as a print book customer, you are entitled to a discount on the eBook copy. Get in touch with us at service@packtpub.com for more details.

At www.PacktPub.com, you can also read a collection of free technical articles, sign up for a range of free newsletters and receive exclusive discounts and offers on Packt books and eBooks.

http://PacktLib.PacktPub.com

Do you need instant solutions to your IT questions? PacktLib is Packt's online digital book library. Here, you can search, access, and read Packt's entire library of books.

Why subscribe?

- Fully searchable across every book published by Packt
- Copy and paste, print, and bookmark content
- On demand and accessible via a web browser

Free access for Packt account holders

If you have an account with Packt at www.PacktPub.com, you can use this to access PacktLib today and view 9 entirely free books. Simply use your login credentials for immediate access.

Table of Contents

Preface

It is said that the most advanced technologies are invisible to the user. This is certainly true in the case of database management systems. Databases are one of the most important invisible technologies that make things happen. They are everywhere around us and we use them several times a day; though we can't see them. For example, we use them when we make a phone call, or reserve a hotel room, or visit a website, or use some electronic device. Sometimes, these databases are big and complex. And, in many cases, they are managed by MySQL or one of its forks such as MariaDB.

MySQL is mainly known for being one of the four components of the LAMP stack, that is, Linux, Apache, MySQL, and PHP — the most common technologies that make websites work. And that's the reason why many people, who aren't even associated with Information Technology, have heard about MySQL. In fact, MySQL development started in the 80s but the software became famous only with the birth of dynamic websites between 2000 and 2001. It is open source, free, and very simple to learn and administrate. It was exactly what the new websites needed.

Despite its substantial simplicity, MySQL's features have grown fast. It was criticized by PostgreSQL supporters because it did not support many key features of DBMSs, such as transactions and foreign keys. In spite of this being true at that time, MySQL had several unique features, which were extremely useful for a large amount of users. For example, it supported replication 10 years before PostgreSQL! It was also reliable and fast. And as time went by, MySQL became a complete, feature-rich relational DBMS.

Why then did Monty Widenius, the creator of MySQL, leave the project to start a fork called MariaDB? That was because, in 2005, Oracle bought the InnoDB storage engine. In 2008, Sun Microsystems bought MySQL, which in turn was bought by Oracle in 2009. Since that acquisition, MySQL belongs to its biggest competitor: a big corporation whose business is mainly proprietary, high-cost software.

To be fair, we must make it clear that Oracle is investing substantial resources on the MySQL technology, and did a great job in some areas, especially InnoDB. However, some uncertainty remains; is Oracle selecting the new features to avoid the users of their main product switching to MySQL? Will Oracle always invest in MySQL and keep it open source? Only Oracle managers know the answers to these questions.

What we know for sure is that MySQL is now less open than it used to be in the past. The public bug database is not used by Oracle employees and contains obsolete information. No information or test cases are released about security holes. The repositories are updated less often. And some community-oriented sites, such as a public wiki edited by the community, that contain vast information about MySQL do not exist anymore.

On the contrary, the strength of MariaDB is its continuous collaboration with the community. Very important new features such as multisource replication and roles have been initially developed by community members. MariaDB's bug tracking and project management software allows us to know which bugs or new features are being processed, what the new versions will look like, and when they will be released. Some developers actively communicate with users via the mailing lists and IRC channel. And while MySQL documentation has always been proprietary, MariaDB documentation has free licenses and can be improved by the community using a public wiki.

Most importantly, MariaDB Foundation exists. It is similar to other foundations related to free software projects such as the Apache Foundation. Monty Widenius himself is a member of the board of directors. The purpose of the foundation is to safeguard the MariaDB source code, and guarantee that it will always remain free. It also promotes MariaDB and its ecosystem, maintaining the *MariaDB Knowledge Base*. The website of the MariaDB Foundation is `https://mariadb.org/`.

The MariaDB and MySQL teams follow diverging roads. The starting point is the same: the state of MySQL in 2009. However, while the MySQL road is going towards a less open zone, MariaDB is a perfectly open project. The results of this openness are positive from a technical point of view, too. MariaDB developers and MariaDB users are both interested in constantly improving the server, and they collaborate to achieve this goal.

This book provides the knowledge needed to administrate the MariaDB server and clusters of servers. It will help you master database development on the MariaDB server. It shows you how to maintain a MariaDB server, taking advantage of its most recent features as well as the battle-tested functionalities inherited from MySQL. The book starts with an overview of the basic features and mechanisms that an advanced user should know. This includes diagnosing and solving most of the real-life problems, such as MariaDB errors, logs, and locks. You will learn how to improve the performance of a server by identifying slow queries. The book then covers how to choose and set up a proper backup plan and recover data when disaster occurs. Sharing your data through several servers using replication, MariaDB Galera Cluster, and the SPIDER storage engine will be dealt in detail. By the end of this book, the reader will be able to configure MariaDB servers, diagnose, as well as troubleshoot the standard transactional problems, and execute database maintenance. Both of these features imported from MySQL, as well as MariaDB's unique features, are covered in the book. Plugins and tools developed by the community are also explained.

MariaDB is ready to make things work, even in situations where high performance and high availability are critical. Get ready to make MariaDB work!

What this book covers

Chapter 1, Understanding the Essentials of MariaDB, discusses some of the key concepts and components of MariaDB, such as storage engines and logging. The most important resources for MariaDB professionals are also listed in this chapter.

Chapter 2, Debugging, explains how to debug SQL statements in MariaDB. It discusses how MariaDB generates errors and logs that can be used to find bugs.

Chapter 3, Optimizing Queries, is an overview on query optimization. First, it shows how to find slow queries that need be optimized. Then, it discusses the most important algorithms used by the MariaDB optimizer to execute a query, such as the index merge and the subquery optimization algorithms.

Chapter 4, Transactions and Locks, deals with concurrency. It explains how MariaDB uses locks to guarantee a proper isolation level for each transaction, and how these locks affect performance.

Chapter 5, Users and Connections, discusses how to manage user accounts and their activities in MariaDB. It covers permissions, the allocation of resources on a user basis, authentication methods, SSL connections, and the pool of threads.

Chapter 6, Caches, explains the caches used by the general purpose storage engines: InnoDB buffer pool, MyISAM key cache, and Aria page cache. Then, it explains the query and subquery caches and discusses alternative methods to cache the results of queries.

Chapter 7, InnoDB Compressed Tables, discusses InnoDB compressed tables. It shows how to create compressed tables and how to monitor their performance. Finally, it compares the different compression solutions available in MariaDB.

Chapter 8, Backup and Disaster Recovery, explains the backup methods provided by MariaDB and some third-party tools. The chapter discusses how to choose a backup plan, how to perform the different backup types, and how to restore backups when needed.

Chapter 9, Replication, illustrates how to set up and maintain a replication environment. The latest features of replication from MariaDB 10.0 are included, namely parallel replication and multisource replication.

Chapter 10, Table Partitioning, shows how to split big tables into multiple partitions, perhaps located on different storage devices. The characteristics of different partitioning types are explained, as well as the optimizations allowed by the different partition types.

Chapter 11, Data Sharding, discusses the main methods to distribute data across multiple disks or servers. The storage engines that allow reading and writing data onto remote servers are illustrated here: SPIDER, FederatedX, and CONNECT.

Chapter 12, MariaDB Galera Cluster, covers the MariaDB distribution of the Galera Cluster technology. It explains how to set up a cluster, add new nodes, monitor performance, and identify the most common problems.

What you need for this book

To put the topics of this book into practice, we need a personal computer running any operating system supported by MariaDB: Linux/UNIX, Mac OS X, or Windows. Linux is preferred because this system is most used for MariaDB and the book focuses on it. However, the commands should run unmodified on any Unix system; Windows is also mentioned where necessary.

MariaDB and MariaDB Galera Cluster can be downloaded from MariaDB's official site. The required third-party software is available on the sites mentioned in the relevant chapters. The mentioned system commands should be included in all the Linux distributions.

Who this book is for

This book is for intermediate MariaDB or MySQL users who need a more thorough comprehension of MariaDB, to administer a MariaDB server, or set of servers. Expert users of other relational DBMSs can also read this book, though they are encouraged to learn MariaDB basics using the *MariaDB Knowledge Base* or a MariaDB or MySQL beginner's book.

In particular, the reader of this book should already know the following topics:

- The basic concepts of a relational DBMS
- SQL language, at least at a basic level
- The syntax and structure of configuration files

Knowledge of the following topics is not necessary to understand the book but is recommended to get the best from it:

- How to write a script to automate tasks on Linux or Windows
- How to write a script or program that interacts with MariaDB
- MariaDB stored programs: stored procedures, events, and triggers

Conventions

In this book, you will find a number of styles of text that distinguish between different kinds of information. Here are some examples of these styles, and an explanation of their meaning.

Code words in text, database table names, folder names, filenames, file extensions, pathnames, dummy URLs, user input, and Twitter handles are shown as follows: "The SHOW PROCESSLIST statement returns information about the active connections."

A block of code is set as follows:

```
EXPLAIN [EXTENDED] <statement>;
```

Any command-line input or output is written as follows:

```
root@this:/usr/local/mysql# mysqldump -uroot -proot test customer
--tab=/tmp --fields-terminated-by=, --fields-enclosed-by="'"
--fields-escaped-by=/
```

New terms and **important words** are shown in bold.

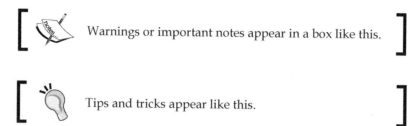

> Warnings or important notes appear in a box like this.

> Tips and tricks appear like this.

Reader feedback

Feedback from our readers is always welcome. Let us know what you think about this book—what you liked or may have disliked. Reader feedback is important for us to develop titles that you really get the most out of.

To send us general feedback, simply send an e-mail to feedback@packtpub.com, and mention the book title via the subject of your message.

If there is a topic that you have expertise in and you are interested in either writing or contributing to a book, see our author guide on www.packtpub.com/authors.

Customer support

Now that you are the proud owner of a Packt book, we have a number of things to help you to get the most from your purchase.

Downloading the example code

You can download the example code files for all Packt books you have purchased from your account at http://www.packtpub.com. If you purchased this book elsewhere, you can visit http://www.packtpub.com/support and register to have the files e-mailed directly to you.

Errata

Although we have taken every care to ensure the accuracy of our content, mistakes do happen. If you find a mistake in one of our books—maybe a mistake in the text or the code—we would be grateful if you would report this to us. By doing so, you can save other readers from frustration and help us improve subsequent versions of this book. If you find any errata, please report them by visiting http://www.packtpub.com/submit-errata, selecting your book, clicking on the **errata submission form** link, and entering the details of your errata. Once your errata are verified, your submission will be accepted and the errata will be uploaded on our website, or added to any list of existing errata, under the Errata section of that title. Any existing errata can be viewed by selecting your title from http://www.packtpub.com/support.

Piracy

Piracy of copyright material on the Internet is an ongoing problem across all media. At Packt, we take the protection of our copyright and licenses very seriously. If you come across any illegal copies of our works, in any form, on the Internet, please provide us with the location address or website name immediately so that we can pursue a remedy.

Please contact us at copyright@packtpub.com with a link to the suspected pirated material.

We appreciate your help in protecting our authors, and our ability to bring you valuable content.

Questions

You can contact us at questions@packtpub.com if you are having a problem with any aspect of the book, and we will do our best to address it.

1
Understanding the Essentials of MariaDB

This chapter provides a generic overview of the MariaDB architecture. Note that this description is not meant to teach MariaDB to new users; some knowledge of the software is necessary to fully understand this book.

The following topics will be discussed in this chapter:

- The MariaDB architecture
- The workflow of SQL statement processing
- Usage and tricks of the command-line client used, in all chapters of this book
- Storage engines and their characteristics
- Logs
- Caches
- User authentication and permissions
- The INFORMATION_SCHEMA and PERFORMANCE_SCHEMA system databases
- Compatibility with MySQL and other DBMS
- Resources on the Web

The MariaDB architecture

MariaDB is a community-driven fork of MySQL that was started in 2009 by Monty Widenius, the original author of MySQL, after the old project was acquired by Oracle. The first version of MariaDB was based on MySQL 5.1, and the improvements to MySQL base code are regularly merged into the MariaDB project. Other features are also merged from the Percona Server, another fork that is very similar to the mainstream product.

The most important Percona feature merged into MariaDB is XtraDB, a fork of the InnoDB storage engine. InnoDB is the default storage engine in modern MySQL and MariaDB versions. XtraDB fixes bugs that are still present in InnoDB before the official bug fixes are released by Oracle. It also has performance improvements and other minor features. The protocol, API, and most SQL statements that work with MySQL also fully work with MariaDB. The plugins that are written for MySQL work with MariaDB too. Thanks to these characteristics, most of the applications for MySQL work with MariaDB, without any modifications required. But, at the same time, switching to MariaDB allows one to use interesting features that are not available with MySQL. If an application's developer ignores these features, the application can use the features of both—MariaDB and MySQL. While the reader is probably familiar with DBMS in general, and particularly MariaDB or MySQL, a quick architecture review might be useful. In this introductory chapter, the main components and operations performed by the server are listed. The details are left for discussion in the remaining chapters.

The following schema represents the architecture of MariaDB:

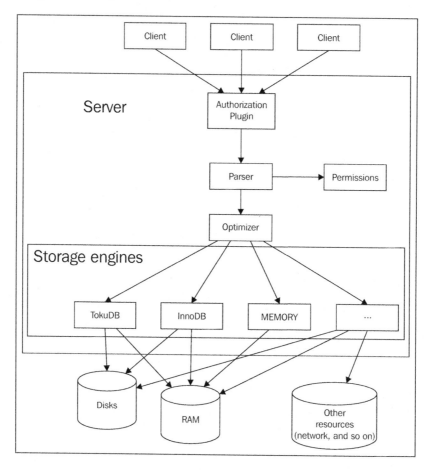

Basically, from a user's point of view, MariaDB receives some SQL queries or statements, elaborates them, and returns a result set. Let's see this process and the components involved in more detail:

- When a client connects to MariaDB, an authentication is performed based on the client's hostname, username, and password. Authentication can optionally be delegated to a plugin.

- If the login succeeds, the client can send a SQL query to the server.

- The parser understands the SQL string.

- The server checks whether the client has the permissions required for the requested action.

- If the query is stored in the query cache, the results are immediately returned to the client.

- The optimizer will try to find the fastest execution strategy, or query plan. This means that the optimizer decides the order in which the tables will be read. It also decides which indexes will be accessed and whether a temporary internal table will be used. A good strategy can greatly reduce the access to the disks and reduce the complexity of the operations by some order of magnitude. This topic will be discussed in *Chapter 3, Optimizing Queries*.

- The storage engines read and write the data and index files and any cache that they may use to speed up operations. Some important features, such as the transactions and foreign keys, are implemented at the storage engine level.

MariaDB and the storage engines maintain a set of logs to keep a track of the received statements, errors occurred, changes to the data, and so on. Most of the logs are optional; however, some logs are necessary for some administrative tasks. For example, the binary log enables backups or replication. Logs will be explained in the later chapters.

MariaDB has several options that affect the server's behavior. Many of them are dynamic, which means that they can be changed at runtime; others are static, which means that the value assigned during a server's startup cannot change. Most of them exist in both—the session level, which means that any individual users can change the value for the current connection, and the global level, which applies to all users who did not set a session value. An option can be specified in several ways, such as server command-line parameters, in configuration files, or if it is dynamic, via a SQL statement. MariaDB reads a set of configuration files in a given order. The exact location and read order are dependent on the operating system. Typically, only one MariaDB instance runs on a machine, so only one configuration file is needed and usually it is `/etc/my.cnf` on Linux and `my.ini` in the MariaDB install directory on Windows, for example, `C:\MariaDB 10.0\my.ini`.

However, this modular configuration system is useful if several MariaDB (and perhaps MySQL) servers are installed on the same machine. Some settings are likely to be valid for all servers, but each server can specify more options or override the generic values. A file can also be placed in a user's `home` directory, so that it will only be read if MariaDB runs with that identity (the `--user` start up parameter). The configuration file patch is listed in *Chapter 8, Backup and Disaster Recovery*. Starting a server with command-line parameters overrides the file's settings. These techniques are useful when testing the behavior of different versions of the server, or with different settings.

This book does not describe all the existing options. The reader should already be familiar with the most important options and server variables. Some of them will, however, be explained when they are relevant to the topics discussed in the book. *MariaDB Knowledge Base* documents all the existing options.

The MariaDB server is the `mysqld` file. On Linux, it is possible to run the server directly but it is usually invoked by another script. The `mysqld_safe` script starts the server and also restarts it in cases where it is terminated abnormally. This is much safer in the production environments. The `mysql.server` script is also available for the System V-like systems, where the runlevel exists. This script is distributed with another name by many Linux distributions. When several installations are present on the same machine, it is possible to manage them using `mysql_multi`.

The command-line client

The code and output examples in this book use the mysql command-line client. Knowing some client commands can greatly increase productivity when this tool is used.

The mysql command-line client knows that a SQL statement is terminated when it finds a semicolon (;), a \g, or a \G terminator. In the first case, the output is printed in a tabular form, shown as follows:

```
MariaDB [(none)]> SHOW DATABASES;
+--------------------+
| Database           |
+--------------------+
| information_schema |
| mysql              |
| performance_schema |
| test               |
+--------------------+
```

Downloading the example code

You can download the example code files for all Packt Publishing books you have purchased from your account at http://www.packtpub.com. If you have purchased this book elsewhere, you can visit http://www.packtpub.com/support and register to have the files e-mailed directly to you.

The mysql client has a prompt that normally appears at the beginning of a new line, as follows:

```
MariaDB [none]>
```

In the prompt, [none] means that no default database is selected. This means that, every time a table is named in a statement, the name of the database where it is located must be specifically specified. The USE statement selects a default database, whose name will appear in the prompt. The following example shows how to use it:

```
MariaDB [(none)]> USE test;
Database changed
MariaDB [test]>
```

When a statement spans on more lines, the lines begin with a different prompt, as shown in the following example:

```
MariaDB [test]> SELECT 1
    -> FROM DUAL;
```

If we forget to type a statement terminator, the modified prompt helps us notice the problem, shown as follows:

```
MariaDB [test]> SHOW TABLES
    ->
```

Here, the mysql client does not know that the statement is finished because a terminator (similar to a semicolon) is missing.

If a quote is open at the end of a line, the quoting character is shown in the prompt of the new line. While one could include a newline character in a string by pressing the *Enter* key, more often this happens by mistake. As we can see in the following example, the prompt helps us notice the problem:

```
MariaDB [test]> SELECT 'hello world FROM DUAL;
    '>
```

The problem here is that the end quote for the "hello world" string is missing. Note that the second line's prompt starts with a single quote.

Sometimes the tabular output is very difficult to read, particularly when output rows are longer than the command-line rows. When this is the case, the \G terminator is more convenient, as shown in the following example:

```
MariaDB [(none)]> SHOW VARIABLES LIKE 'char%' \G
*************************** 1. row ***************************
Variable_name: character_set_client
        Value: utf8
*************************** 2. row ***************************
Variable_name: character_set_connection
        Value: utf8
*************************** 3. row ***************************
Variable_name: character_set_database
        Value: latin1
...
```

On Linux systems, it is possible to use a **pager** program to read long outputs. Pagers provide the ability to scroll the output using the keyboard, or the mouse wheel, or any other method supported by the selected pager. Examples of good pagers are **less**, **more**, and **lv** (not installed by default on many distributions). To use less, run the following command:

```
MariaDB [(none)]> \P less
PAGER set to 'less'
```

The following queries will be seen with less. To disable the pager, run the following command:

```
MariaDB [(none)]> \P
Default pager wasn't set, using stdout.
```

Sometimes an output is long, but the user is only interested in a few rows, or even one row. In this case, it is possible to use the grep command as a pager with an option. The following example shows how to run the SHOW ENGINE InnoDB STATUS administrative statement, and get the rows that show the thread's status (the ones containing the string 'I/O thread'):

```
MariaDB [performance_schema]> \P grep 'I/O thread'
PAGER set to 'grep 'I/O thread''
MariaDB [performance_schema]> SHOW ENGINE InnoDB STATUS \G
I/O thread 0 state: waiting for completed aio requests (insert buffer
thread)
I/O thread 1 state: waiting for completed aio requests (log thread)
I/O thread 2 state: waiting for completed aio requests (read thread)
...
```

Another interesting option is to set the `md5sum` program as a pager. As a result, when a query is executed, the MD5 hash of the query will be shown. This is useful to compare the results of two queries, for example, to check that two tables are identical, shown as follows:

```
MariaDB [(none)]> \P md5sum
PAGER set to 'md5sum'
MariaDB [(none)]> SELECT * FROM test.t1;
3ec930f74d6ec7d7bdd7aa8544440835  -
MariaDB [(none)]> SELECT * FROM test.t2;
3ec930f74d6ec7d7bdd7aa8544440835  -
```

In the preceding example, the queries are passed to `md5sum`, and their MD5 values appear in the command line. Since the values are identical, we can be reasonably sure that the queried tables (`t1` and `t2`) are identical.

The `\tee` command can be used to log the current client session into a text file. On Windows, this can be used to save long outputs to a file and open it with a text editor, since the `\P` command does not work. To stop the logging, the `\notee` command can be used.

SQL warnings are not printed on the command prompt by default; only a warning count is showed. This can be a problem because warnings often indicate that a statement did not work as expected. To see all the warnings, the `\W` (uppercase) client command can be used. To suppress all the warnings and obtain a cleaner output, the `\w` (lowercase) command is used:

```
MariaDB [(none)]> \W
Show warnings enabled.
MariaDB [(none)]> SELECT 1/0;
+------+
| 1/0  |
+------+
| NULL |
+------+
1 row in set, 1 warning (0.00 sec)
Warning (Code 1365): Division by 0
MariaDB [(none)]> \w
Show warnings disabled.
MariaDB [(none)]> SELECT 1/0;
+------+
| 1/0  |
+------+
| NULL |
+------+
1 row in set, 1 warning (0.00 sec)
```

In the preceding example, we first enable the printing of warnings. The following SELECT query generates a warning. Then, we disable the printing of warnings. The same query does not show a warning anymore, but a warning count is still seen.

Sometimes, while using the command line, one needs to write a complex query. Using a good editor will be convenient. On Linux, it is possible to switch to an editor such as **vi** or **Emacs** by typing the edit command. The editor specified in the EDITOR environment variable is used. When the user exits the editor, the statement he/she wrote will appear in the command line.

In MariaDB 10.0, it is possible to stop the server from the command line without exiting or opening a new console to call mysqladmin. The SQL command to stop the server is SHUTDOWN. Unlike most administrative statements that require the SUPER privilege, this command requires the SHUTDOWN privilege. Normally, only the root user has these privileges. The client command to exit the client is \q. The following example shows how to terminate both the server and the client:

```
MariaDB [(none)]> SHUTDOWN;
Query OK, 0 rows affected (0.00 sec)
MariaDB [(none)]> \q
Bye
```

The mysql client can also be used to execute a batch file, that is, a text file containing a list of SQL statements. This can be done to restore a logical backup or to create a database required by an application. The results of the execution can be written into a text file. This is done using a Unix-like syntax, which works on all systems (including Windows) for the mysql client, shown as follows:

```
mysql < input_file > output_file
```

To quickly execute a single statement and see the results, it is not necessary to run the entire program. It is possible to use only one simple invocation:

```
federico@this:/usr/local/mysql/bin$ ./mysql -e "SELECT version();"
+---------------------+
| version()           |
+---------------------+
| 10.0.5-MariaDB-log  |
+---------------------+
```

Storage engines

As explained in the previous section, storage engines implement data handling at the physical level. They handle the data files, the data, and the index caches if they exist, and whatever is necessary to efficiently manage and read the data.

The .frm files are an exception. For each table, one .frm file exists. These files contain the definition of the table, and are created and used by the server.

Using the SHOW ENGINES statement or querying the information_schema.ENGINES table, it is possible to see the available storage engines. The following output is obtained with a standard MariaDB 10.0.6 installation:

```
MariaDB [(none)]> SELECT ENGINE, SUPPORT FROM information_schema.ENGINES
\G
*************************** 1. row ***************************
 ENGINE: FEDERATED
SUPPORT: YES
*************************** 2. row ***************************
 ENGINE: MRG_MyISAM
SUPPORT: YES
*************************** 3. row ***************************
 ENGINE: CSV
SUPPORT: YES
*************************** 4. row ***************************
 ENGINE: BLACKHOLE
SUPPORT: YES
*************************** 5. row ***************************
 ENGINE: MEMORY
SUPPORT: YES
*************************** 6. row ***************************
 ENGINE: MyISAM
SUPPORT: YES
*************************** 7. row ***************************
 ENGINE: ARCHIVE
SUPPORT: YES
*************************** 8. row ***************************
 ENGINE: InnoDB
SUPPORT: DEFAULT
*************************** 9. row ***************************
 ENGINE: PERFORMANCE_SCHEMA
SUPPORT: YES
*************************** 10. row ***************************
 ENGINE: Aria
SUPPORT: YES
```

A list of available engines will be displayed along with a SUPPORT column that indicates whether the engine is available.

When a table is created, a storage engine should be specified. If not, the default storage engine will be used. The default storage engine is specified in the `storage_engine` system variable, as showed in the following example:

```
MariaDB [(none)]> SELECT @@global.storage_engine;
+-------------------------+
| @@global.storage_engine |
+-------------------------+
| InnoDB                  |
+-------------------------+
```

The `TABLES` table in the `information_schema` database has a column called `ENGINE`, which can be read to check which storage engine is used for a particular table, shown as follows:

```
MariaDB [(none)]> SELECT ENGINE FROM information_schema.TABLES WHERE
TABLE_SCHEMA='test' AND TABLE_NAME='t1';
+--------+
| ENGINE |
+--------+
| InnoDB |
+--------+
```

A brief description of the available storage engine follows the preceding code.

XtraDB and InnoDB

InnoDB became the default engine with MariaDB 5.5 and MySQL 5.5. Percona maintains an InnoDB fork called XtraDB; it is InnoDB with bug fixes applied by Percona, and some unique features (mainly for performance and monitoring). By default, MariaDB uses XtraDB. For compatibility with InnoDB and MySQL, the commands still mention InnoDB but the XtraDB fork is used instead. However, this behavior can be changed by compiling the server with InnoDB, instead of XtraDB. This is not necessary since any new code can come with new bugs or unexpected performance problems, and XtraDB is not an exception.

 In this book, the default engine will generally be called InnoDB. In some cases, the XtraDB name will be used, to indicate that we are talking about a feature that is not supported by the mainstream InnoDB.

InnoDB is a high-performance, general-purpose storage engine that supports transactions with savepoints, XA transactions, and foreign keys. Savepoints are intermediate states that can be saved in the middle of a transaction and can then be restored if necessary. XA is a special type of transaction designed for operations that involve multiple resources, not necessarily SQL databases. In most cases, InnoDB performance is better than other engines. For this reason, this book will focus on XtraDB, which will be used for examples where another engine is not explicitly specified. For simplicity, XtraDB will be generally called InnoDB, except when describing features that are not supported by InnoDB.

InnoDB transactions are implemented via a complex locking system and undo logs. Each lock involves a single row or a range of rows; rows are identified using index records. Undo logs are used to rollback transactions when necessary, and can be stored in the system tablespace or elsewhere.

TokuDB

This storage engine is developed by Tokutek and has been included in MariaDB since Version 5.5, though it must be installed and enabled separately. It supports transactions with savepoints, XA transactions, but not foreign keys and full-text indexes. It is very different from InnoDB. Its main peculiarity is the use of a new data structure for indexes: the fractal trees. They are very similar to the commonly used B-trees, but each node has a buffer. This buffer contains the changes that need to be applied to the nodes that are more in-depth. Only when the buffer is full are the changes applied altogether. If the changes need to be written to disk, this is an important optimization, because writing fewer and bigger blocks is usually much faster. Also, this is not a problem with fractal trees fragmentation.

Another important feature of TokuDB is data compression. Of course, its compression level depends on the dataset, but it is generally much higher than the one provided by other storage engines. This happens because the write operations are grouped together. Data compression is always used in TokuDB and cannot be disabled.

Fractal trees and compression make TokuDB suitable to work with datasets that are too big to be entirely stored in memory. For such workloads, TokuDB can be faster than InnoDB. For most purposes, TokuDB offers reduced performance and has fewer features.

MyISAM and Aria

MyISAM was historically the default storage engine for MySQL and MariaDB, before Version 5.5. It is a relatively simple engine, optimized for read-heavy workloads where there are just a few writes or no writes at all. In practice, MyISAM is good for data warehousing and more generally for data reporting where data can be appended to tables, but not modified or deleted.

MyISAM writes two files for each table: a `data` file and an `index` file. The `index` file can always be rebuilt if it gets damaged for some reason. Copying `data` files (and the `.frm` files), even across different machines, is sufficient to back up and restore MyISAM tables.

Three data formats are available: `FIXED`, `DYNAMIC`, and `COMPRESSED`. The `FIXED` data format assigns a fixed length to columns, while `DYNAMIC` saves space when possible. The `FIXED` data format is faster, more reliable, and harder to fragment. The `COMPRESSED` data format is used to create small read-only tables.

Aria is designed to be MyISAM's successor. It uses logs that allow data recovery after a crash. Data changes are atomic in Aria; they are applied entirely, or the table is damaged. Aria uses a different data format called `PAGE` that is generally faster and never fragments too much, but it is possible to use the `FIXED` or `DYNAMIC` formats for compatibility with MyISAM (where the table will not be crash-safe).

Aria can be better than MyISAM in environments where there is concurrency, and the *MariaDB Knowledge Base* suggests using Aria for new applications. Yet, users should be aware that bulk writes are slower in Aria, particularly where duplicate indexed values exist.

Both MyISAM and Aria do not support transactions and foreign keys, but as explained previously, each statement on an Aria table can be considered a transaction. Even full-text indexes are supported by MyISAM and Aria.

The `MRG_MyISAM` storage engine, also called `MERGE`, can be used to build a table on multiple MyISAM identical tables, to work around the file size limit of the operating system.

Other engines

The storage engines described up to this point are of general purpose, even if some of them are only suitable for some particular workloads. Other storage engines use non-standard input or output methods, or process queries in a non-standard way, and thus are used for very specific purposes described as follows:

- The **OQGRAPH** storage engine is developed by **OpenQuery**. It is meant to handle tree and graph data structures. Trees can be handled in several ways in SQL databases but, whichever method is used, there are some drawbacks because the relational theory does not suit tree structures. OQGRAPH solves this problem by translating SQL queries into tree-specific requests. OQGRAPH was introduced in MariaDB 5.2, temporarily disabled in 5.5, and then reintroduced in MariaDB 10.

- The **BLACKHOLE** storage engine is inherited from MySQL. BLACKHOLE tables are always empty. Modifications have no effect on them and queries always return an empty result set.

- The **SPIDER** storage engine is developed by Kentoku Shiba. It reads and writes data into other instances of MariaDB. XA transactions are supported. SPIDER has been designed for data sharding and will be discussed in more detail in *Chapter 11, Data Sharding*.

- The **CONNECT** storage engine is a MariaDB-specific storage engine that allows reading and writing data from and to external sources. The data sources can be MariaDB or MySQL connections, ODBC connections, files, and directories. Files can use several formats, including but not limited to CSV, HTML tables, and binary data. An API exists to develop additional formats. Data can also be compressed with the `gzip` format. A `CONNECT` table can also be used to transform data contained in other tables, for example, to merge tables or reorganize data into a pivot table. This storage engine will probably obsolete some older storage engines: **CSV**, which accesses the CSV files; **FEDERATED**, an engine inherited from MySQL, which can access tables from other MariaDB or MySQL instances; and **FEDERATEDX**, added in MariaDB because FEDERATED was no longer maintained.

- The **ARCHIVE** storage engine handles compressed tables. It has several limitations, such as the inability to modify or delete data after an insertion, and is quite slow. Nowadays, compressed InnoDB, MyISAM, or TokuDB tables are always preferable.

- The **CassandraSE** storage engine connects to the Apache Cassandra NoSQL server to read and write data. It converts MariaDB's data types and logic into Cassandra and vice versa. It is a MariaDB-specific storage engine because it uses MariaDB's dynamic columns to emulate Cassandra's column families.

- The **SphinxSE** storage engine is used to allow MariaDB to access a table that is stored in the Sphinx database server. Sphinx is mainly used and known for its good full-text searches.

- The **mroonga** storage engine is specifically designed for full-text searches. These involve the Japanese, Chinese, or Korean character sets and languages. It also includes fast geometric indexes for geolocation.

- The **SEQUENCE** storage engine cannot be used to physically create a table. If it is enabled, queries can involve virtual tables whose names follow a certain pattern. Based on the name, the SEQUENCE storage engine returns an integer series. For example, the `seq_1_to_10` virtual table returns a result set with numbers from 1 to 10. The `seq_1_to_10_step_2` virtual table returns a similar series, but with an increment of 2.

- The **performance_schema** storage engine is only used internally for the tables in the `performance_schema` databases. The only reason why a **database administrator (DBA)** should be aware of it is that a specific statement exists to check how much memory is consumed by the `performance_schema` by using the `SHOW ENGINE performance_schema STATUS` command.

Logs

A MariaDB server maintains the following logs:

- **Error log**: This log contains the error occurred during the server execution. This includes both server problems (such as errors that stop a plugin from starting) and SQL errors.

- **SQL_ERROR_LOG**: This is a plugin introduced in MariaDB 5.5 that logs the errors generated by the SQL statements into a file. This is more specific than the error log, because it only logs SQL errors. Using this plugin is the easiest way to see the errors that occur in a stored routine or trigger.

- **General query log**: SQL statements are logged into this file.

- **Slow query logs**: This log can be configured to store the queries that take more than a given amount of time or do not use any index. It is useful for finding out why an application or database is slow.

- **Binary log (binlog)**: Depending on the chosen format, this log contains data that is changed to a binary form, or the SQL statements that caused the change. It is necessary for implementing incremental backups, replication, or a database cluster.

- **Relay log**: This log only exists on replication slaves and it contains the data received by the master. Each entry in a slave's relay log matches an entry in a master's binary log.

InnoDB also has two logs named undo log and redo log. The undo log is used to keep track of the changes performed by the active transactions and roll them back if necessary. The redo log tracks data of the requested data changes and is used to recover tables after a crash.

Aria has a log (the Aria log) that contains the data not applied to the data files, and is used at startup to recover tables that were not closed properly. Changes to MyISAM tables are stored in the MyISAM log.

Each log consists of a set of files, stored in the installation directory and in the data directory, or in a different location determined by the user. However, some logs can be written in the system tables, which are located in the `mysql` database. The write process is slower in this case, but this allows querying such logs using SQL statements. Also, the CSV storage engine can be used, which allows you to import the logs into external programs using a well-known format.

Since logs are written very often, they have a buffer to improve performances (writing data in chunks has an overhead, which can be reduced by writing data together). Of course, logs are more reliable if they are written more often. Some variables control the use of the buffer, and the DBA can adjust them according to the need for reliability and speed.

Logs also need to be periodically rotated, which means that the new entries will be written in a new file, and the oldest file will probably be removed. The rotation can be automatic (for the binary log), or can be requested by the user via the FLUSH LOGS statement or the `mysqladmin` utility.

For each log that the user may need to read, there is a utility to show its contents. The log rotation can be done via the `mysql-log-rotate` script on Red Hat Linux.

MariaDB caches

MariaDB has several caches that can be adjusted using system variables and start-up options to adapt them to the specific workload. Usually, only a few caches should be regulated. By changing just a few options, the overall performances might greatly change. Other caches solve more specific problems.

The InnoDB buffer pool is usually the most important cache. It contains the data and keys of the InnoDB tables. On a dedicated server, usually the buffer pool should be at least 70 percent of the available RAM. Of course, this percentage is purely indicative: the optimal value depends on a wide variety of factors. The buffer pool has two sublists: the new list and the old list. It is possible to set the sublist sizes, as well as a minimum age the data pages must have before populating the new list. These settings determine how often a recent read data populates the new list, or remains in the old list until it is evicted. To improve concurrency, more instances of the buffer pool can be used. Different instances never contain the same data.

The change buffer, an area of the buffer pool, stores the data changes that are not yet flushed to disks. For write-intensive workloads, the percentage of the buffer pool occupied by the change buffer can be increased; for read-heavy workloads, the change buffer can be decreased or even disabled. It can also be configured to store only some types of changes, which is useful for some workloads.

MyISAM uses a buffer called key cache. It does not store data; it stores only indexes. More instances of the key cache can be created and individually configured.

Aria uses a cache called page cache that is similar to MyISAM's key cache. The Aria page cache is faster for data of a fixed length. Currently, Aria does not support multiple instances of this cache.

If MyISAM or Aria is mainly used, the key cache or the page cache should ideally be as large as your frequently accessed indexed data.

The table opens the cache and stores the handles for the physical table files. MyISAM and Aria use two files for each table (because indexes and data are stored separately). This cache reduces the file access overhead.

The host cache contains the association between the IP addresses and the hostnames of the clients that are connected to the server, and when the account is blocked.

InnoDB data structures

In MariaDB, by default, InnoDB is mapped to XtraDB, a compatible InnoDB fork maintained by Percona.

InnoDB tables are contained in tablespaces. A tablespace is a file that contains data and indexes for one or more tables. In old MariaDB and MySQL versions, all the tables are created in a system tablespace. If the `innodb_file_per_table` system variable is set to `1`, which is the default since the 10.0 Version, each table is stored in a separate tablespace. This variable is dynamic, so it is possible to store some tables in separate files, and others in the system tablespace.

The system tablespace, by default, also contains InnoDB's data dictionary, the undo logs, the change buffer, and the doublewrite buffer. The data dictionary is a metadata collection of all InnoDB tables, columns, and indexes. The system tablespace is stored in the `data` directory, in the `ibdata` files (by default, two files).

A portion of a tablespace is called a segment. Regular tablespaces have one segment for data and one segment for each index. The system tablespace has several segments.

A page is a small data unit stored in a tablespace or in the buffer pool. Pages have a fixed size that can be configured. A page contains one or two rows and usually some empty space. The non-empty space ratio is called the fill factor.

A page that has been modified in the change buffer is called a dirty page.

In some cases, for example for a consistent read process, InnoDB sequentially reads several pages together, with a total size of 1 MB. Such groups of pages are called extents.

InnoDB indexes are important not only for reads, but also for locks. Each lock points to an index record.

An InnoDB index can be a clustered index or a secondary index. Primary keys are clustered indexes. If a table does not have a primary key, the first `UNIQUE` index, which only contains `NOT NULL` columns, will be used as a primary key. If no such index exists, a hidden cluster index is automatically created. All secondary index records point to a clustered index record, so we can say that all secondary indexes contain the clustered index.

Authentication and security

MariaDB authentication is based on a username, a password, and the client's hostname (or its IP address). The username and the hostname form the account, for example:

```
user_01@localhost
```

Each user can be authenticated by a different plugin. This is helpful when using external login systems, for example, operating system users. MariaDB or a plugin checks the password provided by the client and accepts or rejects the connection.

Permissions can be assigned to individual accounts or to accounts that match a pattern. Patterns are specified using the syntax for the LIKE operator. Several permissions exist. Each of them allows executing a single statement type, or a limited set of statements. Permissions can be applied to the whole server, to databases and the object they contain (tables and stored procedures), to individual objects, or even to individual columns in a table or view. This allows great granularity and flexibility when deciding what actions can be performed on what objects, and who can perform those actions.

MariaDB 10 also supports roles. Permissions can be granted to roles instead of accounts. Roles are assigned to accounts. If a user has a role assigned, he can use that role and perform all the actions whose permissions the role has to execute. Roles improve permission management in systems with many users, where a good security policy is required.

Additional options are available. For example, the DBA can require a user to always connect using SSL encryption. The DBA can also limit the resources used by a user, or can decide whether a user can use multiple connections simultaneously.

The information_schema database

The information_schema database (often called I_S for brevity) is a virtual database that contains informative tables. These tables can be divided into several groups:

- **Metadata tables**: Tables such as SCHEMATA, TABLES, and COLUMNS contain information about the structure of databases, tables, columns, and so on.

- **Status and variables tables**: The GLOBAL_VARIABLES and SESSION_VARIABLES tables list the values of the server's system variables. The GLOBAL_STATUS and SESSION_STATUS tables provide information about the operations performed by the server.

- **Privilege tables**: The tables whose names end with _PRIVILEGES indicate users that have various permissions on objects.

- **The PROFILING table**: This table can be used to monitor the queries executed during the current session, and see which low-level operations are performed by the server.

- **The PROCESSLIST table**: This table shows the active sessions and their status.

Several tables provide information about InnoDB. Some of them are XtraDB-specific. These table names begin with INNODB_ or XTRADB_ if they only exist for XtraDB, discussed as follows:

- **InnoDB locks tables**: The INNODB_LOCKS, INNODB_LOCK_WAITS, and INNODB_TRX tables contain information about active locks, waits, and transactions that acquired a lock or are waiting for a lock, respectively.

- **InnoDB buffer pool tables**: Tables whose names start with INNODB_BUFFER_ are the buffer pool contents and page usage.

- **The INNODB_METRICS table**: This table provides information about some low-level operations performed by InnoDB.

- **InnoDB compression tables**: Tables whose names start with INNODB_CMP provide information about the performance of compressed pages.

- **InnoDB full-text tables**: Tables whose names start with INNODB_FT_ provide information about full-text indexes in InnoDB tables.

- **InnoDB data dictionary tables**: Tables whose names start with INNODB_SYS_ provide metadata about InnoDB tables, columns, and foreign keys. They are similar to the more generic tables that contain metadata, but these tables are specific to InnoDB. They also contain statistics and information about files.

Generally, the information that can be read from information_schema can also be obtained with the SHOW statements and vice versa. Querying information_schema is a more flexible and standard way to retrieve such information, but is also more verbose.

Information on the InnoDB activities can also be obtained in a human-readable form via the SHOW ENGINE InnoDB STATUS and SHOW ENGINE InnoDB MUTEX statements.

To answer the queries of information_schema, the server opens and reads the database files, which can be a slow operation. For this reason, the queries that are often executed on a production server should be optimized to only read the necessary files. This can usually be done with a good WHERE clause.

The performance_schema database

In the most relevant parts of MariaDB code, instrumentations can be found that allow detailed performance monitoring. The results of such monitoring are written into a special database called performance_schema. Since the monitoring activity sensibly slows down the server performance, it is possible to disable it in the configuration file, by setting the performance_schema variable to 0.

The `performance_schema` variable is based on the following concepts:

- **Actors**: An actor is a thread that is currently monitored. It can be a user connection or a background MariaDB thread.
- **Consumers**: Consumers are tables that are populated with performance data.
- **Instruments**: These are used in instrumented MariaDB activities such as knowing the server's internals where the instruments names are intuitive. For example, `wait/io/file/sql/binlog` is a wait to acquire a lock on the binary log.
- **Objects**. These are the tables whose activities must be monitored.

To determine what the server must monitor, the `performance_schema` setup tables can be modified: `setup_actors`, `setup_consumers`, `setup_instruments`, and `setup_objects`. When a low-level operation takes place and `performance_schema` is enabled, if the involved actor, consumer, instrument, and object is monitored, new information is written into the `performance_schema`. A `setup_timer` table determines the granularity of the timers that are used to monitor various events (microseconds, nanoseconds, and so on).

The `performance_schema` setup table consists of several tables. However, the names of the most important ones follow a pattern, based on a prefix and suffix. The prefix indicates what type of information the table provides. The most important prefixes are:

- `events_statements_`: This means that the table refers to SQL statements.
- `events_stages_`: This means that the table refers to the stages of a SQL statement execution (such as parsing and table opening).
- `*_instances_`: This means that the table refers to a certain type of lock. For example, `mutex_instances_` refer to mutexes.
- `events_waits_`: This means that the table refers to threads that are waiting for a lock to be released.

The suffix indicates how the information is aggregated, shown as follows:

- `_current`: This means that only the current server activities are in the table
- `_history`: This means that some limited historical information is stored
- `_history_long`: This means that more historical information is present

Other suffixes exist, but are self-explanatory.

For example, the `events_waits_current` table lists the threads that are currently waiting for an event. The `events_statements_history` table shows information about the recently executed statements.

Compatibility with MySQL and other DBMS

Each MariaDB tree uses a MySQL tree as a codebase. For example, MariaDB 5.5 is based on MySQL 5.5. When the MySQL tree is updated, MariaDB imports the bug fixes and new features. MariaDB should be fully compatible with the corresponding MySQL tree. This means that all the SQL statements, API calls, and configuration settings that work with MySQL will produce the same results on MariaDB. If an undocumented compatibility is found, it is treated as a bug. Of course, MariaDB develops new features on top of the MySQL codebase; thus what works with MariaDB will not work on MySQL if the MariaDB-specific features are used.

In a replication environment, it is safe to replicate MySQL on a compatible version of MariaDB. The opposite is only safe if the queries do not use MariaDB-specific features.

MariaDB also imports several features from the Percona Server, which also uses MySQL as a codebase. This means that programs that use features specific to the Percona Server can work with the corresponding tree of MariaDB.

The following table shows the correspondence between MySQL and MariaDB trees:

MariaDB tree	MySQL tree
5.1	5.1
5.2	5.1
5.3	5.1
5.5	5.5
10.0	5.5, partly 5.6

Each MariaDB tree till 5.5 is compatible with the MySQL tree having the same number, or (if such a tree does not exist) with the latest version having a lower number. MariaDB 10.0 breaks this pattern because it just implements a part of the MySQL 5.6 features; thus, it is not fully compatible. The complete list of incompatibilities is available in *MariaDB Knowledge Base*. Most users should not be affected, unless they want to use MySQL 5.6 and MariaDB 10.0 in the same replication environment. Also, MySQL 5.6 allows InnoDB tables to be used as a bridge to **memcache**, but this feature is not currently available in MariaDB.

MariaDB and MySQL use a syntax called executable comments to improve compatibility with other DBMS. Executable comments can be used to execute a part of a SQL statement on MySQL and MariaDB, but not on other DBMS; or just on MariaDB but not on MySQL; or again, on recent versions of MariaDB but not on older versions.

The most generic executable comment allows a part of a query to be executed on MariaDB and MySQL, shown as follows:

```
SELECT 1 /*! , VERSION() */;
```

By adding M, the comment will only be executed on MariaDB:

```
SELECT 1 /*M! , 'You are using MariaDB!' */;
```

It is possible to specify a minimum version number. This number must consist of five or six digits in the following form: the first number or the first two numbers are the major version, the following two numbers are the minor version, and the final two numbers are the patch number. For example:

```
SELECT 1
  /*!50510 , 'MySQL 5.5.10 or newer' */
  /*M!100006 , 'MariaDB 10.0.6 or newer' */;
```

Note that MariaDB 10.0 always executes executable comments for MySQL 5.6, which is mostly compatible, but it ignores executable comments for MySQL 5.7.

Also, the SQL_MODE system variable has some flags that make the general syntax more compatible with older versions of MySQL, or with other database systems.

MariaDB resources

The primary source of documentation is the *MariaDB Knowledge Base*, also called KB, that contains information about related open source tools. It is also a good place to ask technical questions about MariaDB and the community will answer. The MariaDB KB can be found at:

* https://mariadb.com/kb/en/

The MariaDB Foundation has a blog that allows users to stay updated with new releases and other important news. It can be found at:

* https://mariadb.org/

Planet MariaDB aggregates blog posts related to MariaDB at:

* http://planetmariadb.org/

MariaDB's project planning tool **JIRA** can be used to report bugs, browse information on known bugs and their fixes, and to know when new releases are scheduled and which bug fixes and features they will contain. It can be found at:

- `https://mariadb.atlassian.net/browse/MDEV`

Summary

In this chapter, we reviewed the general MariaDB architecture. Many features of the `mysql` client were explained. They increase productivity of the DBA and reduce the need for a GUI.

We discussed the storage engines that are included in MariaDB's binaries or sources. An overview of InnoDB, TokuDB, MyISAM, and Aria was presented. InnoDB will be used in this book and in most practical cases. For this reason, special attention has been dedicated to this engine and its data structures. However, uncommon use cases could benefit from other engines, for one reason or another. Also, a brief description of all the minor storage engines was presented. These engines can be used to solve specific problems. For example, Spider will be discussed in a later chapter, while the chapter about replication will show how BLACKHOLE can be used to avoid replicating some data.

The logs used by the server were briefly introduced. Some of them are essential to use some MariaDB features, such as physical backups, replication, or recovering after a `DELETE` statement that erased too much data. The details about how to use, configure, and maintain the logs will be explained in the later chapters, when the logs will be used for practical purposes.

The most important concepts about caches and security were reviewed. More details will be discussed in the chapters entirely dedicated to these topics.

The `INFORMATION_SCHEMA` and `PERFORMANCE_SCHEMA` databases contain a lot of useful information. This book does not explain all the tables in detail, because exhaustive information about them can be found in the MariaDB's KB. However, in the later chapters, some of these tables will be explained and used to demonstrate how they can be of help for practical purposes.

Since MariaDB is a fork of MySQL, the compatibility between different versions of MariaDB and MySQL was discussed. This topic is important while gradually replacing MySQL servers with MariaDB, while using a replication environment where MariaDB and MySQL coexist, or while developing an application that must work with both the DBMS (particularly if the developers want to take advantage of MariaDB's unique features).

Finally, this chapter presents a list of the most useful MariaDB resources. All advanced users should check them regularly to keep themselves updated with new releases and never stop learning!

In the next chapter, we will learn how to use some logs to find the errors that occurred in MariaDB, and how to debug SQL statements. This information is important for troubleshooting, and we will use it to deal with the more complex topics that will be discussed in the following chapters.

2
Debugging

In this chapter, we will discuss the basic techniques that can be used to find problems in the MariaDB server and in SQL statements. The following are some of the basic tools and techniques used:

- Error conditions
- The diagnostics area
- The error log
- The general query log
- Maintaining logs
- The `SQL_ERROR_LOG` plugin
- Debugging of stored programs

Understanding error conditions in MariaDB

Before discussing the database debugging techniques, it is important to understand the most important tools used by MariaDB that notify us about error conditions, that is, when something goes wrong.

An error in MariaDB consists of the following types of data:

- A `SQLSTATE` value
- An error number
- An error message

While conditions are usually generated by the server, the user can raise them using the `SIGNAL` and `RESIGNAL` SQL statements.

To get information about errors, the C API provides three methods: `mysql_sqlstate()`, `mysql_errno()`, and `mysql_error()`. Most MariaDB or MySQL APIs have corresponding methods with almost identical names. These methods and statements will be discussed later in this chapter. Now, let's discuss the MariaDB errors.

The SQLSTATE value

The `SQLSTATE` value is an alphanumerical string of five characters. The first two characters represent a class and provide general information about the problem. The last three characters represent a subclass and indicate an exact error or a set of possible errors. If a subclass is not indicated, then the value is `000`. All characters are digits or uppercase English letters.

The special value `00000` represents a success. This is the only value in the `00` class, and this value cannot be raised by the user. The `01` class represents a warning that the requested action was performed, but some parts of it have been skipped or if some problem has occurred. The `02` class represents the **not found** conditions; this is not strictly an error. It is a condition that the user should expect, for example, if a cursor iterates a set of rows, after it reads the last rows, a not found condition will be produced.

Other classes represent errors. If an error occurs, the requested action cannot be completed. For nontransactional engines, this could mean that the actions have been partly executed. For example, if you try to insert two rows, and the second row contains a duplicated value for the primary key.

Some conditions do not have a dedicated `SQLSTATE` value in the current versions of MariaDB. These conditions use the `HY000` value, which is sometimes called the **general error**. This value is used for many errors inherited from MySQL, and for most MariaDB-specific errors.

The error number

The error number, or code, is a `SMALLINT SIGNED` value (the maximum value is 32767), which only identifies a condition. The value `0` implies success and cannot be used for conditions raised by the user.

A MariaDB version shares the errors of the MySQL version it is based on. MariaDB-specific error codes start from `1900`. A MariaDB-specific error is usually an error related to a MariaDB-specific feature such as the virtual columns or the dynamic columns.

The error message

The error message is a human readable VARCHAR(128) string. In the simplest of cases, it is just a way to recognize an error without searching its number in the MariaDB documentation. Sometimes, it also contains additional details such as the name of a table or column involved in an operation that failed.

Usually, the error message is enough to understand which error has occurred. However, if an error message is too vague or misleading, if the problem is not immediately clear, the user should refer to the error number and search for it in the MariaDB documentation.

The custom errors

A custom error is an error explicitly generated by the user with the SIGNAL or RESIGNAL statements. The SQLSTATE value, error code, and error message of such errors is defined by the user. The difference between these commands is that SIGNAL creates and raises a new error, while RESIGNAL modifies an error's properties before raising it again.

The main reason to raise a custom error is to provide a better interface to a stored program. For example, if an incorrect parameter is passed to a stored procedure, it is possible to raise an error that clearly states the problem. However, SIGNAL also works out of stored programs. For this reason, it is also possible to use it to write an error in SQL_ERROR_LOG, where the message could have a meaning for a DBA or a tool that will read the log.

The 45000 value is suggested for user-generated custom errors. MariaDB, MySQL, and all other forks cannot use this value even in future versions. However, any SQLSTATE value is safe if the generic 000 subclass is used because such values are not meant to identify a single error. For the same reason, the general error is also acceptable.

 For more details, refer to the *MariaDB Error Codes* page at https://mariadb.com/kb/en/mariadb-error-codes/.

There could be valid reasons to use different SQLSTATE values; for example, a custom error in the 01 class is not fatal, and continues the execution. Another reason is mapping a custom error to a built-in error; for example, a custom error can be raised in a particular case when a duplicate key error occurs. A custom error is created to provide the DBA or the applications with useful information on how to debug the problem. However, you also probably want the application to take actions that it normally takes when a duplicate key error occurs. So, the custom error can use the same 23000 SQLSTATE value.

> The default error number depends on the SQLSTATE value: 1642 for warnings, 1643 for not found conditions, and 1644 for errors. These values are dedicated to user-generated errors. In these cases, the default error message informs whether the condition is a user-generated warning or an error. Otherwise, the default error message is an empty string.

Other condition properties exist in SQL standard and are partially supported in MariaDB. Such condition properties contain additional information about the cause of errors. They can be set for custom errors via SIGNAL and RESIGNAL, and they can be read via GET DIAGNOSTICS. However, these properties are not set for built-in conditions and are never returned to the client; so, developers normally ignore them.

The SHOW WARNINGS and SHOW ERRORS statements

MariaDB errors and warnings, collectively known as conditions, are stored in a container called the **diagnostics area**. Generally, the diagnostics area contains the warnings and errors generated by the last executed statement. However, the exact mechanism that determines how the diagnostics area is populated or emptied is a bit more complex and will be explained in the next section. MariaDB provides some SQL statements that allow us to inspect the contents of the diagnostics area.

The SHOW WARNINGS statement returns all the conditions that are currently populating the diagnostics area. The SHOW COUNT(*) WARNING statement returns the number or count of such conditions. This number is also assigned to the warning_count session variable.

In the following example, we will execute a query that generates two warnings:

```
MariaDB [(none)]> CREATE TABLE test.t1 (col INT) ENGINE = xxx;
Query OK, 0 rows affected, 2 warnings (0.29 sec)
MariaDB [(none)]> SHOW WARNINGS;
+---------+------+------------------------------------------+
| Level   | Code | Message                                  |
+---------+------+------------------------------------------+
| Warning | 1286 | Unknown storage engine 'xxx'             |
| Warning | 1266 | Using storage engine InnoDB for table 't1' |
+---------+------+------------------------------------------+
2 rows in set (0.00 sec)
```

The output contains three columns. You can see the error codes, the error messages, and a level. The level indicates the condition type: it can be a note (just an informative message from the server), a warning, or an error. Notes can be excluded from the output of SHOW WARNINGS by setting the @@sql_note variable to 0.

Some SQL clauses and system variables can change the type of some conditions. For example, the IF EXISTS and IF NOT EXISTS options can be added to several DDL statements such as CREATE TABLE and DROP TABLE. They turn an error into a note, in case an object cannot be created because it already exists, or the object cannot be dropped because it does not exist.

The following example shows how the Level column helps to indicate the relevance of a problem:

```
MariaDB [(none)]> DROP TABLE test.t;
ERROR 1051 (42S02): Unknown table 'test.t'
MariaDB [(none)]> SHOW WARNINGS \G
*************************** 1. row ***************************
  Level: Error
   Code: 1051
Message: Unknown table 'test.t'
1 row in set (0.00 sec)
MariaDB [(none)]> DROP TABLE IF EXISTS test.t;
Query OK, 0 rows affected, 1 warning (0.00 sec)
MariaDB [(none)]> SHOW WARNINGS \G
*************************** 1. row ***************************
  Level: Note
   Code: 1051
Message: Unknown table 'test.t'
1 row in set (0.00 sec)
```

In the preceding example, we executed two very similar statements. In the first case, DROP TABLE generates an error because we are trying to erase a table that does not exist. In the second case, we added an IF EXISTS option to DROP TABLE, which means that we do not want MariaDB to generate an error if the table is not present. However, a note is still generated because you may want to know that no such table exists. This example shows the importance of the Level column. The SHOW WARNINGS statement returns a very similar output in these cases, with the level note being the only difference.

As explained previously, the DBA can decide whether warnings are written to the error log or not. For this reason, using SQL clauses that change the error behaviors (such as IF EXISTS and IF NOT EXISTS and IGNORE for the DML statements) or changing the value of the SQL_MODE system variable can help to log more possible problems. They can also help to keep the log files smaller if you think that some kinds of problems are not relevant in your case.

The SHOW ERRORS and SHOW COUNT(*) ERRORS statements are very similar to the statements explained in the previous section, but they only show and count the errors, not warnings or notes. The number of errors in the diagnostics area is also assigned to the error_count session variable.

The following example shows the usage of SHOW COUNT(*) WARNINGS and SHOW COUNT(*) ERRORS:

```
MariaDB [(none)]> CREATE DATABASE IF NOT EXISTS test;
Query OK, 1 row affected, 1 warning (0.00 sec)
MariaDB [(none)]> SHOW COUNT(*) ERRORS \G
*************************** 1. row ***************************
@@session.error_count: 0
1 row in set (0.00 sec)
MariaDB [(none)]> SHOW COUNT(*) WARNINGS \G
*************************** 1. row ***************************
@@session.warning_count: 1
1 row in set (0.00 sec)
```

In the preceding example, trying to create a database with the IF NOT EXISTS clause generates a note. The number of errors is therefore 0, while SHOW COUNT(*) WARNINGS returns 1 because the sql_notes variable is ON by default.

The diagnostics area

The diagnostics area consists of two subareas: the statement information and the condition information.

The statement information contains two values:

- NUMBER: This is the number of conditions stored in the condition area.
- ROW_COUNT: This is the number of rows modified by the statement it refers to. The same value is returned by the ROW_COUNT() SQL function and by the mysql_affected_rows() API function.

The diagnostics area is populated and emptied by following the exact rules. Knowing these rules is very important to debug single statements without falling for some common pitfalls, and it is more important to debug the stored programs.

Whenever a statement generates at least one condition (notes, warnings, or errors), the diagnostics area is populated with such conditions. Any condition present previously in the diagnostics area is deleted. However, there is an exception. If the new statement is RESIGNAL or GET DIAGNOSTICS, the old conditions are not deleted. This is to help the developers. Such statements are used to handle errors and even if they are unsuccessful, the user still needs to read the older conditions. However, if the statement cannot be correctly parsed (because of a syntax error), MariaDB does not know that the statement is RESIGNAL or GET DIAGNOSTICS; thus, the diagnostics area is empty.

If a statement does not produce any conditions and does not access any tables, the old contents of the diagnostics area are preserved. If the statement accesses a table, the old contents are always deleted, even if the statement does not produce any conditions.

The max_error_count system variable represents the maximum number of conditions that can be included in the diagnostics area.

Let's see some examples of how the diagnostics area works. In all the following examples, SHOW WARNINGS is used as a simple way to show the whole diagnostics area. As an easy way to generate an error, we will try to set the SQL_MODE server variable to x, which is not a valid value.

Consider the following example where we will first generate an error and visualize the diagnostics area that contains this error:

```
MariaDB [(none)]> SET sql_mode = 'x';
ERROR 1231 (42000): Variable 'sql_mode' can't be set to the value of 'x'
MariaDB [(none)]> SHOW WARNINGS \G
*************************** 1. row ***************************
```

```
   Level: Error
    Code: 1231
Message: Variable 'sql_mode' can't be set to the value of 'x'
1 row in set (0.00 sec)
MariaDB [(none)]> SET sql_mode = 'STRICT_ALL_TABLES';
Query OK, 0 rows affected (0.00 sec)
MariaDB [(none)]> SHOW WARNINGS \G
*************************** 1. row ***************************
   Level: Error
    Code: 1231
Message: Variable 'sql_mode' can't be set to the value of 'x'
1 row in set (0.00 sec)
```

After visualizing the diagnostic area that contains the error, we will execute a correct statement that does not access any table. No error is produced, and the old contents of the diagnostics area remain.

Consider the following example where we will generate an error with the SET statement and then another error with the DROP TABLE statement:

```
MariaDB [(none)]> SET sql_mode = 'x';
ERROR 1231 (42000): Variable 'sql_mode' can't be set to the value of 'x'
MariaDB [(none)]> DROP TABLE information_schema.COLUMNS;
ERROR 1044 (42000): Access denied for user 'root'@'localhost' to database
'information_schema'
MariaDB [(none)]> SHOW WARNINGS \G
*************************** 1. row ***************************
   Level: Error
    Code: 1044
Message: Access denied for user 'root'@'localhost' to database
'information_schema'
1 row in set (0.00 sec)
```

In the preceding example, because DROP TABLE accesses the referred table, the second statement clears the diagnostics area. Thus, SHOW WARNINGS visualizes only the second error.

Consider the following example where we will generate an error and then execute a RESIGNAL statement that generates another error:

```
MariaDB [(none)]> SET sql_mode = 'x';
ERROR 1231 (42000): Variable 'sql_mode' can't be set to the value of 'x'
MariaDB [(none)]> RESIGNAL;
ERROR 1645 (0K000): RESIGNAL when handler not active
MariaDB [(none)]> SHOW WARNINGS \G
*************************** 1. row ***************************
   Level: Error
```

```
   Code: 1231
Message: Variable 'sql_mode' can't be set to the value of 'x'
*************************** 2. row ***************************
   Level: Error
   Code: 1645
Message: RESIGNAL when handler not active
2 rows in set (0.00 sec)
```

In the preceding example, since a correctly parsed RESIGNAL statement never clears the diagnostics area, SHOW WARNINGS returns both the errors. Consider the following example, where we will generate an error, and then we will execute a correct statement that reads a table:

```
MariaDB [(none)]> SET sql_mode = 'x';
ERROR 1231 (42000): Variable 'sql_mode' can't be set to the value of 'x'
MariaDB [(none)]> SELECT COUNT(*) FROM mysql.user \G
*************************** 1. row ***************************
COUNT(*): 11
1 row in set (0.00 sec)
MariaDB [(none)]> SHOW WARNINGS \G
Empty set (0.00 sec)
```

In the preceding example, even if the second statement does not produce any warning, the diagnostics area is emptied.

The GET DIAGNOSTICS statement

The GET DIAGNOSTICS statement is a good way to show the structure of the diagnostics area because it can copy each value into a variable.

It has a verbose and an error-prone syntax, but it is the only way to analyze the diagnostics area within a stored program. In fact, SHOW WARNINGS returns a result set to the client but does not allow the SQL code to access it. The HANDLER block is executed when an exact error or a class of errors occurs, but it does not provide information about the problem. The reader is expected to be familiar with the stored programs. However, some examples of the use of GET DIAGNOSTICS are useful to demonstrate the contents of the diagnostics area.

First, let's populate the diagnostics area with two errors. For this, we will use the same statements of the previous example:

```
MariaDB [(none)]> SET sql_mode = 'x';
ERROR 1231 (42000): Variable 'sql_mode' can't be set to the value of 'x'
MariaDB [(none)]> RESIGNAL;
ERROR 1645 (0K000): RESIGNAL when handler not active
```

Now, let's use GET DIAGNOSTICS to copy the number of conditions in the diagnostics area into a variable, and SELECT to show these values. Consider the following example:

```
MariaDB [(none)]> GET DIAGNOSTICS @num_errs = NUMBER;
Query OK, 0 rows affected (0.00 sec)
MariaDB [(none)]> SELECT @num_errs;
+-----------+
| @num_errs |
+-----------+
|         2 |
+-----------+
1 row in set (0.00 sec)
```

Now, we know that there are two conditions. Let's visualize the SQLSTATE value, the condition number, and the message of the two conditions, as shown in the following code:

```
MariaDB [(none)]> GET DIAGNOSTICS CONDITION 1 @sqlstate =
RETURNED_SQLSTATE, @errno = MYSQL_ERRNO, @error = MESSAGE_TEXT;
Query OK, 0 rows affected (0.00 sec)
MariaDB [(none)]> SELECT @sqlstate, @errno, @error;
+-----------+--------+----------------------------------------------------
---+
| @sqlstate | @errno | @error
|
+-----------+--------+----------------------------------------------------
---+
| 42000     |   1231 | Variable 'sql_mode' can't be set to the value of
'x' |
+-----------+--------+----------------------------------------------------
---+
1 row in set (0.00 sec)
```

The error log

The error log contains information about a server's startup and shutdown as well as any critical errors that the server encounters. This includes problems that stop the server or prevent a plugin from starting as well as data corruptions. The log can be enabled or disabled.

 The error log is a file and is located in the data directory by default. Its default name is the server's hostname with the .err extension. Using the default name may not be a good idea in a replication environment as all servers have different hostnames, and the administrator may prefer to have identical names for all log files.

On Windows, the error log is enabled by default. If it is explicitly disabled, the errors can be shown on the console using the --console option. Note that this does not work if the --log-error option is present.

 On Linux and Unix systems, the error log is disabled by default. In this case, the errors are written on stderr unless the output is redirected to another file.

On all systems, --log-error explicitly enables the log. It is possible to specify a filename and a path (optionally) using the --log-error=filename syntax. If only a filename is specified, without a path, the error log is placed in the data directory.

If a file is used, the path and name of the file can also be read from the log_error server variable, which is a read-only variable.

 The error log can be disabled on Windows using the console option, but it cannot be disabled on Linux. If a configuration file used by several servers enables the error log, the log files used by an individual server cannot disable it. A trick to do this is specifying the /dev/null special file as an error log, and all writes will simply be suppressed.

If the log_warnings dynamic variable is greater than 0, warnings are logged in to the error log. If the value is greater than 1, all connection errors are logged.

The error log format

The error log file contains a row for each entry. When the server starts, an empty line is left after the last shutdown message.

Let's see a sample entry and analyze its format:

```
131231 17:17:38 [ERROR] Event Scheduler: [root@localhost]
[dataset1.populate_t01] Table 'dataset1.t01' doesn't exist
```

The first data we see in the preceding example is the date when the error occurred. It is written in the **YYMMDD** format. After a space, the time is written in a human-readable format.

Then, there is the entry type. The `[Note]`, `[Warning]`, and `[ERROR]` values have the same meaning just like they do in the `Level` column of `SHOW WARNINGS`. An additional value is `mysqld_safe`, which means the entry has been recorded by the `mysqld_safe` script. Such rows inform us about server startups and automatic restarts.

Some informative rows do not follow this format because it is not necessary. This happens on startup and after a crash. Such information is never written in the system table.

On some systems, the error log file also includes a stack trace after an abnormal shutdown. This can be used for server debugging.

A troubleshooting example with the error log

Suppose that your MariaDB server, on a Linux system, does not start. The first thing to do is to check the error log. Of course, the error must be in the last part of the log. You also know that a fatal error should contain the `[ERROR]` label.

You can start searching for that label in the final 10 lines of the error log from the command line. You need two Linux utilities: `tail`, which returns the last lines of a file; and `grep`, which returns lines that match a given regular expression. On a typical configuration, you also need `sudo` to gain the permissions to access the file. These programs are all part of the GNU project. All Unix systems have similar tools. On Windows, open source ports of these tools can be installed separately. The most widely used tool is called **Cygwin** and is available at `www.cygwin.com`.

Let's execute the proper command, shown as follows:

```
federico@this:~$ sudo tail -20 /usr/local/mysql/data/this.err | grep
ERROR

140101 18:11:21 [ERROR] /usr/local/mysql/bin/mysqld: unknown variable
'base_dir=/usr/local/mysql'

140101 18:11:21 [ERROR] Aborting
```

The first returned line tells you the exact problem—you set an invalid option in a configuration file (the exact typing is `basedir`, not `base_dir`). The second line just informs you about the server shutdown, but you already know that. All you have to do is open the file with an editor and fix the problem.

The problem was simple. However, this example shows the procedure to find the problem that you need to solve.

System logs

If `mysqld_safe` is invoked with the `--syslog` option, the errors are also logged in the **system log** (**syslog**). This feature works only if the system has the logger program, which is usually present on Linux systems, and in such cases, the **daemon** facility is used. By default, each syslog entry has a `mysqld` or `mysqld_safe` tag, depending on the program that generated its entry. If multiple instances of MariaDB (or MySQL) are running on the same system, it is advisable to add a different suffix for each instance to find out which particular instance logged a particular error. To do this, you can start `mysqld_safe` with the `--syslog-tag` option, as shown in the following example:

```
mysqld_safe --syslog --syslog-tag=serv1
```

In this case, the errors will be logged in the syslog, and the tags will be `mysqld-serv1` and `mysqld_safe-serv1`. However, this option is usually set in the `my.cnf` file in the server's directory. In this case, the `syslog` and `syslog_tag` options must be written in the `[mysqld_safe]` options group, as shown in the following example:

```
[mysqld_safe]
syslog
syslog_tag=maria10
```

On Windows, there is no syslog, but errors are always recorded in the **Windows Event Log** in the Application log. This cannot be avoided. The source of entries is the name of the service or MySQL. Warnings, notes, and informational entries that do not follow the standard format are logged as informational messages.

The general query log

All statements sent to MariaDB are logged in the general query log or general log. They are written in the same order they were received. This order is never identical to the order of execution on multithread environments (because statements often need to wait for a lock to be released). Connections and disconnections are also written to the general log.

The general log is often suitable for finding problems that are caused by the application's bugs.

The general query log depends on the **binary log** format. This log will be described in *Chapter 8, Backup and Disaster Recovery*. While the general log is designed to be read by humans, the binary log is read by programs. A human can read its contents using the **mysqlbinlog** tool. This tool tracks the changes to databases and does this in different formats such as STATEMENT (SQL statements are logged), ROW (binary data is logged), or MIXED (both methods can be used). The reason for this will be clear in the later chapters, but it is important to remember that the general log only works properly if the binary log uses the STATEMENT format. If the MIXED format is used, some statements will not be logged.

The general log can be enabled with the `--general_log` startup option and disabled with `--general_log=0`. By default, it is disabled. It can also be enabled or disabled at runtime using the `general_log` dynamic system variable.

If the general log is enabled, by default it is written to a file. The default filename is the server's hostname with a `.log` extension. The default path for that file is the data directory. So, specify a different filename, and optionally a different path, to use the `--general_log_file=filename` option. In a replication environment, assigning identical names to log files for all servers is good practice.

The `--log-output` option determines the destination of both the error log and the general query log (which will be discussed later in this chapter). Note that this variable affects both these logs. It has three allowed values that can be combined in a variety of ways. The values are FILE (the logs are recorded into files), TABLE (the logs are written into a table in the MySQL database), and NONE (logging is suppressed). To log the errors in both a file and a system table, the syntax is as follows:

```
--log_output=FILE,TABLE
```

If NONE is specified, other values are ignored.

A system variable called `log_output` also exists. It is dynamic, which means that the destination of the error log and the general query log can be changed at runtime. It only exists at the global level, so it is not possible to change the destination of the log for the current session only.

Sometimes, a **superuser** may want to disable the logging of his/her queries. The most common reason to do this is to change a password (having a clearly written password in a text file or a table makes it less secure). However, whatever the reason, users with the SUPER privilege can disable the general query log and the slow query log for the current session by setting the sql_log_off server system variable to 1, shown as follows:

```
SET @@session.sql_log_off = 1;
```

This variable exists at both the session and global levels, so it can also be used to temporarily disable logging of all the queries, if it is necessary for some reason.

The file format of the general query log

The general query log starts with three lines shown as follows:

```
/usr/local/mysql/bin/mysqld, Version: 10.0.7-MariaDB-log
(MariaDB Server). started with:
Tcp port: 0  Unix socket: (null)
Time                Id Command     Argument
```

After general information about the server, you see the headers for four columns. The contents of the following lines are aligned with these headers.

These lines are rewritten at each server restart and each time the logs are flushed. (**Logs' flushing** is explained later in this chapter.)

The following is a sample entry:

```
140103 18:14:47      4  Query    SHOW TABLES
```

The Time column contains a date, in the **YYMMDD** format, and a time, in the **HH:MM:SS** human-readable format. In some cases, these values can be missing.

The Id column contains the connection's ID. This is the same value used in several information_schema and performance_schema tables and returned by the CONNECTION_ID() function.

The Command argument indicates what kind of action the user performed. Possible values are: Connect, Init DB, Query, and Quit.

The contents of the Argument column depend on the value of Command. In the previous example, since the user sent a statement, the Argument column contains the text of such a statement.

Let's see another example shown as follows:

```
140103 18:14:31          4 Connect   root@localhost as anonymous on
```

In the preceding statement, the Connect value means that a connection is established. The Argument value indicates the account used.

Consider the following statement:

```
140103 18:14:42        4 Init DB      test
```

In the preceding statement, the Init DB value means that the user selected a default database (typically via the USE statement). The Argument indicates the name of the selected database.

Consider the following statement:

```
140103 18:14:57        4 Quit
```

In the preceding statement, the Quit value means that the user closed the connection. If a Quit action has not been performed by a connection, it could mean the connection is still open, or another thread killed the connection.

The general_log table

As explained previously, the general query log can be written in the form of a table called general_log in the MySQL database. Its columns are as follows:

- event_time: This column refers to the Time column in the file
- user_host: This column contains the account that executed a statement
- thread_id: This column refers to the Id column in the file
- server_id: This column contains the ID of the server needed to set up the replication
- command_type: This column refers to the Command column in the file
- argument: This column refers to the Argument column in the file

A sample row from the table is shown as follows:

```
MariaDB [mysql]> SELECT * FROM general_log ORDER BY event_time
DESC LIMIT 1 \G
*************************** 1. row ***************************
  event_time: 2014-06-17 08:34:25.864270
   user_host: root[root] @ localhost []
   thread_id: 4
   server_id: 1
command_type: Query
    argument: SET @@session.sql_log_off = 1
1 row in set (0.01 sec)
```

The preceding example from the table has the following characteristics that also apply to the `slow_log` table.

The log tables have several restrictions. The most important restriction is that these tables cannot be modified by the user because DML statements that involve log tables produce an error. Only a few operations are allowed. Also, such tables cannot be locked by the user. A `FLUSH TABLES WITH READ LOCK` option can be safely used to lock all other tables. A `LOCK TABLES` option on those tables will produce an error.

The `general_log` table is a CSV table (that stands for comma separated values). This table allows users to open the data file (`general_log.CSV` present in the `data` directory) with external programs because CSV is a widely supported format. However, this slows down SQL queries because CSV tables do not support indexes.

It is possible to convert the table to the **MyISAM** format. This will be faster, but still sensibly slower than file-based logging. No other storage engine can be used for this table. Note that before you change the storage engine, it is necessary to disable the log. The following code can be used for this purpose:

```
MariaDB [(none)]> SET GLOBAL general_log = 0;
Query OK, 0 rows affected (0.06 sec)
MariaDB [(none)]> ALTER TABLE mysql.general_log ENGINE = MyISAM;
Query OK, 12 rows affected (0.28 sec)
Records: 12  Duplicates: 0  Warnings: 0
MariaDB [(none)]> SET GLOBAL general_log = 1;
Query OK, 0 rows affected (0.00 sec)
```

Log tables can periodically be emptied with the `TRUNCATE TABLE` command if you do not care about the entry of the old log. However, since DML statements are not supported, there is no way to delete only a portion of the rows from the table. Thus, usually, a better way to prevent the log tables from growing too much is to rotate them. This operation is easy and relatively fast because the `RENAME TABLE` command is supported. All these operations require that the general log be temporarily disabled, as shown in the previous example. After you rename a log table, it doesn't have the restrictions of a log table anymore.

The `CHECK TABLE`, `OPTIMIZE TABLE`, and `REPAIR TABLE` commands are also supported. Since a repair operation can be slow, if a table is damaged, it would be a good idea to rename it and create a new one, before you start the recovery. In this way, queries will still be logged to the process.

Since the ALTER TABLE command works (with the general log disabled), it is possible to add one or more indexes to a table, after converting it to MyISAM. This will make the SELECT operations much faster. However, this will also slow down insertions, which can be a major problem. However, if you rotate the general log tables, you may choose to add indexes to the historical tables. Depending on the size of the new historical table, this operation might be very slow, and the required space might be a problem for us. However, the queries will also be much faster.

Debugging examples with the general query log

The following two examples use SQL tables to show the cross-platform code that can be executed within MariaDB. This does not mean that tables are the best way to store logs. The default destination is FILE, and each DBA will decide whether changing the default destination makes sense for this particular case. As discussed previously, *The error log* section shows how to investigate a log file using a Linux command line.

As a first example, let's suppose you just realized that someone dropped a table named orders history, which was still in use. You also know that this deletion happened no more than one week ago. The first thing to do is to restore the table, and *Chapter 8, Backup and Disaster Recovery*, shows you how to do this. However, the table could be dropped again, and you don't want this to happen. There is probably a permissions problem or a bug in the application. To find out the exact problem, you need to know who dropped the table, and probably when this was done. The SQL table to do this is quite simple, as shown in the following code snippet:

```
SELECT user_host, event_time, argument
    FROM mysql.general_log
    WHERE
        event_time >= NOW() - INTERVAL 1 WEEK
        AND command_type = 'Query'
        AND argument LIKE '%drop%table%orders\_history%'
    ORDER BY event_time DESC
    LIMIT 20;
```

In the previous code snippet, the first condition specifies that event_time must not be older than one week. The second condition does not add anything (as the third condition will be sufficient), except that it should filter out many records in a fast way. The third condition is the most interesting. You do not know the exact string that was received by the server; for example, it could contain spaces, or the database name, or back ticks around the table name. With the % sign, this is not a problem—each query that contains the tree terms you indicated is returned. Also, note that LIKE is case insensitive.

You could obtain a lot of results and, theoretically, it would be weird but still possible. For this reason, you need to order the results: the last row is the statement that most recently dropped the table. And, while you may be interested in seeing who executed similar statements and when, we will limit the results to 20 rows.

The second example follows up the first one: we found that the connection with the ID 100 executed the DROP TABLE statement this morning. Now we want to know why it did this. Probably, the connection also executed other statements, and so, we want to know its history. There are other cases when you may want to know a connection's history. For example, sometimes it may be the easiest way to debug a web application that has a bug in its SQL statements. In any case, getting the log records that involve that ID is quite easy, shown as follows:

```
SELECT event_time, command_type, argument
    FROM mysql.general_log
    WHERE thread_id = 100
    AND event_time > NOW() - INTERVAL 1 DAY
    ORDER BY event_time \G
```

These are the general log's most commonly used use cases. Of course, since they provide detailed information that can be read in a flexible way, many other use cases are possible. For example, all clients should close their connections with the MariaDB server as soon as they are no longer needed, in order to free memory. However, the problem here is MariaDB maintains some per-thread buffers and the temporary MEMORY tables until a connection is closed. Having multiple open connections can be a waste of memory. The general log can be used to see which connection did not issue a Quit command, that is, to determine those clients who did not close the connection properly. Note that if a connection is now closed, but it never executed a Quit command, then it probably has been terminated by the root user with the KILL statement. However, usually most of these connections expire because they exceed the timeout that has been set (using the @wait_timeout server variable). In other words, the application that created them did not close them, so they have been inactive for a longer period of time, wasting some memory. For example, the execution of the following query will be slow:

```
CREATE TABLE tmp.g_log ENGINE = MEMORY
    SELECT thread_id, command_type, COUNT(*)
        FROM mysql.general_log
        WHERE event_time > NOW() - INTERVAL 1 DAY
        AND command_type IN ('Connect', 'Quit')
        GROUP BY thread_id, command_type
        ORDER BY thread_id, command_type;
```

The result of this query is used to create a new table. The execution will be faster if you create indexes for the table; however, you only need to query it twice, so it would be a waste of time in this case. When querying such tables, you will obtain an output shown as follows:

```
+-----------+--------------+----------+
| thread_id | command_type | COUNT(*) |
+-----------+--------------+----------+
|        10 | Connect      |        1 |
|        10 | Quit         |        1 |
|        11 | Connect      |        1 |
|        12 | Connect      |        1 |
|        13 | Connect      |        1 |
|        13 | Quit         |        1 |
|        14 | Connect      |        1 |
|        14 | Quit         |        1 |
|        15 | Connect      |        1 |
|        15 | Quit         |        1 |
+-----------+--------------+----------+
23 rows in set (0.01 sec)
```

This output is very easy to inspect. The rows are sorted by thread_id; if a Quit command is missing for a certain thread_id, or if it has a lower COUNT(*) than the matching Connect command, then that thread has not been properly closed. Unless the server is restarted, the thread IDs are hardly reused within the same day, so you can expect the value to be 1 or to be missing. In the previous example, the 11 and 12 threads IDs never issued a Quit command. So, we want to know who these threads belonged to.

The following query returns the accounts used by these threads:

```
SELECT m.thread_id, m.user_host
    FROM mysql.general_log m LEFT JOIN tmp.g_log g
    ON m.thread_id = g.thread_id
    AND g.command_type = 'Quit'
    WHERE m.event_time > NOW() - INTERVAL 1 HOUR
    AND g.thread_id IS NULL;
```

In the previous example, the JOIN command returns the rows in the general log that do not have a matching Quit row in the tmp.g_log table we previously created. The time limit here is very important because you do not want to use rows that have been written before the last server restart. For each row we obtain, we see the used account:

```
+-----------+-------------------------------+
| thread_id | user_host                     |
+-----------+-------------------------------+
|        11 | [arancia] @ localhost []      |
|        12 | [arancia] @ localhost []      |
+-----------+-------------------------------+
```

Now, you know which user has not closed his connections. If it is used by an application, you can ask its developers to fix the problem.

Maintenance of the server logs

All server logs require some maintenance. We will start with the FLUSH statements, which can be used occasionally, to ensure that the last information is written to the files. Then, we will discuss how to rotate both the file- and table-based logs to the free space available on the disk.

Flushing logs

After performing certain operations, or before performing a backup, you may want to flush the contents in the logs. Flushing a log means that its files are closed and reopened, and all the buffered information is written to the file during the process. For file-based logs, the FLUSH LOGS statement can be used. To flush all logs, simply run the following command:

```
FLUSH LOGS;
```

The following flavors are available to selectively flush only one log:

```
FLUSH ERROR LOGS; -- error log
FLUSH GENERAL LOGS; -- general query log
FLUSH SLOW LOGS; -- slow query log
FLUSH BINARY LOGS; -- binary log
FLUSH ENGINE LOGS; -- storage engines logs
FLUSH RELAY LOGS; -- replication slaves log
```

By default, these statements are replicated by the slaves, if any. To execute them only on the masters, the LOCAL keyword (or NO_WRITE_TO_BINLOG, which is a synonym) can be used, as shown in the following code snippet:

```
FLUSH NO_WRITE_TO_BINLOG LOGS;
FLUSH LOCAL ERROR LOGS;
```

Note that this has no effect on the general_log and slow_log tables, if they exist. The flushing of all tables can be done using the FLUSH TABLES command, which closes the data files and reopens them. This forces the cached changes to be applied to the files. However, there is no way to specifically flush only the logs or the tables—all tables in all databases will be flushed, as shown in the following code snippets:

```
FLUSH TABLES;
FLUSH LOCAL TABLES;
```

The mysqladmin utility can also be used to flush logs or tables, shown as follows:

```
mysqladmin flush-logs
mysqladmin flush-tables
```

Rotating the file-based logs

MariaDB does not automatically rotate the logs.

The only exception is the binary log, which rotates when it reaches a certain size. Also, when the binary log is flushed, a new file is created automatically. The binary log rotation will be discussed in *Chapter 8, Backup and Disaster Recovery*.

The rotation of all other logs must be implemented by the user, which can be done by renaming the current file periodically or when the files reach a certain size. Red Hat Enterprise Linux and the derived Linux distributions provide a tool that can be used to perform the rotation automatically.

Let's see an example of how to rename the general log files from a Linux shell.

First, you may want to obtain a list of the error files, their size, and some more related data. Suppose that the current file is called maria.log.01, and the older files have different numeric suffixes (such as 02 and 03), shown as follows:

```
root@this:/usr/local/mysql/data# ls | grep "maria\.log\."
maria.log.01
maria.log.02
maria.log.03
```

This means that one of the MariaDB configuration files contains the following options:

```
general_log=1
general_log_file="query"
```

Now, you want to rename the files. If the server is running, first you need to disable the general log using the following SQL statement:

```
MariaDB [(none)]> SET GLOBAL general_log = 0;
Query OK, 0 rows affected (0.07 sec)
```

You can delete the last file and rename the other files, shown as follows:

```
root@this:/usr/local/mysql/data# rm maria.log.03
root@this:/usr/local/mysql/data# mv maria.log.02 maria.log.03
root@this:/usr/local/mysql/data# mv maria.log.01 maria.log.02
```

To re-enable the general query log, use the command shown as follows:

```
MariaDB [(none)]> SET GLOBAL general_log = 1;
Query OK, 0 rows affected (0.00 sec)
```

Now let's flush the logs as follows:

```
root@this:/usr/local/mysql/data# ../bin/mysqladmin flush-logs -uroot -p
```

Since the `maria.log.01` file does not exist anymore, the server recreates this file. In order to be sure, let's check whether everything worked fine using the following command:

```
root@this:/usr/local/mysql/data# ls | grep "maria\.log\."
maria.log.01
maria.log.02
maria.log.03
```

In Windows, the command to delete a file is `del`, the command to rename a file is `rename`, and the command to get a list of files is `dir`. So, the correct sequence of the commands to be used is shown as follows:

```
del maria.log.03
rename maria.log.02 maria.log.03
rename maria.log.01 maria.log.02
dir maria.log.*
```

Of course, we will never do this manually on a production server. Instead, you need a well-tested script that does this automatically.

The Red Hat Linux distribution has a script that does this. It is called `mysql-log-rotate`.

Rotating the table-based logs

As mentioned in the previous section, it is possible to rotate a table-based general query log, as well as a table-based slow query log. In order to do this, we will create a stored procedure. This procedure can be called by an event, which is described at the end of this section.

Let's look at the following code and discuss how it works:

```
CREATE PROCEDURE '_'.'rotate_general_log'()
BEGIN
    DECLARE old_general_log TINYINT DEFAULT @@global.general_log;
    SET @@global.general_log = 0;
    DROP TABLE 'mysql'.'general_log03';
    RENAME TABLE
        'mysql'.'general_log02' TO 'mysql'.'general_log03',
        'mysql'.'general_log' TO 'mysql'.'general_log02';
    CREATE TABLE 'mysql'.'general_log' LIKE 'mysql'.'general_log02';
    SET @@global.general_log = old_general_log;
END;
```

Since all procedures must belong to a database, we have a commodity database called '_' for general purpose routines. A short name allows you to call the procedure quickly from the command line.

The first action the event takes is to delete the oldest log table. Then, with a `RENAME TABLE` statement, log tables are renamed: `general_log` becomes `general_log02` and `general_log02` becomes `general_log03`. The `RENAME TABLE` statement is always an atomic operation, and so, if one renaming fails, all rename operations will fail. In this case, the procedure will recreate the `general_log` table using the same definition as `general_log02`.

The `general_log` table is disabled at the beginning of this procedure. However, it is possible that it was already disabled, so the value of the `general_log` variable is copied to a temporary variable and is restored at the end of the procedure.

This procedure is just a very basic example. A good procedure is beyond the purpose of this book. However, it should be flexible and error-proof. To improve it, the reader could implement the following ideas:

- The number of archived logs should not be fixed: it should be read from a table. So, the RENAME TABLE statement should not be hardcoded, but it should be composed in a string and executed as a prepared statement (this technique can be tricky, but it is very common in prepared statements, because SQL is not flexible).

- Each part of the statement (the old_name TO new_name parts) should be added only if the source table really exists. While we could see no reason why it could be erased, we must remember that, if it is not found, the whole rotation operation will fail. Of course, in this case an IF EXISTS clause should be added to DROP TABLE.

- You could return a result set that tells the user whether the operation was successful, though this would lead to an error if the procedure is called within an event (because events cannot return a result set); so, you may want to record this information to a table.

Writing this code as a procedure is useful for at least two reasons: it is easier to debug and it can be called manually at any time. However, you also want the rotation to happen at regular time intervals, and so you need to write an event that calls the routine, shown as follows:

```
CREATE EVENT 'event_db'.'rotate_general_log'
    ON SCHEDULE
        EVERY 1 WEEK
        STARTS '2014-01-05 00:00:00'
    COMMENT 'Rotates general_log'
DO BEGIN
    CALL '_'.'rotate_general_log'();
END;
```

The event should be executed when none of the server's workload is too high. In the previous example, it is activated at midnight, between Sunday and Monday.

The SQL_ERROR_LOG plugin

While the error log stores the SQL errors, it may be useful to keep such errors in a separate log, which will then be used to debug the applications. This can be done via SQL_ERROR_LOG, a plugin introduced in MariaDB 5.5.

The SQL_ERROR_LOG plugin is not installed by default. To install this, you can run the following SQL statement:

```
MariaDB [(none)]> INSTALL SONAME 'sql_errlog';
Query OK, 0 rows affected (0.04 sec)
```

 Note that it is not necessary to reinstall the plugin at every server restart.

MySQL users will probably notice that we used a MariaDB extension to the INSTALL statement. This syntax allows installing all plugins contained in the sql_errlog library, not only a specific plugin. In this case, the library contains only one plugin, so the only advantage is that the command is shorter. However, there is another difference: we did not include the file extension (.so or .dll), because it is optional in MariaDB. This makes the command independent from the system.

If SQL_ERROR_LOG is installed, some server system variables will be available. They can be used to control the behavior of this log. Let's check whether such variables exist using the following code snippet:

```
MariaDB [(none)]> SHOW VARIABLES LIKE 'sql_error_log%';
+-------------------------+----------------+
| Variable_name           | Value          |
+-------------------------+----------------+
| sql_error_log_filename  | sql_errors.log |
| sql_error_log_rate      | 1              |
| sql_error_log_rotate    | OFF            |
| sql_error_log_rotations | 9              |
| sql_error_log_size_limit| 1000000        |
+-------------------------+----------------+
5 rows in set (0.01 sec)
```

If you uninstall the plugin, these variables will disappear.

Let's describe these variables so that you can properly use the plugin:

- sql_error_log_filename: This is the name of the log file, which is located in the data directory. This variable is a read-only variable.

- sql_error_log_rate: This is the number of errors that will occur before all cached errors are written to the log file. The value 1 means that all errors are immediately logged. The value 10 means that the errors are logged after 10 errors occurred. The value 0 disables the log. Incrementing this value is useful to reduce the overhead caused by the disk writes, in case many SQL errors occur in the server.

- `sql_error_log rotate`: This is always OFF. Setting this variable to ON (or any other permitted value) forces a log rotation.

- `sql_error_log_rotations`: This is the number of old files that are kept after rotations. The value 9 means that nine old files are placed after rotations. This variable is a read-only variable.

- `sql_error_log_size_limit`: This is the maximum size (in bytes) of the log file. After this size has been reached, the log files are rotated. This variable is a read-only variable.

Rotation happens when the value in `sql_error_log_size_limit` is reached, or the user sets `sql_error_log_rotate`. Old files have the same name as the log file, plus a numeric extension. Let's see a file list, shown as follows:

```
MariaDB [(none)]> \! ls /usr/local/mysql/data | grep errors
sql_errors.log
sql_errors.log.1
sql_errors.log.2
sql_errors.log.3
sql_errors.log.4
sql_errors.log.5
sql_errors.log.6
sql_errors.log.7
sql_errors.log.8
sql_errors.log.9
```

Forcing the rotation can be useful to debug a script or a stored program. This avoids us having to read a large file to find new errors.

Comments are logged with the statements they belong to. However, this is not possible if the client eliminates the comments from statements before sending them to the server to optimize network traffic. The `mysql` command-line client strips them, unless the `--comments` option is specified. Logging comments is useful to make statements easier to search. For example, suppose you are not sure whether a given statement produces an error in some situations. You can add a unique ID to this statement, shown as follows:

```
CALL test.p(5, 0) /* test01 */ ;
```

Then, we will be able to search for the lines that contain the following comment:

```
cat /usr/local/mysql/data/sql_errors.log | grep test01
```

The SQL error log format has been designed to be read by humans, not programs. Here is an example of a typical record:

```
2014-01-09 17:31:07 root[root] @ localhost [] ERROR 1062: Duplicate entry
'1' for key 'a' : INSERT INTO t VALUES (1, 1)
```

In the preceding record, there is a human-readable date and time value, the account that issued the query, the error that occurred, and the statement as it was received. The new line characters and spaces are preserved.

Tips on debugging stored programs

Debugging a stored program can be tricky in MariaDB. There are several reasons. The most obvious is that MariaDB does not have any native debug API. Some debuggers exist, but they use dirty techniques to emulate the debugger process. Some of them parse the stored programs code and transparently add some statements that emulate a checkpoint, or keep track of the call stack, or return information to the debugger. This technique heavily modifies the code, thus it is not always reliable. Other debuggers execute the code internally to be able to implement debugging features. However, they cannot reproduce the exact behavior of MariaDB and MySQL in all circumstances, especially if you consider that several versions exist, and that they necessarily have bugs in both the program and the documentation. Of course, this is true for all existing software, not only for MariaDB!

To debug stored programs, a developer needs to use some tricks, which consist of adding some informational statements in various parts of the stored program's code. When the debug process ends, these informational statements must be deleted or commented for future use.

If the developer just wants to know whether a branch of an `IF` statement is executed, a `SELECT 1;` is enough, like in the following example:

```
IF @a > 1 OR @b IS NOT NULL THEN
    SELECT 1; -- debug code
    ...
END IF;
```

More often, a developer may want to `SELECT` a table row or a variable to check his/her values. Before executing a dynamic prepared statement, checking the text of the statement is often a good idea, as shown in the following example:

```
SET @sql := /* some string expression here */ ;
SELECT @sql; -- debug code
PREPARE stmt FROM @sql;
```

However, debugging based on SELECT statements only works in stored procedures because other stored programs (such as stored functions, triggers, and events) cannot return a result set. In the development stage, it is often a good idea to implement them as a stored procedure.

For events, this is simple: no modifications are needed to turn an event into a procedure. However, events should generally be written in a table whether they succeed or not. This is often important because if they encounter problems, the errors are not returned to a client.

For functions, it is easy. Functions have more limitations than procedures, so it is important to remember that some features cannot be used (for example, prepared statements). The only modification required is that a procedure cannot return a value. So the RETURN statements need to be turned into SELECT statements.

For triggers, the conversion can be hard. This is because triggers can access a table row's values—both OLD values (the values as they were before the statement execution) and the NEW values (the values modified by the statement). Turning the required values into procedure parameters can be a convenient solution in simple cases. However, in complex cases, this is an error-prone technique because the values must be passed manually. A better solution might be using the INSERT statement instead of the SELECT statement. The values will not be returned to the client; they will be written to a debug table. The drawback of this technique is that writing and reading such values will require more code.

Debugging stored programs using the SQL_ERROR_LOG plugin

The SQL_ERROR_LOG plugin is particularly useful to log errors of the stored programs. For example, consider the following procedure:

```
CREATE PROCEDURE backups.backup_table(IN db_name CHAR(64),
IN table_name CHAR(64))
BEGIN
    DECLARE EXIT HANDLER FOR SQLEXCEPTION
    BEGIN END;

    SET @sql = CONCAT('TRUNCATE TABLE backups.', table_name);
    PREPARE stmt FROM @sql;
    EXECUTE stmt;

    SET @sql = CONCAT('INSERT INTO backups.', table_name,
                    'SELECT * FROM ', db_name, '.', table_name);
```

```
    PREPARE stmt FROM @sql;
    EXECUTE stmt;
    DEALLOCATE PREPARE stmt;
    SET @sql = NULL;
END;
```

The preceding procedure is very simple. It just copies a table to a backup database, after deleting the old rows in the backup table. You can think of it as a quick way to run the TRUNCATE TABLE and INSERT ... SELECT statements.

However, many problems may occur. For example, the backup table may not exist yet. Or, the source table may not exist, or its structure may be changed. There may also be privilege problems. If any of these problems (or any other problem) occur, an SQL error is produced. In that case, the execution moves to the DECLARE EXIT HANDLER block, which does nothing, except suppress the error. This block may look useless, and probably it is; however, in real use cases, there are several good reasons why a HANDLER block might be used, and it always suppresses the error (unless a RESIGNAL statement is issued). When debugging a stored program, this means that the error is not sent to the client, and the developer may not notice the error that has occurred.

An empty handler can be useful in a program. It can suppress warnings or errors that are expected and do not cause any problem. The most obvious example is when a stored procedure tries to create tables with the IF NOT EXISTS clause. If tables exist, a note will be issued. However, in most cases, this is not useful or is even annoying and thus, you may want to suppress the note. In case of the EXIT handlers, the execution of the program will still stop. In case of a CONTINUE handler, the execution will continue normally, and the warning or error will simply be ignored. While this could be the desired behavior, it is also a potential source of problems: if we use a generic class such as SQLEXCEPTION, the handler could suppress an error that was not expected, making the debugging harder.

Of course, a quick way to see that an error occurred is using the SHOW WARNINGS statement. But this statement can only work in a stored procedure, not in stored programs that cannot return a result set.

The SQL_ERROR_LOG plugin is generally a better way to see errors. Let's execute the previously discussed procedure:

```
MariaDB [test]> CALL backups.backup_table('shop', 'customer');
Query OK, 0 rows affected (0.62 sec)
```

On executing the procedure, we see that no error is reported but we want to check whether an error has occurred. If we take a look at the last lines of the SQL error log, we can find one of the following entries depending on the error that occurred:

- If the backup table still does not exist:

```
2014-01-10 12:26:43 root[root] @ localhost [] ERROR 1146: Table
'backups.customer' doesn't exist : TRUNCATE TABLE backups.customer
```

- If the source table's structure is changed:

```
2014-01-10 13:12:06 root[root] @ localhost [] ERROR 1146: Table
'shop.customer' doesn't exist : INSERT INTO backups.customer
SELECT * FROM shop.customer
```

- If the source table has been dropped:

```
2014-01-10 13:09:13 root[root] @ localhost [] ERROR 1136: Column
count doesn't match value count at row 1 : INSERT INTO backups.
customer SELECT * FROM shop.customer
```

If everything worked fine, of course, we will see no errors.

Summary

This chapter focused on logging, finding, and understanding the errors that occur in a MariaDB installation.

We analyzed the information available in a single error condition. These conditions populate the diagnostics area. We discussed how the diagnostics area is populated or emptied by the statements we execute. We also discussed and tried the SQL statements that show information from the diagnostics area: SHOW WARNINGS, SHOW ERRORS, and GET DIAGNOSTICS. The SQL errors are also logged in a file if the SQL_ERROR_LOG plugin is enabled. We learned how to use that plugin efficiently. Some further notes were dedicated to the debugging of stored programs, which is often a difficult task.

The general query log is also useful to debug applications or find problematic statements. While it does not contain information about errors which occurred, it keeps a track of all the statements that were sent to the server. This log can be written to a file or to a SQL table called general_log.

SQL errors are not the only type of errors that can occur. The error log contains other types of errors, including the ones that prevent the server from starting, or a plugin from loading, or the data corruption problems. This log is always written to a file.

We also discussed the format of both the error log and the general query log. We discussed some simple examples, where we used the Linux command line to find the log entries we needed. We also learned how to rotate the logs, and to prevent individual files from growing too much.

We did not analyze all MariaDB logs, still. However, with this information, we have the necessary knowledge to find the problems that may occur while using the advanced MariaDB techniques that are discussed in the following chapters.

In the next chapter, we will learn how to use the slow query log to find slow SQL statements, and how to optimize queries to make them faster.

3
Optimizing Queries

This chapter explains the basics of how to improve the performance of the queries that are executed on a MariaDB server. First, the important tools required to find slow queries are described. Once we find such queries, we will need to find out why they are slow. Thus, a description of how MariaDB uses indexes follows. Then, we will discuss the EXPLAIN command, which shows how MariaDB executes a query. Contextually, we will also discuss the main execution strategy.

The topics covered in this chapter are:

- The slow query log
- The pt-query-digest command from Percona Toolkit
- Indexes
- Table statistics
- The EXPLAIN statement
- Important MariaDB optimizations

The slow query log

The slow query log (or simply slow log) stores SQL statements that take too long to execute. To enable it, the slow_query_log variable or the --slow-query-log startup option can be set to 1. To explicitly disable the log, the --slow-query-log startup option must be set to 0. Without passing any arguments, the --slow-query-log startup option enables this log. As the slow_query_log variable is dynamic, the slow query log can be enabled or disabled at runtime.

The default filename of the slow query log is the server's hostname followed by the -slow.log suffix.

Just like the general query log, the slow query log can be a file, table, or both. The log output server variable can be used to specify if the log is a table or file. The allowed values to be set are FILE, TABLE, and NONE (which disables both the slow query log and the general query log). A combination of these values (separated by a comma) is allowed. The NONE value overrides other values.

For example, if the hostname is hal, hal-slow.log will be the default name for the slow query log. A different name can be specified using the slow_query_log_file server variable, or using the --slow-query-file option. In a replication environment, using the same file name for all logs is a good practice, because it may be necessary to execute the same scripts on all the servers.

If the slow query log is written into a table, the table is called slow_log and it can be found in the mysql database. In *The general query log* section in *Chapter 2, Debugging*, we have described in detail what can or cannot be done with the general_log table. These sections also apply to the slow_log table. As explained previously, in the slow query log we can find the queries that were executed too slowly. But what does this depend on? This depends on our workload, of course. For this reason, the rules that determine what queries are written in the slow query log depend on some of the server's system variables.

First, we may want to log queries that do not use indexes at all. To do this, we can set the log_queries_not_using_indexes variable (or the --log-queries-not-using-indexes startup option) to 1, as its default value is 0. This variable is dynamic, but only exists at the global level.

Even if a query uses indexes, we may want to log it if it exceeds a time-out. This can be done via the long_query_time variable, or the --long_query_time startup option. If the value is 0, there is no time-out and the slow queries are not logged. This value is expressed in seconds. Decimal values are allowed with a precision of microseconds (up to six decimal digits); however, for table-based logs, the decimal part is ignored. The query execution time is counted from the time the thread acquires the necessary locks. This means that, if a query takes too much time just because it is blocked by a slow query, it is not logged. This variable is dynamic and exists at both the global and session levels. This allows connections that execute more complex queries to set a greater time-out.

A query can also have other problems that we may want to log. The classes of problems that must be logged are listed in the log_slow_filter variable, separated by a comma. The allowed values are described as follows:

- full_scan: This value means that the query has performed a full table scan (same as log_queries_not_using_indexes)
- full_join: This value means that the query performed a join operation, which does not use indexes

- `filesort`: This value means that the query performed a sorting operation, which requires an internal, temporary in-memory table

- `filesort_on_disk`: This value means that the query performed a sorting operation, which requires a temporary on-disk file

- `tmp_table`: This value means that the query created an implicit temporary table

- `tmp_table_on_disk`: This value means that the query created an implicit temporary table written on the disk

- `query_cache_miss`: This value means that a query search was performed but the query was not found in the query cache

By default, the `log_slow_filter` variable contains all these values. It is dynamic and exists at both the session and global levels.

Even if a query matches the criteria defined by the `log_queries_not_using_indexes` and `long_query_time` system variables, the `min_examined_row_limit` variable can prevent it from being logged. Queries that examined fewer than the described number of rows are never written into the slow query log. A value of `0` allows all queries to be logged. The maximum value is platform-dependent, but is always very high. This variable is dynamic and exists at both the global and session levels. This setting is usually useful because, if a query examines only a few rows, it would not benefit from the use of an index in any case (and the optimizer takes this into account). If the query exceeds the time-out, it is still possible that it does not examine many rows, for example, if the query requires complex ordering or grouping operations, or if it calls slow functions (including stored functions).

Sometimes, logging all the queries that do not use indexes can be a heavy task for a busy server. For this reason, it is possible to limit the logging of such queries using the `log_throttle_queries_not_using_indexes` system variable. If the value of the system variable is `0` (the default), there is no limit. If its value is higher than `0`, it will determine the number of queries that do not use indexes and that can be logged in a minute. When this limit is reached, further queries will not be logged. A minute after the last query that does not use indexes is logged, a summary of the suppressed queries is written into the log.

By default, administrative queries (such as CHECK TABLE or ANALYZE TABLE) are not written to the slow query log. To change this behavior, the `log_slow_admin_statements` variable can be set to `1`. This variable is dynamic, but only exists at the global level.

In a replication environment, usually, slaves do not log replicated slow queries, because such queries can be found in the master's slow query log. Normally, a slow query is logged only if it was directly sent to the slave. However, this behavior can be changed by setting the `log_slow_slave_statements` variable to 1. This variable is dynamic, but only exists at the global level. If the workload on the master is heavy and the workload on the slaves is light, using the slow query log on a slave instead of the master could be an optimization. Of course, it will still be necessary to explicitly enable the slow query on a slave and disable it on the master.

To produce a less verbose slow query logfile, the `--log-short-format` startup option can be used. In the configuration files, it can be specified as `log-short-format`. This option also affects the binary log.

The counterpart of the `--log-short-format` startup option is `log_slow_verbosity`, which can be used to add information to the slow query logfile. It is a comma-separated list of values, where each value adds some information. The allowed values are described as follows:

- `microtime`: This value means that the variable uses microtime precision
- `query_plan`: This value means that the variable logs information about the query execution plan
- `innodb`: This value means that the variable logs the InnoDB statistics
- `profiling`: This value means that the variable enables query profiling
- `profiling_use_getrusage`: This value means that the variable logs the results of the `getrusage` function
- `explain`: This value means that the variable prints the output of the EXPLAIN statement (discussed in the next section)

To enable `profiling` and `profiling_use_getrusage`, it is necessary to use XtraDB. The default value is `'query_plan'`. Both `log_short_format` and `log_slow_verbosity` affect the file-based slow query log but not the table.

To summarize, the following variables determine the queries that should be written in the slow query log:

- `log_queries_not_using_indexes`
- `log_throttle_queries_not_using_indexes`
- `long_query_time`
- `log_slow_filter`

The following variables can filter out the variables that match the previous criteria:

- `min_examined_row_limit`
- `log_slow_admin_statements`

The following variables determine what information is logged (and the overhead caused by the slow query log):

- `log-short-format`
- `log_slow_verbosity`

Queries that examine tables with no rows or a single row are always excluded from the slow query log.

The file format of the slow query log

When the server starts, lines similar to the following command are written into the slow query log:

```
/usr/local/mysql/bin/mysqld, Version: 10.0.7-MariaDB-log (MariaDB
Server). started with:
Tcp port: 0  Unix socket: (null)
Time                   Id Command     Argument.
```

Now, let's see an entry made into a slow query log. The following example shows how a query is written in the slow query log, with a default configuration:

```
# Time: 140116 11:19:05
# User@Host: root[root] @ localhost []
# Thread_id: 4  Schema: test  QC_hit: No
# Query_time: 0.059419  Lock_time: 0.000340  Rows_sent: 1  Rows_examined:
66620
SET timestamp=1389867545;
SELECT COUNT(*) FROM t
 WHERE a > b;
```

The commented lines provide general information about the cost of the query, discussed as follows:

- `Time`: This is the date and time the query execution was started. It follows the same format used by the logs, as we have already discussed, with a human-readable time.
- `User@Host`: This is the account that executed the query.

- `Thread_id`: This is the ID of the connection, and is the same value that is displayed in the `information_schema` and `performance_schema` tables, or returned by the `CONNECTION_ID()` function. On the same line, we also see `Schema`, which is the default database that was selected (as a result of the `USE` statement). It is written even if the default database is not used by the query.

- `QC_hit`: This informs us if the query is found in the query cache.

The last commented line is the most important. The `Query_time` value is the execution time in seconds. If the slow query log is written to a file, the `Query_time` value is a floating point number with a microsecond precision. If the log is written to a table, this value is an integer. The `Lock_time` value is the amount of time that the query had to wait before relevant locks were released by other sessions. If a statement takes a lot of time because of long-running queries executed in concurrent sessions, we probably will not need to optimize it. The `Rows_sent` value is the quantity of data sent by the server to the client, that is, the number of rows in the result set. The `Rows_examined` value is the number of lines read by the query. The server must examine the number of rows before deciding if they must be included in the result set or used to join tables. If the used indexes are not selective enough, or no indexes are used, this value is higher than necessary. This is usually the most expensive part of the query cost.

Then, we find the statements to be executed to repeat the procedure. First, we can find a `SET timestamp` statement, which is sometimes necessary (for example, if functions such as `CURRENT_TIMESTAMP()` are used in a `WHERE` clause). A `USE` statement can only be found for the first slow query issued by the connection. Of course, despite these lines, it may be impossible to repeat the procedure with a copy and paste operation; for example, if a query involves temporary tables or user-defined variables, or it may be nondeterministic. Finally, we find the slow query, as it was received from the client.

If the `log-short-format` startup option is active, a much shorter format is used by the slow query log, shown as follows:

```
# Thread_id: 5  Schema: test  QC_hit: No
# Query_time: 0.230296  Lock_time: 0.000302  Rows_sent: 1  Rows_examined:
263337
SET timestamp=1389869887;
SELECT COUNT(*) FROM t WHERE a > b;
```

These lines are a subset of the former example; thus, they do not need any further explanation.

Depending on the `log_slow_verbosity` variable, more information can be added to the slow query log. The output of `EXPLAIN` is the most useful information we may need to find out the reason why a query is slow, but we usually prefer to execute this statement manually.

The slow_log table

The `slow_log` table contains information that is very similar, but not identical, to the information contained in a default slow query logfile. This table contains the following columns:

- The `start_time` column matches the `Time` column
- The `user_host` column matches the `User@Host` column
- The `query_time` column matches the `Query_time` column
- The `lock_time` column matches the `Lock_time` column
- The `rows_sent` column matches the `Rows_sent` column
- The `rows_examined` column matches the `Rows_examined` column
- The `db` column matches the `Schema` column
- The `last_insert_id` and `insert_id`, columns that contain information about the `AUTO_INCREMENT` columns in the future
- The `server_id` column gives the server's `server_id` variable, which is always set in a replication environment
- The `sql_text` column, which is the original query
- The `thread_id` column matches the `Thread_id` column

Explaining the pt-query-digest command from Percona Toolkit

The `pt-query-digest` command is a tool included in the Percona Toolkit project (formerly known as Maatkit). This command can read the queries from the slow query log, general query log, binary log (to be discussed later), and `SHOW PROCESSLIST` statement.

To use `pt-query-digest`, Percona Toolkit needs to be installed. The package is included in several Linux distributions. The latest version can be downloaded from Percona's website as the `.deb` or `.rpm` package. It is compatible with all versions of MariaDB and MySQL starting from MySQL 5.0. It does not work on Windows and requires Perl.

Usually, we prefer to analyze the slow query log first because the queries it contains are likely to be problematic. This is what we will do in the next example. We have not discussed the slow log yet but it does not matter much. A user can just pass `pt-query-digest`, which is the name of the general query log, instead of the slow log. We will not discuss every single datum that is reported by `pt-query-digest`; we will comment the following example instead, highlighting the most important details.

As an example, we will just run the following:

```
root@this:~# pt-query-digest /usr/local/mysql/data/slow_query
```

Assuming that the `slow_query` file exists, the first part of the `pt-query-digest` output will look like the following:

```
# 460ms user time, 40ms system time, 27.54M rss, 110.14M vsz
# Current date: Fri Jan 17 12:58:56 2014
# Hostname: this
# Files: /usr/local/mysql/data/slow_query
# Overall: 63 total, 23 unique, 0.00 QPS, 0.00x concurrency
```

```
# Time range: 2014-01-09 09:14:22 to 2014-01-17 10:57:22
# Attribute          total     min     max     avg     95%  stddev  median
# ============     =======  ======  ======  ======  ======  ======  ======
# Exec time           628s   391us    189s     10s     60s     30s     2ms
# Lock time          157ms       0   139ms     2ms   366us    17ms   273us
# Rows sent          1.86M       0   1.23M  30.29k   19.46 170.63k    0.99
# Rows examine      10.35M       0   3.70M 168.18k 245.21k 668.95k   36.69
# Query size         2.39k      11      92   38.78   84.10   22.19   33.28
```

We will generally be interested in the detailed statistics about the query's execution time, lock time, examined rows, and sent rows. For every data, we will consider the maximum, minimum, and average—the standard deviation will tell us how significant the average is. The total is also important, if it is compared to the `95%` column. In our example, five percent of the queries take a huge amount of time. This tells us that a small number of queries definitely need to be optimized (if possible). In other cases, the comparison may suggest that most queries are poorly optimized. A good average with a low standard deviation is the ideal result.

The 95 percent ratio is not arbitrary; although in the example we have used the default value, it can be changed with the `--limit` option. We may want to start with the default value and, if necessary, again call `pt-query-digest` with a different limit to find out the ratio of queries that consumes most resources.

Then, we see a summarized query profile, shown as follows:

```
# Profile
# Rank Query ID             Response time   Calls R/Call   V/M    Item
# ==== ================== =============== ===== ======= =====
=============
#    1 0x9DEBB548615A0927 518.7809 82.6%  1679 86.4635 25.03
#    2 0xB4C4971837CA7647  72.6882 11.6%     6 72.6882  0.00
#    3 0xED8BDB15894993C6  10.6332  1.7%     5 10.6332  0.00 CALL test.
rotate
# MISC 0xMISC              26.1711  4.2%    55  0.4758   0.0 <20 ITEMS>
```

The `pt-query-digest` command shows the most problematic statements first, by default. In fact, in the preceding example, the first query appears to be dramatic; it has a huge response time and has been used several times.

The statements that are almost irrelevant (when compared to the most problematic ones) are grouped in the final row. Such statements are what statisticians call **outliers**: the values that are not used to compute the average, because they do not represent whole set of values. The `--outliers` option defines the bound between the outliers and the other statements. This bound is based on the query time by default, but can also be based on other values. It also specifies the number of times a statement must appear to be excluded from the outliers.

A detailed explanation of `--limit` or `--outliers`, as well as other useful options, is beyond the purpose of this book. Detailed information can be found in the documentation on Percona's website.

Next, the single queries are reported. Let's take a look at the first one:

```
# Query 1: 0.00 QPS, 0.41x concurrency, ID 0x9DEBB548615A0927 at byte
11399
# This item is included in the report because it matches --limit.
# Scores: V/M = 25.03
# Time range: 2014-01-14 15:06:35 to 15:27:39
# Attribute    pct   total    min    max    avg    95% stddev
median
```

```
# ============= === ======= ======= ======= ======= ======= =======
=======
# Count          9      6
# Exec time     82    519s    45s    189s    86s    184s    47s
83s
# Lock time      1     2ms  249us   371us  289us  366us   40us
273us
# Rows sent      0      0      0      0      0      0      0
0
# Rows examine   3 368.15k         0 200.48k  61.36k 192.13k  84.74k
0
# Query size     2     66     11     11     11     11      0
11
# String:
# Databases     test (5/83%), mysql (1/16%)
# Hosts         localhost
# Users         root
# Query_time distribution
#    1us
#   10us
#  100us
#    1ms
#   10ms
#  100ms
#    1s
#   10s+  ################################################################
CALL test.p\G
```

Introducing indexes

Before discussing the EXPLAIN statement and how the MariaDB optimizer chooses an execution plan, it is important to understand how MariaDB uses indexes.

An index can be defined on one or more columns and their order is relevant. An index that involves string columns can be defined on their prefixes (the leftmost part of the data). For the TEXT and BLOB columns, the index is mandatory.

Rarely can the use of an index prefix speedup queries. However, sometimes we may want to reduce the disk space occupied by indexes. If only the leftmost characters of a string column are used in WHERE clauses, we can choose to use a partial index on it; for example, this can be feasible if a column contains codes, where each character or group of characters has a special meaning. However, we will probably only save a considerable amount of space if we have a very high number of rows, or if several column prefixes can be indexed.

There are two important index types: BTREE and HASH. Another type, RTREE, is only used for geometric data. The FULLTEXT indexes are used to execute full-text queries. These types will not be discussed in this book.

The HASH type can only be used for equality comparisons: the ones involving the = or <=> (NULL-safe equal) operators. It cannot be used to order or group rows. Where the index type is relevant, all examples in this book use BTREE indexes, and so the type is not specified.

The BTREE type can be used with many comparison operators, such as <, <=, =, >=, >, LIKE, BETWEEN, and IN. It can be used to order and group rows.

Thus, any statement can take advantage of a BTREE index if it is built on the relevant columns. HASH can typically be used for queries that search for an exact index entry. For such queries, HASH indexes can be faster than BTREE indexes. But remember that, for different query types, these indexes will simply be ignored. Even in such cases, though, using a BTREE index is not generally considered a major performance problem.

The BTREE index is the default type for most storage engines. However, since the MEMORY storage engine is often used to cache data (thus, to search one exact entry), its default index type is HASH. Remember to explicitly define the BTREE indexes if HASH is not suitable for some of your queries. As explained later, in the *Storage engines and indexes* section, InnoDB can optionally use an adaptive algorithm to silently convert the BTREE indexes to HASH, if the latter option seems to be more effective for the server's workload.

MariaDB is able to use the leftmost part of an index. For example, if an index is defined on a column called col1, a query involving the initial part of the column will usually take advantage of the index:

```
SELECT * FROM t WHERE col1 LIKE 'begin%';
```

However, if we execute a query that only reads the rightmost, or central, part of the index, the index will not be used. For example, the following query will not use the index:

```
SELECT * FROM t WHERE col1 LIKE '%end';
```

For the same reason, if an index involves multiple columns, it can speedup queries that use the leftmost columns in the index, but not queries that do not involve the leftmost part. For example, if an index is defined on two columns called col1 and col2, the following query can take advantage of it in this order:

```
SELECT * FROM t WHERE col1 = 10;
```

The following query cannot use such index:

```
SELECT * FROM t WHERE col2 = 10;
```

The ORDER BY and GROUP BY clauses can use an index even if the column's order does not match. However, this requires a two-pass sort; the data will be copied into a temporary table or file, and then ordered. The I/O required by such operations can be a performance killer and should be avoided whenever possible. For example, the following query can use our index and does not require extra sorting operations:

```
SELECT * FROM t ORDER BY col1, col2;
```

However, the following query requires a temporary table or file:

```
SELECT * FROM t ORDER BY col2, col1;
```

An index is usually of great help if it can avoid any access to data for a query. This happens if the SELECT statement only returns columns from the index, and all the other clauses can take advantage from the index. In this case, it is called a covering index.

Table statistics

Even if a query can use an index, the optimizer can decide if the use of an index is not of great help, and thus use another index or a full table scan. The general rule is that indexes are useful when they help reduce read operations. What reduces read operations is the index cardinality, that is, the number of unique values in an index. If an index is unique, its cardinality is equal to the difference in the number of rows and the NULL values. If an index only has a few possible values (for example, it is an ENUM field, or TINYINT used as a boolean), its cardinality will be very low. The selectivity is a correlated term that indicates how many rows can be excluded if an index is used to satisfy a WHERE clause.

To determine whether an index is useful, the optimizer takes into account factors such as the index cardinality, index length, and number of rows in the table. For example, if a table contains only a few rows, there is no point in using an index to avoid reading the data.

The problem with cardinality is that MariaDB does not know its exact value; it is just an estimated value. While in most cases the cardinality is accurate enough, this value can sometimes be out of sync with the real data. This can lead the optimizer to exclude an index (and maybe choose a full table scan) for a query, which would greatly benefit from the use of an index. To recalculate a table's index cardinality, the ANALYZE TABLE statement can be used. The estimate index cardinality is reported in the output of the SHOW INDEX statement.

Index statistics are collected by storage engines and, optionally, by the server. The statistics are based on groups of identical values stored in each index. The most important value is the average number of elements present in groups. Some storage engines have a variable that determines whether NULL values should be considered like any other value (in this context) or not. These variables are innodb_stats_method, aria_stats_method, and myisam_stats_method. They all accept the same values. A nulls_equal value means that the average number of elements should be calculated considering the group of NULL values as any other group. A nulls_unequal value means that each individual NULL value should be considered a group. Both these options affect the statistics in a different way; the first value should be preferred if there are a few NULL index records, while the latter value is preferable when there are several NULL index records. A nulls_ignored value also exists, which causes the NULL values not to be counted. For InnoDB and MyISAM, nulls_equal is the default value, while for Aria, nulls_unequal is the default value.

InnoDB has a variable called @@innodb_stats_on_metadata. It is disabled by default. If it is set to 1, the InnoDB statistics are collected each time the user executes SHOW KEYS, or a corresponding query on the information_schema database. This helps to have updated statistics, but can take a long time on big tables.

Since MariaDB 10, the server can also collect statistics. Such statistics are collected not only for the indexed columns, but also for nonindexed columns. The main problem with this feature is that recalculating statistics for a table always requires a full table scan. Engine-independent statistics are disabled by default, and can be configured using the @@user_stat_tables server system variable. A value never disables the feature, whereas other values enable the engine-independent statistics; with complementary, the features will be used only when the storage engine does not provide the required information, while preferably uses the server statistics whenever possible.

Storage engines and indexes

An InnoDB table always has a clustered index. A clustered index is a column containing sorted values that uniquely identify each row. Each row in secondary indexes contains the indexed values, followed by the clustered index value from the same table row. Only the clustered index contains pointers to the position of the physical rows in the files. This technique is much more complex than the index structure used in MyISAM. All MyISAM keys (the primary key and all other indexes) contain the offset of each row in the data file. The use of clustered indexes makes InnoDB much faster when searching for a specific value in the primary key.

InnoDB uses the primary key as a clustered index, if it exists. If a table does not have a primary key, a unique index is used. If there are no unique keys, a cluster index is created by InnoDB. In such cases, the cluster index is a unique value of 6 bytes that is invisible to the user. Such clustered indexes imply more locks than a normal clustered index based on the primary key. For these reasons, with InnoDB, it is important to explicitly define small primary keys.

The AUTO_INCREMENT values generally imply a lock that prevents two concurrent connections from using the same value. The working of this lock depends on the value of the innodb_autoinc_lock_mode system variable. The allowed values, for the innodb_autoinc_lock_mode system variable are discussed as follows:

- 0: This value describes that all the INSERT statements hold a table lock until the end of the operation. This was the only available mode in the older InnoDB versions. It is slow, but can be used if a problem arises with value 1.

- 1: This value describes that the multirow INSERT statements and LOAD DATA INFILE still require a table lock. For a single row INSERT statements, a lighter lock is used. This is the default process because it is the most scalable mode that can be safely used with a statement-based replication.

- 2: This value denotes that no table locks are ever held. This is not safe with the statement-based replication. This value is, however, safe with row-based replication, and is mandatory with Galera, as explained in *Chapter 12, MariaDB Galera Cluster*.

If the innodb_adaptive_hash_index server variable is set to 1 (the default), InnoDB can automatically convert BTREE indexes to HASH, and vice versa. This is generally useful for tables whose data is stored in the buffer pool, queried by statements that use the = operator in the WHERE clause. To decide which type of index should be used, InnoDB collects statistical data about how the tables are used. Increasing the value of the innodb_adaptive_max_sleep_delay system variable reduces the overhead due to such operations, which can be useful on busy servers.

With Aria and MyISAM, indexes store the minimum and maximum value of each field they contain. Thus, a SELECT command without any optional clauses, and that returns only maximum and minimum values, is immediately executed.

Index limits (number of indexes per table, number of columns per index, index length, prefix length, and so on) may vary depending on the storage engine. However, the limits are very high.

Some special storage engines, such as CSV, do not support indexes or have a very limited support for them.

Working with the EXPLAIN statement

The EXPLAIN statement is the main tool to understand how a statement is executed within a server. In MariaDB 10, this works not only with the SELECT statements, but also with the UPDATE and DELETE statements. The syntax of the EXPLAIN statement is:

```
EXPLAIN [EXTENDED] <statement>;
```

The EXTENDED clause adds a column to the output and generates a note (which can be seen with the SHOW WARNINGS command) containing statement as it has been internally rewritten by the optimizer.

After MariaDB 10, another property of this command was added, shown as follows:

```
SHOW EXPLAIN FOR <thread_id>;
```

This command allows us to obtain the execution plan from a running statement. This is useful when a statement is taking a lot of time and we want to know the reason. To see the running queries and related thread IDs, SHOW PROCESSLIST can be used.

For example, to check how a query is executed and then see how it is rewritten, we can run the following code:

```
MariaDB [test]> EXPLAIN EXTENDED SELECT a, b FROM t WHERE a = 1 ORDER BY
a DESC \G
*************************** 1. row ***************************
           id: 1
  select_type: SIMPLE
        table: t
         type: ref
possible_keys: idx_a
          key: idx_a
```

```
      key_len: 5
          ref: const
         rows: 1165569
     filtered: 100.00
        Extra:
1 row in set, 1 warning (0.00 sec)


MariaDB [test]> SHOW WARNINGS \G
*************************** 1. row ***************************
  Level: Note
   Code: 1003
Message: select 'test'.'t'.'a' AS 'a','test'.'t'.'b' AS 'b' from
'test'.'t' where ('test'.'t'.'a' = 1) order by 'test'.'t'.'a' desc
1 row in set (0.00 sec)
```

To see which queries are running, and then check how one of them is executed:

```
MariaDB [(none)]> SHOW PROCESSLIST \G
*************************** 1. row ***************************
      Id: 12
    User: root
    Host: localhost
      db: NULL
 Command: Query
    Time: 0
   State: Table lock
    Info: SHOW PROCESSLIST
Progress: 0.000
*************************** 2. row ***************************
      Id: 37
    User: root
    Host: localhost
      db: test
 Command: Query
    Time: 1
   State: Sending data
    Info: SELECT a, b FROM t WHERE a = 1 ORDER BY a DESC
```

```
Progress: 0.000
3 rows in set (0.00 sec)


MariaDB [(none)]> SHOW EXPLAIN FOR 37 \G
*************************** 1. row ***************************
           id: 1
  select_type: SIMPLE
        table: t
         type: ref
possible_keys: idx_a
          key: idx_a
      key_len: 5
          ref: const
         rows: 1165569
        Extra:
1 row in set, 1 warning (0.00 sec)


MariaDB [(none)]> SHOW WARNINGS;
+-------+------+-------------------------------------------------+
| Level | Code | Message                                         |
+-------+------+-------------------------------------------------+
| Note  | 1003 | SELECT a, b FROM t WHERE a = 1 ORDER BY a DESC |
+-------+------+-------------------------------------------------+
1 row in set (0.00 sec)
```

If the statement execution ends after we send the SHOW EXPLAIN command, we will see an error similar to the following:

```
MariaDB [(none)]> SHOW EXPLAIN FOR 37 \G
ERROR 1933 (HY000): Target is not running an EXPLAINable command
```

This is worth mentioning because it may be confusing. The SELECT, UPDATE, and DELETE statements are always EXPLAINable. The INSERT statements do not cause this error, but they do not produce a useful result.

Understanding the output of EXPLAIN

In this section, we will analyze the output of the EXPLAIN command. In the meantime, we will also discuss how some queries are executed, and the most important optimization strategies used by MariaDB.

For the JOIN and UNION queries, the output of EXPLAIN contains one row for each simple SELECT or UNION operation. It consists of the following columns:

- id: This column defines a unique identifier for each row.
- select_type: This column defines the type of the SELECT command.
- table: This column defines the table read by the SELECT command.
- partitions: This column defines a list of partitions that will be accessed.
- type: This column defines the type of JOIN.
- possible_key: This column defines a list of keys that can be used to execute a statement.
- key: This column defines the key that the optimizer decides to use. If this value is NULL, a full table scan is done.
- key_len: This column defines the length (size) of the selected key, in bytes.
- ref: This column defines the columns used to join two tables.
- rows: This column gives an estimate of how many rows will be examined.
- filtered: This column gives an estimate of the percentage of rows that will not be returned (shown only with EXPLAIN EXTENDED).
- Extra: This column defines some additional information.

Now, let's see how to interpret these columns in some practical cases.

Simple SELECT statements

Let's start our series of practical examples with a simple SELECT statement that involves only one table. Here is the table that we will use:

```
CREATE TABLE 'user' (
  'email' char(100) NOT NULL,
  'username' char(20) NOT NULL,
  'password_md5' binary(32) NOT NULL,
  'first_name' char(30) NOT NULL,
  'last_name' char(30) NOT NULL,
  'birth_date' date DEFAULT NULL,
```

```
'id' smallint(6) NOT NULL AUTO_INCREMENT,
'sex' char(1) NOT NULL,
PRIMARY KEY ('id'),
UNIQUE KEY 'email' ('email'),
UNIQUE KEY 'username' ('username'),
KEY 'idx_birth' ('birth_date'),
KEY 'idx_birth_sex' ('birth_date','sex')
) ENGINE=InnoDB
```

After creating the table, we will run a simple query shown as follows:

```
MariaDB [test]> EXPLAIN SELECT birth_date, sex, COUNT(*) FROM user GROUP
BY birth_date, sex\G
*************************** 1. row ***************************
          id: 1
 select_type: SIMPLE
       table: user
        type: index
possible_keys: NULL
         key: idx_birth_sex
     key_len: 7
         ref: NULL
        rows: 6
       Extra: Using index
1 row in set (0.00 sec)
```

The value of `type` is `index`, which means that an index is used to execute the query. The used index is `idx_birth_sex`, as showed in the `key` column. The `possible_keys` column tells us that there were no alternatives. The used index contains all the columns that need to be read to execute the query, so it is a covering index; this is what the `Extra` column tells us.

The `idx_birth` index was not considered useful here, because it does not contain all the columns referenced in the `GROUP BY` column. Since all the data contained in `idx_birth` is also contained in `idx_birth_sex`, we should probably drop `idx_birth_date`. Remember that each index causes an overhead for the `write` operations and for the query optimization stage; so, they should not exist if they are useless.

Internal temporary tables or files

Sometimes, MariaDB needs to transparently create an internal temporary table to execute a query. If data needs to be read more than once, copying it into a temporary table allows the release of table locks immediately after the copy operation. However, if the data to be copied is too big, this can cost a lot, which MariaDB tries to avoid.

Internal temporary tables are used in the following cases:

- For views that aggregate data, or are defined with the TEMPTABLE algorithm
- For UNION operations
- If both the ORDER BY and GROUP BY clauses are specified and they are not equal
- If a JOIN clause is used and the ORDER BY or GROUP BY clause contains columns that are not located in the first read table
- If both DISTINCT and ORDER BY are present
- When a subquery or derived table needs to be materialized

If a temporary table is used, the Extra column of the EXPLAIN output contains Using filesort or Using temporary.

By default, temporary tables use the Aria storage engine; this usually speeds up the GROUP BY and DISTINCT operations. If the compile option of aria_used_for_temp_tables is set to 0, the temporary tables use the MyISAM storage engine. We may want to do so if an Aria bug affects us, or if this storage engine is not efficient enough for some of our queries. But these cases will be rare.

Usually, temporary tables are stored in memory. If its size exceeds the tmp_table_size or max_heap_table_size server variables, the temporary table is written on disk. There are also some cases when the internal temporary tables are always stored on disk, as follows:

- When a TEXT or BLOB column is read.
- When a GROUP BY or DISTINCT clause contains a column larger than 512 bytes (not characters). This also applies to UNION DISTINCT.
- For UNION ALL operations.

The UNION queries

The UNION queries are not very different from the simple SELECT commands that we discussed earlier. Each SELECT statement in the UNION query is optimized independently. Let's see how the UNION queries are explained, as shown in the following code:

```
MariaDB [test]> EXPLAIN (SELECT first_name, last_name, birth_date FROM
user WHERE last_name LIKE 'A%') UNION (SELECT first_name, last_name,
birth_date FROM user WHERE last_name LIKE 'C%');
+------+--------------+------------+-------+---------------+----------+---------+------+------+----------------------+
| id   | select_type  | table      | type  | possible_keys | key      | key_len | ref  | rows | Extra                |
+------+--------------+------------+-------+---------------+----------+---------+------+------+----------------------+
|    1 | PRIMARY      | user       | range | idx_last      | idx_last | 90      | NULL |    1 | Using index condition |
|    2 | UNION        | user       | range | idx_last      | idx_last | 90      | NULL |    1 | Using index condition |
| NULL | UNION RESULT | <union1,2> | ALL   | NULL          | NULL     | NULL    | NULL | NULL |                      |
+------+--------------+------------+-------+---------------+----------+---------+------+------+----------------------+
3 rows in set (0.00 sec)
```

We see three records in this output. The first row is of type PRIMARY; this is the first executed SELECT command. Then, we have a row of type UNION; this type is used for all the subsequent queries. The last row is of type UNION RESULT; this refers to the UNION operation.

Simple index access methods

MariaDB can use several index access methods. One of them is called **range**. It is used to extract intervals of values from an index. The following two examples use the range access method:

```
MariaDB [test]> EXPLAIN SELECT first_name, last_name, birth_date FROM
user WHERE birth_date BETWEEN '1994-01-01' AND '1994-12-31' \G
*************************** 1. row ***************************
           id: 1
  select_type: SIMPLE
        table: user
         type: range
```

```
possible_keys: idx_birth,idx_birth_sex
          key: idx_birth
      key_len: 4
          ref: NULL
         rows: 2
        Extra: Using index condition
1 row in set (0.00 sec)
MariaDB [test]> EXPLAIN SELECT first_name, last_name, birth_date FROM
user WHERE last_name LIKE 'B%' \G
*************************** 1. row ***************************
           id: 1
  select_type: SIMPLE
        table: user
         type: range
possible_keys: idx_last
          key: idx_last
      key_len: 90
          ref: NULL
         rows: 2
        Extra: Using index condition
1 row in set (0.00 sec)
```

As we can see, the `type` column tells us if the range method is used.

The HASH indexes allow the range access method too, but each range of values can only consist of a single value, and the comparison must be expressed with the = or IN operators.

Another index access method is `index_merge`. It is used to scan ranges of values from more than one index. When this method is used, `index_merge` is displayed in the `type` column.

Index optimizations of the JOIN clause

When performing a JOIN clause between two or more tables, the order in which the tables are read is often important. For example, if a table contains 10,000 rows, and another table consists of only 1,000 rows, it is preferable that the smaller table be read first. If the WHERE clause excludes some rows, the matching rows on the greater table will not be searched. The order in which tables are read is the same in which they appear in the output of EXPLAIN.

Engine-independent statistics can help the optimizer to choose the best order. MariaDB stores histograms representing the distribution of values of indexed and nonindexed columns. Thus, sometimes, the optimizer knows how much a certain comparison is selective; for example, `qty=1` may be much more selective than `qty=100`, and the histograms are stored to detect this.

It is also possible to force MariaDB to read the tables in the same order they appear in a `JOIN` clause by using the `STRAIGHT_JOIN` clause.

Optimization of subqueries

In relational theory, a semi-join is a `SELECT` statement that contains a subquery in the `WHERE` clause. Usually, such subqueries are better executed as `JOIN` statements, which extract only columns from a table. For example, if we want to know the average of the price of products in a certain category, the following syntax is probably the most intuitive:

```
SELECT AVG(price) FROM product WHERE cat_id =
  (SELECT id FROM category WHERE id = 42);
```

The same result can be obtained with a `JOIN` query:

```
SELECT AVG(p.price)
  FROM product p
  LEFT JOIN category c
  ON p.cat_id = c.id
  WHERE c.id = 42;
```

A MariaDB optimization known as **table pullout** consists of translating semijoins into a complete `JOIN`. If this optimization is not applied, the query can be very slow. Table pullout was not supported in MariaDB versions older than 5.3. In modern MariaDB versions, if a subquery is slow, we should check whether the optimizer rewrites it as a `JOIN`. If this does not happen, we should try to do it ourselves.

Another important optimization is the **FirstMatch** strategy. It is used for `IN` subqueries, where the subquery execution may stop as soon as a record is found. This optimization is used when the `EXPLAIN` command shows `FirstMatch(tableNumber)` in the `Extra` column.

LooseScan is a strategy used for particular `IN` subqueries, used to read groups of records from a table. For example:

```
SELECT * FROM Country
WHERE Country.code in (SELECT country_code FROM Satellite);
```

This subquery retrieves all the values of `country_code` from `Satellite`, many of which are probably identical. This optimization consists of grouping such values, and joining them with the left table. This avoids the production of duplicate record combinations. If this strategy is applied, the `Extra` column of the `EXPLAIN` output contains `LooseScan`.

Older versions of MariaDB as well as MySQL are used to materialize all the derived tables, that is, the subqueries used in a `FROM` clause. This may be very slow, especially if the materialized data is large. This is generally avoided in MariaDB whenever possible. In this case, the query is transformed to read the same data without using any derived tables. If the optimization is not possible, the `Extra` column of the `EXPLAIN` output shows `Using temporary` as a result. Even in this case, another optimization is still possible in recent versions of MariaDB by adding a key to the materialized table.

Summary

In this chapter, we covered the process of finding slow queries and optimizing them.

First, we analyzed how the slow query log can be configured to find queries that we want to be faster. Its options allow defining useful criteria. We also discussed the `pt-query-digest` tool, from the Percona Toolkit, that gave us an overview about the performance of slow queries.

We discussed how MariaDB uses indexes. This is very important to know because a fast query is generally a query that makes good use of a proper index. Then, we discussed an important feature of MariaDB 10.0 called engine-independent statistics, which collects statistics about data in the indexed and non-indexed columns. These statistics can be used by the optimizer to choose a query execution plan.

In the last part, we analyzed the `EXPLAIN` statement. This command provides information about the strategy the optimizer decided to use to execute a query. While discussing `EXPLAIN`, we also analyzed the main execution plans that MariaDB uses to execute queries.

Based on the `EXPLAIN` output and knowledge of the possible execution plans, we can adjust the indexes or the query so that MariaDB can use a better plan.

Of course, in an environment where concurrency exists, individually optimizing the queries can be insufficient. The next chapter discusses how transactions prevent sessions from colliding, and how to minimize the overhead caused by the isolation of these transactions.

4
Transactions and Locks

The SQL-99 specification defines transaction in this way:

> *"An SQL-transaction (transaction) is a sequence of executions of SQL-statements that is atomic with respect to recovery. That is to say: either the execution result is completely successful, or it has no effect on any SQL-schemas or SQL-data.*
>
> *The SQL Standard"*

So, a transaction is an important feature that guarantees the integrity of data. It is useful to prevent the data from remaining in an inconsistent state when an operation fails. Suppose, for example, we are administering a database for an e-commerce website. We have several tables; one of them stores the orders, and the others store the available products and their quantity. When a customer buys a product, a new order must be written in the appropriate table and the quantity of that product must decrease. These operations must occur within the same transaction. In this way, if a server crashes after the order has been written but before the product's quantity decreases, the whole transaction never becomes effective. Only, if all the operations succeed, will the transaction be finalized.

But, transactions have another important property: they are isolated from each other. Many isolation levels exist, and each one implements different types of isolation. Anyway, the idea is that the operations performed by one transaction should never interfere with concurrent transactions. Let's again consider the example of the e-commerce website. When a customer buys a product, the application checks whether the desired product is available and then decreases its quantity. This happens within a transaction and avoids malfunctioning if two customers try to buy the same product at the same time. One of the customers will begin a transaction and lock the table row corresponding to the product he/she wants to buy. The second customer will have to wait until the first transaction ends. In this way, if the first customer buys the last stocked product, the second customer will not buy a "phantom" product. In MariaDB, transactions may only be used on storage engines that support them, such as InnoDB, TokuDB, and SPIDER.

The basic mechanisms that allow storage engines to guarantee data consistency are **locks**. We will analyze them in this chapter.

We will also discuss some aspects of the ALTER TABLE statement, which can lock big tables for a long period of time.

The InnoDB locks

A lock is a data structure that is acquired by a user and associated to a resource. Until the lock is held, other users will not be able to modify that resource or, depending on the lock type, they would not be able to read it. Typically, concurrent operations will be queued. InnoDB can lock rows and entire tables to prevent the concurrent operations from colliding.

In order to understand how the InnoDB locks work, it is necessary to understand how the concurrent transactions work. Also, this allows us to diagnose and fix problems, such as the transactions that have to wait for too long or the frequent deadlocks between the transactions.

When a transaction needs to access a row that is locked, it is put on hold until the transaction that holds the lock **commits** or **rolls** back. The wait has a limit, which is determined by the innodb_lock_wait_timeout server variable, expressed in seconds. The default value is 50 and can usually be decreased. If this timeout exceeds, the transaction terminates and an error is produced, shown as follows:

```
ERROR 1205 (HY000): Lock wait timeout exceeded; try restarting
transaction
```

The lock modes

InnoDB has two main lock modes: **shared** and **exclusive**. A shared lock prevents other connections from writing to a row, but allows them to read it. An exclusive lock prevents other connections from reading a row; the isolation level (explained in the *Transactions isolation levels* section) determines whether other transactions can write in the row. Shared locks are acquired before reading a row, and exclusive locks are acquired before writing a row. Before a transaction can acquire a shared or exclusive lock, it needs to acquire an intention shared lock or an intention exclusive lock. In other words, an intention lock indicates that a transaction is waiting to acquire a shared or exclusive lock, and prevents two connections from acquiring a lock on the same rows.

Shared and exclusive locks are commonly abbreviated as **S** and **X**. Intention shared locks and intention exclusive locks are abbreviated as **IS** and **IX**.

A lock on a record can only be acquired if an incompatible lock does not already involve the same record. If such a lock exists, the connection is put on hold. The following table shows which lock modes block the other lock modes:

Lock mode	Lock modes that will be blocked
X	X, S, IX, IS
S	X, IS
IX	X, S
IS	X

Lock types

InnoDB supports both table-level locks and record-level locks.

Table-level locks lock a whole table. They can be acquired explicitly with LOCK TABLES, but this is not good practice with InnoDB and it is normally disabled. To enable this locking mode with InnoDB, the innodb_table_locks server variable can be set to ON. The LOCK TABLES command is designed to guarantee the consistency of non-transactional tables, such as Aria and MyISAM. Its performance is poor, because it locks a whole table, not just the rows involved in a transaction. Note that some information_schema InnoDB-specific tables (that are discussed in the *Diagnosing locks* section) store information about the existing locks, but they do not contain information about the locks that are created using the LOCK TABLES command.

Record-level locks lock one or more records. InnoDB has the following types of record-level locks: record locks, gap locks, and next-key locks.

- A record lock involves a single index record. If no index has been explicitly created for the table, record locks involve records in the clustered index (which is described in the previous chapter).

- A next-key lock involves an index record and all the records that precede it. This prevents other connections from inserting or modifying the records that have already been accessed by the current transaction. Next-key locks are used with the REPEATABLE READ isolation level.

- A gap lock is a lock on a set of records. This set can be composed by one record, multiple records, or it can be empty. This lock type is not used for a single row search on a UNIQUE index, unless the index is composed of multiple columns.

A particular case of gap lock is the insertion gap lock. It is acquired before the insertion of a new row. If another connection tries to insert a row with the same index values, it will be put on hold until the current transaction commits or rolls back the changes.

Gap locks are not used with the READ COMMITTED isolation level.

Diagnosing locks

While locks are necessary to guarantee the consistency of data, they can cause performance problems. Each lock can cause one or more sessions to wait, slowing down the applications. If sessions have to wait too long or too often, we have to find out the reason and fix the problem.

The SHOW ENGINE INNODB STATUS statement is usually the fastest way to get human-readable information about locks. Its output is quite long, but fortunately it is human-readable, friendly for regular expressions, and divided into some useful sections. The section which lists existing locks is TRANSACTIONS. Here is an example:

```
------------
TRANSACTIONS
------------
Trx id counter 14488
Purge done for trx's n:o < 14477 undo n:o < 0 state: running but idle
History list length 230
LIST OF TRANSACTIONS FOR EACH SESSION:
...
---TRANSACTION 14509, ACTIVE 3 sec inserting
mysql tables in use 1, locked 1
LOCK WAIT 2 lock struct(s), heap size 376, 1 row lock(s), undo log
entries 1
MySQL thread id 5, OS thread handle 0x7f5d48554700, query id 161
localhost root update
INSERT INTO t VALUES (1)
------- TRX HAS BEEN WAITING 3 SEC FOR THIS LOCK TO BE GRANTED:
RECORD LOCKS space id 48 page no 4 n bits 72 index `a` of table
`test`.`t` trx id 14509 lock mode S waiting
Record lock, heap no 2 PHYSICAL RECORD: n_fields 2; compact format; info
bits 0
 0: len 4; hex 80000001; asc       ;;
 1: len 6; hex 000000000601; asc         ;;
```

```
-----------------

---TRANSACTION 14486, ACTIVE 9 sec
2 lock struct(s), heap size 376, 1 row lock(s), undo log entries 1
MySQL thread id 4, OS thread handle 0x7f5d4859d700, query id 154
localhost root cleaning up
```

For each transaction, an ID is shown. The last listed transaction has been active for nine seconds. We know its thread ID is 4, which is important to debug. By executing SHOW PROCESSLIST, we can find out what thread 4 is doing. The operating system thread ID is also shown, in the hexadecimal format. It can be converted to a decimal number by using the UNHEX() function. We know it holds a lock on 1 row.

Another transaction is shown in this example. It has been active for three seconds. The transaction has been blocked for three seconds from inserting a row by the existing lock.

To get more specific information about one or more locks, the INNODB_LOCKS table in the information_schema database can be queried. Note that locks appear in that table only if they are blocking a transaction. The table consists of the following columns:

- LOCK_ID: This is a string ID. Its format may change in the future.
- LOCK_TRX_ID: This is the transaction ID that appears as a result of SHOW ENGINE INNODB STATUS.
- LOCK_MODE: These are the possible values: S, X, IS, IX; for gap locks: S_GAP, X_GAP, IS_GAP, IX_GAP; for autoincrement locks: AUTO_INC.
- LOCK_TYPE: This column shows whether the lock type is RECORD or TABLE.
- LOCK_TABLE: This is the name of the table that is involved by the lock. It includes the database name and the table name, both quoted.
- LOCK_INDEX: For record locks, this column shows the name of the index whose record is locked.
- LOCK_SPACE: For record locks, this column shows the name of the tablespace involved by the lock. The INNODB_SYS_TABLESPACES table shows which table this tablespace belongs to.
- LOCK_PAGE: For record locks, this is the page number.
- LOCK_REC: For record locks, this is the record number within the page.
- LOCK_DATA: For record locks, this is the clustered index value for the locked record.

The `INNODB_LOCK_WAITS` table shows which transactions are waiting to obtain a lock, and which transactions are holding the locks which are blocking them. Its columns are:

- `REQUESTING_TRX_ID`: The ID of the waiting transaction
- `REQUESTED_LOCK_ID`: The ID of the requested lock
- `BLOCKING_TRX_ID`: The ID of the blocking transaction
- `BLOCKING_LOCK_ID`: The ID of the lock that is blocking the requesting transaction

The `INNODB_TRX` table holds information about a transaction's activities.

The following example shows a `JOIN` query between `INNODB_LOCKS` and `INNODB_LOCK_WAITS`, which shows all the transactions that are blocking another transaction, as well as the detailed information about the blocking lock:

```
MariaDB [test]> SELECT * FROM information_schema.INNODB_LOCK_WAITS lw
LEFT JOIN information_schema.INNODB_LOCKS l ON lw.BLOCKING_LOCK_ID =
l.LOCK_ID \G
*************************** 1. row ***************************
requesting_trx_id: 14512
requested_lock_id: 14512:48:4:2
  blocking_trx_id: 14486
 blocking_lock_id: 14486:48:4:2
          lock_id: 14486:48:4:2
       lock_trx_id: 14486
        lock_mode: X
        lock_type: RECORD
       lock_table: `test`.`t`
       lock_index: a
       lock_space: 48
        lock_page: 4
         lock_rec: 2
        lock_data: 1
1 row in set (0.00 sec)
```

Note that `information_schema` related to InnoDB does not show information about the locks obtained using `LOCK TABLES`. The reason is that those locks are handled by the MariaDB server itself, not by the InnoDB storage engine.

Locks used by various SQL statements

The UPDATE and DELETE statements lock all scanned index records, including the ones that do not satisfy the WHERE condition. Locking reads can free the locks on the index records that do not satisfy a WHERE condition but sometimes this cannot be done.

 When a statement which modifies data does not use any index, all the rows in the table need to be locked. The same happens with locking using the SELECT statement.

The UPDATE and DELETE statements acquire an exclusive next-key lock for each scanned record.

The INSERT statement acquires an insertion gap lock on the index values it is going to insert. Transactions that insert different values do not need to wait for each other. After the insertion, an exclusive record lock is placed on all the new rows until the end of the transaction. If a duplicate error occurs, normally the transaction does not rollback and a shared record lock is placed on the existing record. If the ON DUPLICATE KEY clause is present, an exclusive next-key lock is put on the existing record.

The INSERT ... SELECT statement is similar to the INSERT statement and is used for the inserted tables, except that no insertion gap lock is set. With the READ COMMITTED isolation level, the SELECT part of the statement performs a consistent read. Otherwise, shared next-key locks are set on the read rows.

Foreign keys need to read some rows to guarantee that the integrity constraints are enforced. On each read record, a shared record lock is acquired.

Reads consistency

In this section we will see which reads are consistent within a transaction, and how InnoDB guarantees this consistency. The consistency of queries is determined by the transaction level, by using the WITH CONSISTENT SNAPSHOT option for START TRANSACTION, and the LOCK IN SHARE MODE or FOR UPDATE options for SELECT. Augmenting the consistency of reads can be important to be sure that applications work properly, while relaxing it improves the concurrency.

The non-repeatable reads

A read is called non-repeatable if repeating the same query twice within the same transaction without modifying the data within the transaction returns different results. This happens because the current transaction is not fully isolated from changes requested by other connections.

Of course, this improves the overall performance in an environment where concurrency exists. But the application developers should be aware that this can happen, and if this represents a problem, it must be avoided.

The mechanisms that make a read repeatable are consistent reads and locking reads. Next-key locks also guarantee protection from the insertions of new values in a given range after a query. These mechanisms will be discussed in the following sections. If none of this is used, the read is non-repeatable.

Phantom rows

The next-key locks avoid a problem called *phantom rows*. What is it? Suppose that a transaction performs a query involving a range of values from a non-indexed column, for example, WHERE column BETWEEN 10 AND 20. The query returns three rows with the values 10, 15, and 20. But then, another connection adds a row with the value 13. If the first connection repeats the same query, it will see that a new row has appeared. This is called a phantom row.

If the column is indexed, InnoDB uses a next-key lock. The second connection will still be able to insert the new row immediately. It will not have to wait until the first transaction ends. But the new row will not be visible for the first transaction. This guarantees a good level of isolation between different transactions.

Let's see an example.

First, let's open a mysql client instance. We will create a table with an indexed column that contains the values 1, 3, and 5. Then, let's start a transaction (we will use the REPEATABLE READ isolation level) and retrieve all values >= 3:

```
MariaDB [test]> CREATE TABLE t (a INT PRIMARY KEY) ENGINE = InnoDB;
Query OK, 0 rows affected (0.40 sec)
MariaDB [test]> INSERT INTO t VALUES (1), (3), (5);
Query OK, 3 rows affected (0.08 sec)
Records: 3  Duplicates: 0  Warnings: 0
MariaDB [test]> START TRANSACTION;
Query OK, 0 rows affected (0.00 sec)
```

```
MariaDB [test]> SELECT * FROM t WHERE a >= 3;
+---+
| a |
+---+
| 3 |
| 5 |
+---+
2 rows in set (0.00 sec)
```

InnoDB uses a next-key lock in this case.

Now, let's open another mysql instance, in the autocommit mode. We will insert a new row with the value 4. This row is in the interval that was requested by the former query:

```
MariaDB [test]> INSERT INTO t VALUES (4);
Query OK, 1 row affected (0.06 sec)
```

Now, let's repeat the query in the first mysql instance, commit the transaction, and repeat the same query for the last time to see whether there is a difference:

```
MariaDB [test]> SELECT * FROM t WHERE a >= 3;
+---+
| a |
+---+
| 3 |
| 5 |
+---+
2 rows in set (0.00 sec)
MariaDB [test]> COMMIT;
Query OK, 0 rows affected (0.00 sec)
MariaDB [test]> SELECT * FROM t WHERE a >= 3;
+---+
| a |
+---+
| 3 |
| 4 |
| 5 |
+---+
3 rows in set (0.00 sec)
```

As expected, the new row is not visible before a commit, so the data remains consistent within the transaction. But after a commit, the row becomes visible.

Consistent reads

A consistent read is a read from a table that is consistent within the current transaction. It uses no locks. When a table is accessed for the first time by the current transaction, a snapshot is created. The snapshot represents the table data in an exact point in time. Changes requested by other connections do not affect the snapshot, even after a COMMIT. If the current transaction performs DML statements on the table, like INSERT, only its own snapshot is modified. So other transactions will not be aware of the changes. When a COMMIT statement is made, the snapshot changes are copied into the real table and become visible for all the connections. Changes made by other connections also become visible for the current connection.

Note that this technique can lead the current transaction to see a table version that never existed. To make the current connection aware of the latest changes made by other connections, one may want to COMMIT the transaction and start a new one.

Consistent reads can be obtained by using the REPEATABLE-READ isolation level and START TRANSACTION WITH CONSISTENT SNAPSHOT. They are also used for the SELECT statements when the isolation level is READ COMMITTED, but remember that in this case, each statement will use a separate snapshot even within the same transaction.

The following example illustrates how consistent reads work in practice.

First, let's open a mysql client instance. We'll create the table we are going to use. Then, we will start a transaction with a consistent read and insert the first record:

```
MariaDB [test]> CREATE TABLE t (a INT UNIQUE) ENGINE = InnoDB;
Query OK, 0 rows affected (0.47 sec)
MariaDB [test]> START TRANSACTION WITH CONSISTENT SNAPSHOT;
Query OK, 0 rows affected (0.00 sec)
MariaDB [test]> INSERT INTO t VALUES (1);
Query OK, 1 row affected (0.00 sec)
```

Then, let's open another myql instance. This will use the `autocommit` mode, for brevity. We will insert another record and then check what records are visible for this connection:

```
MariaDB [test]> INSERT INTO t VALUES (2);
Query OK, 1 row affected (0.05 sec)
MariaDB [test]> SELECT * FROM t;
+------+
| a    |
+------+
|    2 |
+------+
1 row in set (0.00 sec)
```

The `SELECT` statement shows that only the record inserted by this connection is visible. The record inserted by the first connection cannot be seen at this point.

Now, let's return to the first mysql instance. Let's commit the transaction and check which rows are visible:

```
MariaDB [test]> COMMIT;
Query OK, 0 rows affected (0.08 sec)
MariaDB [test]> SELECT * FROM t;
+------+
| a    |
+------+
|    1 |
|    2 |
+------+
2 rows in set (0.00 sec)
```

As expected, after the commit, the record inserted by the first connection becomes visible.

Now let's repeat the SELECT command on the second connection:

```
MariaDB [test]> SELECT * FROM t;
+------+
| a    |
+------+
|    1 |
|    2 |
+------+
2 rows in set (0.00 sec)
```

Since the first connection was committed, the record it inserted became visible to everyone.

We can also open another mysql instance and check for InnoDB locks at any point during the former example. Since consistent reads do not imply any locks, we will always get an empty result set:

```
MariaDB [(none)]> SELECT * FROM information_schema.INNODB_LOCKS;
Empty set (0.00 sec)
```

A more complex example could show that the effects of DELETE and UPDATE statements are also not visible for other connections with consistent reads.

If we execute the previous statements without the WITH CONSISTENT SNAPSHOT clause, each row inserted by the second connection will be immediately visible to the first one.

Locking reads

Locking reads are another way to guarantee the consistency of data within a transaction. It is stronger than consistent reads because it locks data so that other connections will not be able to access them at all, or will only be able to read them, until the current transaction ends.

Locking reads can be obtained with two clauses of the SELECT statement: LOCK IN SHARE MODE and FOR UPDATE. The type of locks that are acquired depends on the used clause.

The LOCK IN SHARE MODE clause prevents other connections from modifying the rows that are returned by SELECT. But the other connections will still be able to read them.

With FOR UPDATE, the SELECT statement acts like an UPDATE; returned rows are locked so that they cannot be modified by other connections. Other connections will not be able to read those rows, unless they use the READ UNCOMMITTED isolation level. Even in that case, those connections will not be able to lock the rows in the shared mode.

If the current transaction's isolation level is SERIALIZABLE, and the autocommit mode is disabled, the LOCK IN SHARE MODE clause is always added to SELECT statements, unless they use LOCK IN SHARE MODE.

The following example shows how LOCK IN SHARE MODE works.

First, open a mysql client instance. Let's create a table with an index; this is very important because InnoDB locks are based on index records. Then, we will start a transaction and select one record in the share mode:

```
MariaDB [test]> CREATE TABLE t (a INT UNIQUE) ENGINE=InnoDB;
Query OK, 0 rows affected (0.54 sec)
MariaDB [test]> INSERT INTO t VALUES (1), (2), (3);
Query OK, 3 rows affected (0.05 sec)
Records: 3  Duplicates: 0  Warnings: 0
MariaDB [test]> START TRANSACTION;
Query OK, 0 rows affected (0.00 sec)
MariaDB [test]> SELECT * FROM t WHERE a = 1 LOCK IN SHARE MODE;
+------+
| a    |
+------+
|    1 |
+------+
1 row in set (0.00 sec)
```

Then, let's open another mysql instance. We will try to select all the records and modify two records, of which only one has been returned by the SELECT command executed by the first connection:

```
MariaDB [test]> SELECT * FROM t;
+------+
| a    |
+------+
|    1 |
|    2 |
|    3 |
+------+
3 rows in set (0.00 sec)
MariaDB [test]> UPDATE t SET a = 300 WHERE a = 3;
Query OK, 1 row affected (0.13 sec)
```

```
Rows matched: 1  Changed: 1  Warnings: 0
MariaDB [test]> UPDATE t SET a = 100 WHERE a = 1;
ERROR 1205 (HY000): Lock wait timeout exceeded; try restarting
transaction
```

As shown in the preceding code, the SELECT command works; the UPDATE command on record 3 worked, but the UPDATE command on record 1, which was locked by the first connection, had to wait because of the lock. In this example, we never committed the first transaction, so after a period of time MariaDB returned an error to the second connection. Usually, connections are supposed to be committed or rolled back, which unlocks all the records.

Deadlocks

Some combinations of locks create a situation where some transactions block each other. Since all the involved transactions are waiting for a lock to be released, they will never unblock naturally. Such situations are called deadlocks. InnoDB (like other storage engines which need to deal with such situations) has an internal mechanism to detect deadlocks. It unblocks the situation by terminating the transaction that inserted, deleted, or updated the least number of rows. Such a transaction is called the victim.

Sometimes, a storage engine that uses table-level locks may be involved in a deadlock, which also involves InnoDB tables. In that case, InnoDB can only detect the deadlock if the innodb_table_locks server variable is ON.

In an environment where concurrency exists, deadlocks are normal. When a deadlock occurs, one or more transactions terminate with a 1213 error; this is not a concern, and applications should simply handle this error by restarting the transaction. Of course, this does not mean that deadlocks are expected to happen often. If many deadlocks occur, something should be done to fix the problem. Some of the solutions to fix the problem are:

- There are some guidelines that one can follow to avoid deadlocks; small transactions are less likely to cause deadlocks. If possible, keeping transactions small is a good idea. Reducing the number of locks also helps, of course. To do this, the statements should use the proper indexes. The previous chapter illustrates how to do this. Different transactions that access the same tables should try to do it in the same order. For example, if a transaction accesses the tables A, B, and C in this order, another transaction should avoid accessing them in the same order (if possible); ideally, C, B, and A would be the perfect order.

- Usually the isolation level is not relevant, but deadlocks which are caused by locking reads can be reduced using the READ COMMITTED or READ UNCOMMITTED isolation levels.

To diagnose the latest deadlocks, the SHOW ENGINE INNODB STATUS statement can be used, as shown in the following example. It is also possible to set the innodb_print_all_deadlocks server variable to ON. This prints all InnoDB deadlocks into the error log.

Now, let's see a deadlock example. Creating a deadlock is easy. We will create two tables (t1 and t2) that contain one record and one UNIQUE index. We will use two different mysql client instances. For the first one, we will use SELECT ... FOR UPDATE to acquire an exclusive record lock on t1. For the second connection, we will acquire the same kind of lock on t2. Then, with the first connection we will try to access the record locked by the second connection; we will do the same with the second connection. At this point, the first connection will wait for a lock held by the second connection, but the lock cannot be free because the second connection will be waiting for a lock held by the first connection. This *circular* set of locks is clearly a deadlock. Here are the commands that perform this action:

Connection 1:

```
MariaDB [test]> CREATE TABLE t1 (a INT PRIMARY KEY, b INT UNIQUE) ENGINE
= InnoDB;
Query OK, 0 rows affected (0.48 sec)
MariaDB [test]> CREATE TABLE t2 (a INT PRIMARY KEY, b INT UNIQUE) ENGINE
= InnoDB;
Query OK, 0 rows affected (0.47 sec)
MariaDB [test]> INSERT INTO t1 VALUES (1, 1);
Query OK, 1 row affected (0.06 sec)
MariaDB [test]> INSERT INTO t2 VALUES (1, 1);
Query OK, 1 row affected (0.06 sec)
MariaDB [test]> START TRANSACTION;
Query OK, 0 rows affected (0.00 sec)
MariaDB [test]> SELECT * FROM t1 WHERE b = 1 FOR UPDATE;
+---+------+
| a | b    |
+---+------+
| 1 |    1 |
+---+------+
1 row in set (0.00 sec)
```

Connection 2:

```
MariaDB [test]> START TRANSACTION;
Query OK, 0 rows affected (0.00 sec)
MariaDB [test]> SELECT * FROM t2 WHERE b = 1 FOR UPDATE;
+---+------+
| a | b    |
+---+------+
| 1 |    1 |
+---+------+
1 row in set (0.01 sec)
```

Connection 1:

```
MariaDB [test]> SELECT * FROM t2 WHERE b = 1 FOR UPDATE;
```

Still no output. The connection is now on hold because the record in t2 is locked.

Connection 2:

```
MariaDB [test]> SELECT * FROM t1 WHERE b = 1 FOR UPDATE;
ERROR 1213 (40001): Deadlock found when trying to get lock; try
restarting transaction
```

InnoDB detected the error and connection 2 was terminated. Connection 1 will now receive the output of its query.

We know exactly what happened, but suppose we want to diagnose the deadlock. The SHOW ENGINE INNODB status contains information about the last detected deadlocks. Let's execute it and look at the LATEST DETECTED DEADLOCK section:

```
------------------------
LATEST DETECTED DEADLOCK
------------------------
2014-02-21 16:05:26 7f5d48554700
*** (1) TRANSACTION:
TRANSACTION 14409, ACTIVE 60 sec starting index read
mysql tables in use 1, locked 1
LOCK WAIT 5 lock struct(s), heap size 1248, 3 row lock(s)
MySQL thread id 4, OS thread handle 0x7f5d4859d700, query id 41 localhost
root statistics
SELECT * FROM t2 WHERE b = 1 FOR UPDATE
```

```
*** (1) WAITING FOR THIS LOCK TO BE GRANTED:
RECORD LOCKS space id 44 page no 4 n bits 72 index `b` of table
`test`.`t2` trx id 14409 lock_mode X locks rec but not gap waiting
Record lock, heap no 2 PHYSICAL RECORD: n_fields 2; compact format;
info bits 0
 0: len 4; hex 80000001; asc     ;;
 1: len 4; hex 80000001; asc     ;;


*** (2) TRANSACTION:
TRANSACTION 14410, ACTIVE 21 sec starting index read
mysql tables in use 1, locked 1
5 lock struct(s), heap size 1248, 3 row lock(s)
MySQL thread id 5, OS thread handle 0x7f5d48554700, query id 42 localhost
root statistics
SELECT * FROM t1 WHERE b = 1 FOR UPDATE
*** (2) HOLDS THE LOCK(S):
RECORD LOCKS space id 44 page no 4 n bits 72 index `b` of table
`test`.`t2` trx id 14410 lock_mode X locks rec but not gap
Record lock, heap no 2 PHYSICAL RECORD: n_fields 2; compact format;
info bits 0
 0: len 4; hex 80000001; asc     ;;
 1: len 4; hex 80000001; asc     ;;


*** (2) WAITING FOR THIS LOCK TO BE GRANTED:
RECORD LOCKS space id 43 page no 4 n bits 72 index `b` of table
`test`.`t1` trx id 14410 lock_mode X locks rec but not gap waiting
Record lock, heap no 2 PHYSICAL RECORD: n_fields 2; compact format;
info bits 0
 0: len 4; hex 80000001; asc     ;;
 1: len 4; hex 80000001; asc     ;;


*** WE ROLL BACK TRANSACTION (2)
```

The most important information we need is quite clear. It says which lock types were used by which transactions. For each transaction, it also says which statements caused the locks. It also says which transactions are waiting for which locks ((2) WAITING FOR THIS LOCK TO BE GRANTED). The last line provides us with information about the connection that was killed to unblock the waits.

Transactions

The user can use a set of SQL statements to control transactions. These statements allow us to explicitly start, commit, or rollback a transaction, but in some cases such operations are implicit. We can also set an isolation level, which determines which locks are acquired and how consistent the reads are. We can also declare in advance that a transaction is read only; this allows InnoDB to execute more internal optimizations.

The transactions life cycle

Usually, MariaDB transactions start with the START TRANSACTION statement and end with COMMIT or ROLLBACK. BEGIN WORK is a synonym for START TRANSACTION, but it does not work within stored programs, because the BEGIN and END keywords are used to enclose code blocks. The general syntax is:

```
START TRANSACTION;
<one or more statements>
COMMIT;
```

The START TRANSACTION AND CHAIN command means that another transaction will immediately start after COMMIT or ROLLBACK, so it is useless to repeat START TRANSACTION.

Some statements are not transactional and implicitly commit the current transaction. The list of such statements is long and varies slightly from version to version. As a general rule, all DML or DCL statements, as well as administrative statements, are not transactional. The DML statements that only involve temporary tables are an exception.

By default, the autocommit server variable is ON. It can be changed at global or session level. If it is enabled, each statement is considered a transaction, unless START TRANSACTION is issued. If it is disabled, an implicit START TRANSACTION is added before the first statement and after each COMMIT or ROLLBACK.

Transactions isolation levels

MariaDB supports four isolation levels: READ UNCOMMITTED, READ COMMITTED, REPEATABLE READ, and SERIALIZABLE. The default isolation level is REPEATABLE READ. To change it, the transaction_isolation server variable or the --transaction-isolation startup option can be set, or the SET TRANSACTION statement can be issued. For example:

```
MariaDB [(none)]> SET @@tx_isolation = 'repeatable-read';
Query OK, 0 rows affected (0.00 sec)
MariaDB [(none)]> SET TRANSACTION ISOLATION LEVEL REPEATABLE READ;
Query OK, 0 rows affected (0.00 sec)
```

Of course, it is not possible to change the isolation level after the transaction has started.

The isolation level determines how the data that is accessed by the current transaction is isolated from other connections. That is, it determines how the accessed rows are locked and whether snapshots are generated. Strong isolation levels block other connections for a longer period of time, so they should only be used if necessary. For example, a strong isolation level may not be necessary to query big quantities of data for statistical purposes where a small error is tolerated.

The READ UNCOMMITTED isolation level

With the READ UNCOMMITTED isolation level, a separate snapshot is created for each read command that is executed in the transaction. Reads use a data snapshot. This snapshot may consist of data from a transaction that has not yet been committed, so it is possible that such data will never exist in the table.

The READ COMMITTED isolation level

Like READ UNCOMMITTED, the READ COMMITTED isolation level sets a different snapshot for each consistent read in the transaction, but it never uses uncommitted data to create a snapshot. The UPDATE and DELETE statements, as well as locking reads, never use gap locks. This means that the insertion of phantom rows is always possible.

The REPEATABLE READ isolation level

With the REPEATABLE READ isolation level, all reads within a transaction use the same snapshot. This guarantees much more consistency than the READ COMMITTED isolation level. The UPDATE and DELETE statements, as well as locking reads, and record locks will be used on the UNIQUE indexes; and other indexes gap locks or next-key locks will be used to block insertions on the scanned range of values.

The SERIALIZABLE isolation level

We can think of the SERIALIZABLE isolation level as a REPEATABLE READ mode where all non-locking SELECTs are automatically converted to LOCK IN SHARE MODE. If we only use locking SELECTs, there is no difference between SERIALIZABLE and REPEATABLE READ. Another situation where these levels are identical is when the autocommit mode is enabled. This is because locks are not acquired if the current transaction will finish with the current query.

In practice, SERIALIZABLE can be used when all the queries in a transaction must acquire at least read locks. For example, let's consider the following transaction:

```
SET TRANSACTION ISOLATION LEVEL REPEATABLE READ;

START TRANSACTION;

SELECT @a := AVG(price) FROM product WHERE category = 10 LOCK IN SHARE
MODE;

UPDATE avg_price SET avg = @a WHERE category = 10;

COMMIT;
```

The same effect can be obtained in this way:

```
SET TRANSACTION ISOLATION LEVEL SERIALIZABLE;

START TRANSACTION;

SELECT @a := AVG(price) FROM product WHERE category = 10;

UPDATE avg_price SET avg = @a WHERE category = 10;

COMMIT;
```

Transactions access modes

MariaDB 10.0 introduces the transactions access mode. Two access modes exist: READ WRITE for transactions that may modify the existing data and READ ONLY for transactions that only read data. An exception is that READ ONLY transactions can modify data in temporary tables, but if they try to modify any other data they produce an error. The access mode can be specified with SET TRANSACTION. It is also possible to specify the access mode and isolation level with the same statement. For example:

```
MariaDB [(none)]> SET TRANSACTION READ ONLY;

Query OK, 0 rows affected (0.00 sec)

MariaDB [(none)]> SET TRANSACTION ISOLATION LEVEL REPEATABLE READ, READ
ONLY;

Query OK, 0 rows affected (0.00 sec)
```

If the `autocommit` mode is enabled, MariaDB always knows the exact access mode of a transaction. If it is disabled, or the transaction starts with an explicit START TRANSACTION statement, READ WRITE is the default access mode.

If the storage engine knows that the access mode is READ ONLY, it can perform some optimizations that improve concurrency.

Metadata locks

Metadata locks are a particular type of lock that has been supported since MariaDB 5.5. Transactions acquire metadata locks when they access a table or view for the first time. This includes non-transactional tables such as Aria tables. Metadata locks prevent transactions from dropping the locked object or modifying the structure. This is very important because if a transaction is using a table, you want to be sure that the table columns (or even the whole table) will not disappear in the middle. In some cases, stored programs are also locked.

If a connection tries to execute a DDL statement (such as ALTER TABLE) on a table that has a metadata lock, the connection will be put on hold until the locks are released. However, metadata locks use a timeout, which is defined by the `lock_wait_timeout` expressed in seconds. Note that the default value is `31536000`, which corresponds to one year. If the timeout expires, the connection receives a 1205 error.

Since, as we mentioned before, metadata locks also work with non-transactional tables and views, it makes sense to use transactions to access any kind of entity. Also, if an application uses DDL statements on the existing tables and views, `lock_wait_timeout` should be set to a low value, and the applications should be prepared to receive a 1205 error.

Since MariaDB 10.0, a plugin called `metadata_lock_info` allows to see the existing metadata locks. The plugin is distributed with MariaDB, but is not installed by default. After installing it, a new table METADATA_LOCK_INFO is created in the `information_schema` database. This table contains the following columns:

- THREAD_ID: This is the ID of the thread that holds the metadata lock
- LOCK_MODE: Metadata locks have several modes that determine which operations are locked
- LOCK_DURATION: This indicates whether the metadata lock is valid for the duration of the transaction or statement

- LOCK_TYPE: This indicates which object type is locked (for example, Table metadata lock or Stored function metadata lock)
- TABLE_SCHEMA: This is the name of the schema containing the locked object
- TABLE_NAME: This is the name of the locked object

In the SHOW PROCESSLIST statement output, connections that are waiting for a metadata lock to be released will appear with the Waiting for table metadata lock string in the Extra column.

Now, let's see a deadlock example. Again, we will use two mysql client instances. The first one will create a table, start a transaction, and insert a row. By doing so, it will acquire a metadata lock. We will use an Aria table to demonstrate that this mechanism also works on non-transactional tables. Then, the second connection will try to execute a RENAME TABLE, but it will have to wait. Next, the first connection will commit the transaction and the RENAME TABLE will be executed.

The code for the first connection is as follows:

```
MariaDB [test]> CREATE TABLE my_tab (a INT) ENGINE = Aria;
Query OK, 0 rows affected (0.28 sec)
MariaDB [test]> START TRANSACTION;
Query OK, 0 rows affected (0.00 sec)
MariaDB [test]> INSERT INTO my_tab VALUES (1);
Query OK, 1 row affected (0.03 sec)
```

The code for the second connection is as follows:

```
MariaDB [test]> RENAME TABLE my_tab TO tab;
```

No output at this point; the connection is waiting for a metadata lock to be freed.

Now, let's see what metadata locks exist. For our convenience, we can do this from a third connection:

```
MariaDB [(none)]> SELECT * FROM information_schema.METADATA_LOCK_INFO \G
*********************** 1. row ***********************
    THREAD_ID: 5
    LOCK_MODE: MDL_INTENTION_EXCLUSIVE
LOCK_DURATION: MDL_STATEMENT
    LOCK_TYPE: Global read lock
 TABLE_SCHEMA:
   TABLE_NAME:
```

```
*************************** 2. row ***************************
    THREAD_ID: 5
    LOCK_MODE: MDL_INTENTION_EXCLUSIVE
LOCK_DURATION: MDL_TRANSACTION
    LOCK_TYPE: Schema metadata lock
 TABLE_SCHEMA: test
   TABLE_NAME:
*************************** 3. row ***************************
    THREAD_ID: 4
    LOCK_MODE: MDL_SHARED_WRITE
LOCK_DURATION: MDL_TRANSACTION
    LOCK_TYPE: Table metadata lock
 TABLE_SCHEMA: test
   TABLE_NAME: my_tab
3 rows in set (0.12 sec)
```

We can see three locks. The first connection is the one with ID 4 and holds a shared write metadata lock on the `test.t` table, which presents other connections by modifying the table. The second connection has ID 5 and it holds two intention exclusive locks; this means that it is waiting to acquire exclusive locks on the metadata.

Now, the first connection can commit the transaction. But before and after that, it will execute a query on the table:

```
MariaDB [test]> SELECT * FROM t;
+------+
| a    |
+------+
|    1 |
+------+
1 row in set (0.00 sec)
MariaDB [test]> COMMIT;
Query OK, 0 rows affected (0.00 sec)
MariaDB [test]> SELECT * FROM t;
ERROR 1146 (42S02): Table 'test.t' doesn't exist
```

The first query works, because RENAME TABLE is waiting. But after the commit, the same query does not work, because the table has been renamed.

Note that when a metadata lock is released, the DDL statements are executed in the order they were queued. Even if the blocking transaction terminates with ALTER TABLE, this command may fail because a similar command was already queued and thus, is executed first. The following example shows this behavior. The second connection queues ALTER TABLE, and the ALTER TABLE executed by the first connection fails. If an application uses DDL statements, this behavior may lead to problems that are difficult to debug.

Connection 1:

```
MariaDB [test]> CREATE TABLE t1 (a INT) ENGINE = Aria;
Query OK, 0 rows affected (0.22 sec)
MariaDB [test]> START TRANSACTION;
Query OK, 0 rows affected (0.00 sec)
MariaDB [test]> SELECT * FROM t1;
Empty set (0.00 sec)
```

Connection 2:

```
MariaDB [test]> ALTER TABLE t1 ADD COLUMN b TINYINT SIGNED;
Stage: 2 of 2 'enabling keys'        0% of stage done
```

The client shows a progress report for certain ALTER TABLE commands on the Aria tables. The progress report stops at the second stage because the connection is waiting for the metadata lock to be released.

Connection 1:

```
MariaDB [test]> ALTER TABLE t1 ADD COLUMN b BIGINT UNSIGNED;
ERROR 1060 (42S21): Duplicate column name 'b' ALTER TABLE locks and
algorithms. Running an ALTER TABLE statement against a big table can take
a long time. It is not uncommon, on some databases, to see the building
of a new index takes some hours. With MariaDB 10.0, some operations take
much less time because they use a different algorithm. In some cases,
a table structure change required a whole copy of the table before
10.0, but can be executed in-place since 10.0. Also, in some cases such
operations used to block all connections from writing to the table, or
even from reading the table. Sometimes, this lock is no more necessary
with 10.0.
```

The operations that do not require a table copy anymore are the following:

- Renaming a table
- Changing a table comment
- Renaming a column
- Changing the display size of an integer, for example, INT(3) to INT(4)
- For the ENUM columns, adding a value at the end of the list; for example, ENUM('a', 'b') to ENUM('a', 'b', 'c')

Also, since MariaDB 5.5, adding or dropping an index on an InnoDB table does not require a table copy.

In MariaDB 10.0, some additional clauses were added to ALTER TABLE. One is ALGORITHM. It can be used to force a table copy (probably useful if we are affected by an ALTER TABLE bug) or require the use of an in-place algorithm. In this case, if the in-place algorithm cannot be used, an error is generated. The allowed values for ALGORITHM are COPY, INPLACE, or DEFAULT (which simply uses the best algorithm).

The ONLINE option is a synonym for ALGORITHM=INPLACE.

The LOCK clause can be used so that no locks are used, or only shared (read) locks or exclusive (write) locks are used. If a better locks strategy is available, it will not be used (probably useful if we are affected by some concurrency-related bug in ALTER TABLE). If the requested lock strategy cannot be used, an error will be issued. The allowed values for LOCK are NONE, SHARED, EXCLUSIVE, and DEFAULT (which uses the less restrictive available strategy).

Consider the following code for example:

```
ALTER ONLINE TABLE t ADD INDEX idx1 (col_name);
ALTER TABLE ALGORITHM = INPLACE, LOCK = NONE ADD INDEX idx1 (col_name);
```

For InnoDB tables, the information_schema INNODB_METRICS details show, among other information, the current status of the ALTER TABLE operations. For Aria tables, the mysql command-line client shows a progress report for some ALTER TABLE operations.

Percona maintains a useful tool called **pt-schema-change**, which is included in the Percona Toolkit. It creates an empty copy of a table, alters the structure of the new table, and then copies data into the new table. At the end of this process, the new table replaces the old one. This procedure requires much more time than a normal ALTER TABLE, but does not lock the existing table. With MariaDB 10.0, in many cases this tool is no longer necessary. However, it is still useful for ALTER TABLE operations that still require long table locks, and with older versions of MariaDB. Before using this tool, the Percona documentation should be read carefully.

Summary

In this chapter, we learned how the InnoDB storage engine guarantees the consistency of data in a concurrent environment. First, we discussed how locks and snapshots work. This low-level understanding of InnoDB mechanisms is necessary to understand how InnoDB transactions work. We discussed the isolation levels and how each isolation level uses locks and snapshots to guarantee a certain level of protection. We discussed how to deal with deadlocks that are normal on a busy database, but a DBA should avoid them becoming a problem. We also discussed metadata locks, which protect transactions from changes in the structures of the tables.

In the final section, we discussed how to avoid ALTER TABLE locking other transactions for a long period of time.

In the next chapter, we will learn how to manage connections and users, how to assign them limited resources, and how to deal with security.

5
Users and Connections

This chapter illustrates the tools that MariaDB provides to control advanced security features and process management. The reader should already have the basic knowledge of MariaDB accounts and permission management, such as the basic syntax of the GRANT and REVOKE statements and how the permissions apply to databases, tables, and columns.

The following topics will be discussed in this chapter:

- User accounts
- Roles
- Secure Socket Layer connections
- Authentication plugins
- Limiting user resources
- Pool of threads
- Monitoring connections

User accounts

The access control layer of MariaDB is based on accounts. An account is composed of a username and the name of the host from which the user connects. The account's syntax is shown as follows (the quotes are optional, if no special characters are used):

```
'username'@'hostname'
```

It is good practice to create new users with the CREATE USER statement. Then, permissions can be assigned to the users with GRANT. By default, MariaDB allows assigning permissions to accounts even if its user does not exist, in which case the server will automatically create it. Though, in this way, unwanted users could be created by mistyping the username in the GRANT statement. The autocreation of users can be disabled by setting the NO_AUTO_CREATE_USER flag in the SQL_MODE system variable, shown as follows:

```
MariaDB [(none)]> SET @@global.sql_mode = CONCAT(@@global.sql_mode,
',NO_AUTO_CREATE_USER');
Query OK, 0 rows affected (0.07 sec)
```

In an account, both the username and hostname can use the same wildcard characters that are used with the LIKE operator. For example, 'user__'@'%' matches usernames such as user01 from whatever host they connect. When a user tries to connect, MariaDB searches for an account that matches its username and hostname (or the IP address) in the mysql.user system table. If an account matches, MariaDB checks the password. The password is encrypted in the system table, and also the client encrypts it before sending it to the server. If the encrypted passwords are not identical, or if no account matches the username and hostname, the connection is rejected with an error.

If we provide an incorrect password, we obtain an error similar to the following:

```
ERROR 1045 (28000): Access denied for user 'root'@'localhost' (using
password: NO)
```

This error provides all details, which can be used to diagnose problems such as the username does not exist, account cannot be accessed from this host, or password is wrong. If the password does not appear and the error message tells us that we have provided it, we can easily know whether we just forgot to enter the password.

> The hash algorithm used for authentication is the same used by the PASSWORD() function. It is derived from an SHA algorithm. Note that while PASSWORD() is used by many applications, it was developed for internal use. It is not recommended to call this function in SQL queries.

Sometimes, multiple accounts can match a username and hostname. In such cases, MariaDB tries to choose the least generic account. For example, 'user01'@'mandarino' will be preferred over 'user__'@'%'. This account will be used by MariaDB to check the permissions every time the user issues a command. Permissions associated to other matching accounts will be ignored.

The USER() function returns the complete username and hostname used by the current connection. The CURRENT_USER() function returns the account that was chosen by MariaDB during authentication. For example:

```
SELECT CURRENT_USER(), USER();

+----------------+-------------------+
| CURRENT_USER() | USER()            |
+----------------+-------------------+
| user01@%       | user01@mandarino  |
+----------------+-------------------+
```

In this example, whenever the user sends a SQL statement, the server will check whether the 'user01'@'%' account has the permissions to execute it. More generic accounts may exist such as 'user__'@'%', but they are ignored.

Setting permissions using roles

Directly managing the accounts for a MariaDB server that has several users can be a pain. We may have 20 users that need permissions to perform the same actions. At some point in time, the structure of the database may change. We will need to update the permissions for 20 users, probably with 20 GRANT statements. This task is error prone and extremely frustrating.

For this reason, MariaDB 10.0 introduces roles following the SQL:2003 specification. If a set of permissions can be set for a role, instead of a single account, then the role itself can be associated to a set of accounts. Each of these accounts will then be allowed to enable one of the roles it is associated with. From this moment, MariaDB will check the role's permissions to determine whether the user has the right to perform the requested action. If something changes in the database, only the role's permissions will need to be updated.

Roles can be created and dropped with the CREATE ROLE and DROP ROLE statements. While creating a role, it is also possible to choose its administrator. Consider the following example:

```
MariaDB [(none)]> CREATE ROLE reviewer WITH ADMIN amanda;
Query OK, 0 rows affected (0.02 sec)
MariaDB [(none)]> DROP ROLE reviewer;
Query OK, 0 rows affected (0.00 sec)
```

If the WITH ADMIN clause is not present, the role administrator is the current user. The administrator can use the GRANT and REVOKE statements to associate roles to accounts, or to drop those associations. Note that a role can even be associated to another role. This is useful if we have many roles, some of which share a set of privileges. Instead of individually granting privileges to each role, common privileges can be assigned to another role. Here is a simple example of the usage of the GRANT and REVOKE statements:

```
MariaDB [(none)]> GRANT reviewer TO amanda, josh, lucy;
Query OK, 0 rows affected (0.00 sec)
MariaDB [(none)]> REVOKE reviewer FROM u3;
Query OK, 0 rows affected (0.00 sec)
```

The GRANT statement can also be used to add permissions to a role. The permissions granted to the role are the ones that the associated user will be able to use. To drop the granted permissions, REVOKE can be used. In both cases, the syntax is exactly the same that is used to grant or revoke account permissions. A simple example is as follows:

```
MariaDB [(none)]> GRANT UPDATE ON TABLE 'news_db'.'article' TO reviewer;
Query OK, 0 rows affected (0.03 sec)
```

Remember that users associated to a role will not automatically use the role when they connect to the server. Instead, they need to explicitly enable the role with SET ROLE. Only one role at a time can be enabled (though if a role is associated to another role, its permissions will be available for the user). The CURRENT_ROLE() function returns an active role. An example is shown as follows:

```
MariaDB [(none)]> SET ROLE r;
Query OK, 0 rows affected (0.00 sec)
MariaDB [(none)]> SELECT CURRENT_ROLE();
+----------------+
| CURRENT_ROLE() |
+----------------+
| r              |
+----------------+
1 row in set (0.00 sec)
MariaDB [(none)]> SET ROLE NONE;
Query OK, 0 rows affected (0.00 sec)
```

```
MariaDB [(none)]> SELECT CURRENT_ROLE();
+----------------+
| CURRENT_ROLE() |
+----------------+
| NULL           |
+----------------+
1 row in set (0.00 sec)
```

The `information_schema` database contains two tables that store information about roles. The `APPLICABLE_ROLES` table contains information about roles that can be selected by the current user with `SET ROLE`, such as to whom these roles are granted to and who can grant these roles. The `ENABLED_ROLES` table contains the name of the enabled roles and the names of the roles that are granted to that role. If one or more roles are assigned to the role that the user has explicitly selected, those roles will also be shown. Consider the following example:

```
MariaDB [mysql]> SELECT * FROM information_schema.APPLICABLE_ROLES;
+----------------+-----------+--------------+
| GRANTEE        | ROLE_NAME | IS_GRANTABLE |
+----------------+-----------+--------------+
| josh@localhost | writer    | YES          |
| writer         | reviewer  | NO           |
+----------------+-----------+--------------+
4 rows in set (0.00 sec)
MariaDB [mysql]> SELECT * FROM information_schema.ENABLED_ROLES;
+-----------+
| ROLE_NAME |
+-----------+
| writer    |
| reviewer  |
+-----------+
2 rows in set (0.00 sec)
```

In this case, the `writer` role can be applied to `josh`, the current user. Also, the `reviewer` role is automatically applied to whoever has the `writer` role enabled. In the `ENABLED_ROLES` table, `josh` can see both roles.

Connecting MariaDB through Secure Socket Layer

MariaDB supports the **Secure Socket Layer (SSL)** connections. In order to use SSL, MariaDB must be compiled with **yaSSL** or **OpenSSL**. Binary packages are built with yaSSL. To check whether our local installation has SSL support, we can look at the `have_ssl` server variable. If its value is `YES`, SSL is supported and configured; if its value is `DISABLED`, SSL is supported but not yet configured; and if its value is `NO`, SSL is not supported. For example:

```
MariaDB [(none)]> SELECT @@global.have_ssl;

+-------------------+

| @@global.have_ssl |

+-------------------+

| DISABLED          |

+-------------------+

1 row in set (0.00 sec)
```

To configure SSL, we first need to create a certificate (released by a Certification Authority also known as CA), and public and private keys for both the server and clients that need to use SSL. The certificate and keys can be generated with the OpenSSL program, which is a free software. It is usually already installed on Unix systems and can be downloaded and installed on Windows.

 This section assumes that the user already knows the concepts behind SSL and has already created the certificate and keys.

A suggestion about the key length: a 4096 long key is obviously much more secure than a 2048 long key, or smaller keys. Of course, a longer key also causes a bigger overhead in network communications. But tests show that the difference between a 4096 long key and a 1024 long key is mostly noticeable during the connection establishing phase, while during normal operations it is very small. So, the maximum key length is a good security choice and sometimes it does not noticeably affect the performance of the database. The difference will be more relevant for workloads with several short-lived connections. However, keep in mind that the overhead caused by SSL itself often represents a half of the total query execution time, or more.

To verify that the certificate and keys are in place and valid, you can check them with the `openssl` command:

```
root@this:/usr/local/mysql# cd /etc/ssl/mysql
root@this:/etc/ssl/mysql# openssl verify -CAfile ca-cert.pem
server-cert.pem client-cert.pem
server-cert.pem: OK
client-cert.pem: OK
```

Now we need to let MariaDB know where the certificates and keys are. Let's add the following variables to the configuration file in the `[mysqld]` section:

```
# SSL
ssl-ca=/etc/ssl/mysql/ca-cert.pem
ssl-cert=/etc/ssl/mysql/server-cert.pem
ssl-key=/etc/ssl/mysql/server-key.pem
```

We can also use the corresponding server startup options:

```
mysql --ssl-ca=/etc/ssl/mysql/ca-cert.pem --ssl-cert=/etc/ssl/mysql/
server-cert.pem --ssl-key=/etc/ssl/mysql/server-key.pem
```

We can also add similar variables for the client in the `[client]` section of the configuration file, or use the corresponding client startup options:

```
# SSL
ssl-cert=/etc/mysql-ssl/client-cert.pem
ssl-key=/etc/mysql-ssl/client-key.pem
```

This allows the client to use an SSL connection with the server.

 Typing the options in the configuration file makes the user's life easier, and prevents him/her from forgetting these parameters.

We will also require an account to use SSL. If the account tries to connect without encryption, the connection will be rejected even if the username and password it provides are correct. To do this, we can again use the GRANT statement:

```
MariaDB [(none)]> GRANT USAGE ON *.* TO u1 REQUIRE SSL;
Query OK, 0 rows affected (0.00 sec)
```

This example simply forces the user u1 to connect using an SSL encryption without any further requirements. It is also possible for the user to require a higher security level. One or more options can be used in a single GRANT statement, after the REQUIRE keyword, optionally separated by AND. These options are stated as follows:

- NONE: This option states that SSL can be used, but is not required
- SSL: This option states that an SSL encryption is required without any requirements about its characteristics
- X509: This option states that a valid X509 certificate is required
- ISSUER 'str': This option states that a valid X509 certificate is required which is released by the specified authority
- SUBJECT 'str': This option states that a valid X509 certificate is required with the specified subject
- CIPHER 'str': This option states that a valid X509 certificate is required, and the connection must use one of the specified encryption methods

The following example shows the usage of the preceding options:

```
MariaDB [(none)]> GRANT USAGE ON *.* TO u1@localhost;

Query OK, 0 rows affected (0.00 sec)

MariaDB [(none)]> GRANT USAGE ON *.* TO 'u1'@'%' REQUIRE ISSUER
'/C=FI/ST=Somewhere/L=City/ O=Some Company/CN=Norman Bates/
emailAddress=n.bates@example.net' AND CIPHER 'RSA-SHA';

Query OK, 0 rows affected (0.01 sec)
```

In this example, the user u1 can connect from a localhost without encryption; but if the user wants to connect from anywhere else, he/she must use an SSL connection with a certificate released by the specified authority, using the **Remote Secure Access (RSA)** authentication or the **Secure Hash Algorithm (SHA)** hashing.

Authentication plugins

MariaDB also supports authentication plugins. These plugins can implement different methods for login and logout. Generally, this is useful to prevent an external program from authenticating users into a MariaDB server. Some plugins require the client to interact with them using appropriate client plugins. The client plugins are dynamically loaded and need not be installed, but this requires the client to be built dynamically.

Currently, MariaDB 10.0 comes with four authentication plugins:

- `mysql_native_password`: This is the default MariaDB authentication plugin
- `mysql_old_password`: This is the old (less secure) password hashing used in MySQL 4.0 and even in MySQL 3.23 (they had 20-byte and 9-byte shadowed passwords, respectively)
- `unix_socket`: This plugin uses the credentials of the Unix user
- `pam`: This plugin uses Unix **Pluggable Authentication Modules (PAM)**

The last two plugins are not installed by default. They can be installed with the following statements:

```
INSTALL SONAME 'auth_socket';

INSTALL SONAME 'auth_pam';
```

Other plugins may be added to the MariaDB packages in the future, or developed by companies that need them and have the internal skills to develop authentication plugins. The exact list of authentication plugins can be obtained with the following query:

```
SELECT PLUGIN_NAME, PLUGIN_STATUS
  FROM information_schema.PLUGINS
  WHERE PLUGIN_TYPE = 'AUTHENTICATION';
```

It is possible that you may require an account to connect MariaDB using a particular authentication plugin. To do this, both CREATE USER and GRANT can be used, like in the following examples:

```
CREATE USER federico IDENTIFIED VIA 'mysql_native_password';

GRANT USAGE ON *.* TO federico IDENTIFIED VIA 'unix_socket';
```

In the preceding example, first the user federico was created specifying explicitly that he uses the default MariaDB authentication (this is not necessary when creating a user, but can be done). Then, we require that the user connects via the unix_socket plugin, shown as follows:

```
MariaDB [(none)]> CREATE USER federico IDENTIFIED VIA
'mysql_native_password';

Query OK, 0 rows affected (0.00 sec)

MariaDB [(none)]> GRANT USAGE ON *.* TO federico IDENTIFIED VIA
'unix_socket';

Query OK, 0 rows affected (0.03 sec)
```

The USAGE command is a virtual permission. It can be specified when we don't want to grant any real permission. Simply omitting the permissions list will cause a syntax error. In the preceding example, we used USAGE so that the user federico connects using unix_socket.

To complete the example, let's see how this user can connect to MariaDB.

Let's use a shell as federico, and start the mysql command-line client:

```
federico@this:/usr/local/mysql$ bin/mysql
Welcome to the MariaDB monitor.  Commands end with ; or \g.
```

It works because we are already logged in as federico. The unix_socket plugin verifies whether the thread belongs to federico and accepts the connection.

Now, let's use the shell as the root, and start mysql:

```
root@this:/usr/local/mysql# bin/mysql
ERROR 1045 (28000): Access denied for user 'root'@'localhost'
(using password: NO)
```

As the user of the current system is root and not federico, the connection is not accepted. However, we can use the --user option, which starts the client as the specified user:

```
root@this:/usr/local/mysql# bin/mysql --user federico
Welcome to the MariaDB monitor.  Commands end with ; or \g.
```

With the client running as the appropriate user, the connection is accepted.

> Note that this feature cannot be used to run mysql as another user if you don't have the permissions to do so. Instead, it is useful if you are logged in as root and need to start mysql as a normal user.

Limiting user resources, MariaDB allows us to limit the amount of system resources an account can consume. This is done with the GRANT statement. The following are the limits that can be set:

- MAX_QUERIES_PER_HOUR: This limit sets the number of queries (statements that return data but do not modify them) that can be executed in an hour. It does not affect queries that use the query cache.

- MAX_UPDATES_PER_HOUR: This limit sets the number of statements that modify the data that can be executed in an hour.

- MAX_CONNECTIONS_PER_HOUR: This limit sets the number of connections that the account can establish in an hour.
- MAX_USER_CONNECTIONS: This limit sets the number of simultaneous connections that the account can establish.

For all these values, the default is 0, which means that the limit does not apply to the account. However, MAX_USER_CONNECTIONS is an exception; if it is set to 0, the limit is set to the global value of the max_user_connections server variable. Its default value is 0, which means that the limit does not apply. The user can query the session value of this variable to know the maximum number of simultaneous connections that this account can establish.

An example of how to assign a resource limit is shown as follows:

```
MariaDB [(none)]> GRANT USAGE ON TABLE *.* TO 'u1'@'%' WITH
MAX_QUERIES_PER_HOUR 100 MAX_UPDATES_PER_HOUR 50;

Query OK, 0 rows affected (0.00 sec)
```

The GRANT statement has some mandatory clauses; this means that we cannot execute a GRANT statement that does not assign any permission. Since our purpose is not to assign permission, we specify USAGE, which is a virtual right; it does not allow us to do anything. Then, we specify the WITH keyword, followed by the resource limits we want to set.

An example of how to know which account we are using and how many simultaneous connections it is allowed to establish is shown as follows:

```
MariaDB [(none)]> SELECT CURRENT_USER(), @@session.max_user_connections;

+----------------+-------------------------------+
| CURRENT_USER() | @@session.max_user_connections |
+----------------+-------------------------------+
| root@localhost |                             0 |
+----------------+-------------------------------+
1 row in set (0.00 sec)
```

If an account has reached one of its limits, and we want to temporarily enable it to continue doing its work, we can reset all hourly resource limits. This does not apply to MAX_USER_CONNECTIONS, which is not an hourly limit. Note that there is no way to reset these limits for a single user. To reset the limits, the FLUSH USER_RESOURCES statement can be used. The FLUSH PRIVILEGES or mysqladmin reload commands can also be used because they entirely reload the privilege tables handling threads.

Traditionally, MariaDB and MySQL create a new thread every time a client connects to the server. This thread handling method is called **one thread per connection**. It is still the default method on most systems, with the only exception of Windows (starting from Vista).

In most cases, MariaDB is used for the workloads described with the **On Line Transaction Processing (OLTP)**. This includes all cases where data is often modified, such as most websites and desktop applications. In such workloads, usually a client connects, executes a few fast statements, and closes the connection. If there are many users, this means that many clients connect to the server for a very short time. The one thread per connection method is not good for such workloads, because creating and destroying a thread has a cost in terms of CPU and memory, and the execution of a small series of fast operations may not be worth that cost.

In MariaDB 5.1, a new thread handling method was added called the **pool of threads**. The idea is that each thread can handle multiple connections. Each thread is part of a group. In MariaDB 5.1, the total number of threads is fixed. The pool of threads method has been refactored in MariaDB 5.5. This method now creates new threads when the current number of threads is insufficient and destroys threads when they are not useful anymore. It always tries to keep the number of threads reasonable; if it is too low, this method is not beneficial and if it is too high, there is a wastage of resources.

Note that the pool of threads method can queue several threads in the same group. This means that while this method avoids the overhead of a thread's creation and destruction, and generally speeds up the global performance of an OLTP workload, the individual statements or transactions may be slower. For example, a trivial query such as SELECT VERSION() should immediately return one row, but with the pool of threads method, it may have to wait for more complex queries to be executed.

The pool of threads is a bit different on Windows, because it uses the native threadpool implementation. On all other systems, MariaDB uses its own threadpool implementation. From a user's point of view, this mainly means that on Windows, the available configuration variables are not the same that are available on other systems. On Windows versions older than Vista, this feature does not work, and the one thread per connection method is always used.

Activating the pool of threads

To enable the pool of threads, the configuration file should contain the following line:

```
thread_handling=pool-of-threads
```

On Windows versions older than Vista, this option is silently ignored. On Vista and more recent versions, the pool of threads is the default method (this differs from all other systems).

If this line is written in a global configuration file, it is possible to override it for an individual MariaDB installation by adding the following line to its own configuration file:

```
thread_handling=one-thread-per-connection
```

Monitoring the pool of threads

To see which connection handling method is used, the `thread_handling` variable can be queried:

```
MariaDB [(none)]> SELECT @@global.thread_handling;
+--------------------------+
| @@global.thread_handling |
+--------------------------+
| pool-of-threads          |
+--------------------------+
1 row in set (0.00 sec)
```

The pool of threads has two status variables that can be used to monitor the threads' activities:

- `threadpool_threads`: This variable helps the thread determine the total number of threads.

- `threadpool_idle_threads`: This variable helps the thread determine the number of threads that are doing nothing—because they are idle, or because they are waiting for a lock to be released. This value is not monitored on Windows.

If the one pool per connection method is used, both these values are `0`, as seen in the following example:

```
MariaDB [(none)]> SHOW STATUS LIKE 'threadpool%';
+--------------------------+-------+
| Variable_name            | Value |
+--------------------------+-------+
| Threadpool_idle_threads  | 0     |
| Threadpool_threads       | 0     |
+--------------------------+-------+
2 rows in set (0.00 sec)
```

Configuring the threadpool implementation

As explained previously, MariaDB uses the Windows' native threadpool implementation and an ad hoc implementation on all other systems. These two implementations expose different details about how the pool of threads works; so the variables that can be used on Windows are different from the variables that can be used on a Unix-like system. The ad hoc implementation exposes more details.

The list of pool of threads configuration variables can be obtained with the following query:

```
SHOW VARIABLES LIKE 'thread_pool%';
```

Configuring the pool of threads on Unix

The following variables can be used to configure the pool of threads on Unix:

- `thread_pool_size`: This variable gives the number of thread groups. Since normally one thread per group is working, this is also the approximated number of concurrent threads. By default, it is equal to the number of server CPUs. Note, however, that MariaDB never executes a single query on multiple CPUs. This is a very important parameter to tune under some circumstances. Incrementing it should not lead to any performance gain. However, if MariaDB does not run on a dedicated server, we may want it to use only a limited number of CPUs. For example, if we have a machine with four CPUs running MariaDB and a web server, we might want MariaDB to only use three CPUs. This can be done by setting `thread_pool_size` to 3.

- `thread_pool_stall_limit`: This variable gives a timeout, expressed in milliseconds, after which a thread is considered stalled. When this happens, the pool of threads will try to wake the thread up, or create another one. This mechanism prevents long running queries from stopping the queued queries for a long time. However, if `thread_pool_max_threads` is also reached, no new thread can be created. The default value is 500.

- `thread_pool_max_threads`: This variable gives the maximum number of threads. It refers to the total number and not a per-group limit. When this limit is reached, no new thread can be created. The default value is 500. This variable is available for all systems.

- `thread_pool_idle_timeout`: This variable gives a time-out, expressed in seconds, after which idle threads are terminated. The default value is 60.

- `thread_pool_oversubscribe`: This variable gives a variable for internal use and should not be changed by the user. It is mentioned here just because it appears in the output of the `SHOW VARIABLES LIKE 'thread_pool%'` statement.

Configuring the pool of threads on Windows

The following variables can be used to configure the pool of threads on Unix:

- `thread_pool_min_threads`: This variable gives the minimum number of threads. Windows can retire threads when they are not needed, unless the minimum limit has been reached.

- `thread_pool_max_threads`: This variable gives the maximum number of threads. It refers to the total number; it is not a per-group limit. When this limit is reached, no new thread can be created. The default value is `500`. This variable is available for all systems.

Tuning the configuration variables

Now, we will list some possible problems that may rise on a server that uses the pool of threads, and explain how to use the configuration variables to improve the performance.

Sometimes, a thread may lock several tables to perform some action. For example, it may issue a `FLUSH TABLES ... WITH READ LOCK` statement to perform a physical backup of non-transactional tables (this technique will be discussed in *Chapter 8, Backup and Disaster Recovery*). In such cases, all threads (or several threads) will be blocked. Usually, it causes the pool of threads to create new threads, but in this case the new threads will not solve the problem and will consume more resources. Setting `thread_pool_max_threads` to a sufficiently low value prevents the creation of such threads.

Some workloads are not equally distributed in time. They may burst for a given period, during which a high number of connections are established. After that period, they may return to a state of very low activity. Such workloads do not benefit from the pool of threads method during the period in which several connections are established because it has to create several threads, which takes some time. To avoid this problem, we want MariaDB to preserve more threads during the low activity periods. On Unix, we can achieve this by increasing `thread_pool_idle_timeout`, so that the timeout is higher than the time that separates the interval between two high activity periods. On Windows, we will simply increase `thread_pool_min_threads`.

While data warehouse workloads are not likely to benefit from the pool of threads method, even on an OLTP database, reports may be periodically generated from a nontrivial quantity of data. Such queries probably don't lock (see *Chapter 4, Transactions and Locks*) but can block the queued statements for an amount of time that is not acceptable. To avoid this problem on Unix, we can set `thread_pool_stall_limit` to a lower value.

Unblocking a blocked pool of threads

What happens if the pool of threads method is used and one client obtains a lock on all the tables to perform a very long operation? The other threads will be blocked. To solve this problem, MariaDB will create more threads, but this does not help because each new thread will still have to wait for the lock to be released. Also, we may reach the `thread_pool_max_threads` limit. In this case, the server will refuse new connections and the DBA will not be able to connect to the server to investigate what is happening. To avoid this, one can consider increasing the limit, but this might lead to a high number of threads in all situations, making the pool of threads useless.

The solution is to reserve an extra port for connections that will use the one thread per connection method. The number of such connections is limited, usually one is enough. The variables that control this feature are as follows:

- `extra_port`: This variable gives the number of the port that will accept connections using the one thread per connection method

- `extra_max_connections`: This variable gives the maximum number of simultaneous connections that the extra port will accept

 Note that this technique can also be used to allow some connections to work in the one thread per connection mode (so that they are never queued in a group), while others run in the pool of threads. However, in this case, `extra_max_connections` should be high enough to always accept an extra connection to solve lock problems.

Monitoring connections

The `SHOW PROCESSLIST` statement returns information about the active connections. The `PROCESSLIST` table in the `information_schema` database contains additional complete information; we will discuss this. Also, the `threads` table in the `performance_schema` database includes the same information returned by `SHOW PROCESSLIST`, plus some extra columns. Normally, `SHOW PROCESSLIST` returns sufficient information and is less verbose. The `PROCESSLIST` table has the advantage that its contents can be used in a stored program.

The following example shows the contents of the `PROCESSLIST` table and the output of `SHOW PROCESSLIST`:

```
MariaDB [(none)]> SELECT * FROM information_schema.PROCESSLIST \G

*************************** 1. row ***************************
```

```
          ID: 5

        USER: root

        HOST: localhost

          DB: NULL

     COMMAND: Query

        TIME: 0

       STATE: Filling schema table

        INFO: SELECT * FROM information_schema.PROCESSLIST

     TIME_MS: 0.652

       STAGE: 0

   MAX_STAGE: 0

    PROGRESS: 0.000

 MEMORY_USED: 82920

EXAMINED_ROWS: 0

    QUERY_ID: 11

1 row in set (0.00 sec)


MariaDB [(none)]> SHOW PROCESSLIST \G

*************************** 1. row ***************************

       Id: 5

     User: root

     Host: localhost

       db: NULL

  Command: Query

     Time: 0
```

```
     State: closing tables

      Info: SHOW PROCESSLIST

Progress: 0.000

1 row in set (0.00 sec)
```

The following table shows the descriptions of the columns of the PROCESSLIST table:

PROCESSLIST table column	SHOW PROCESSLIST statement column	Description
ID	Id	This shows the connection ID.
USER	User	This shows the username as it appears after SELECT USER(). The event_scheduler variable is displayed for the process that executes events.
HOST	Host	This shows the hostname as it appears after SELECT USER().
DB	db	This shows the default database (that changes after the USE statement).
COMMAND	Command	This shows the type of the issued command (see the next table for the possible values).
TIME	Time	This shows the seconds elapsed since the process switched to the current state.
STATE	State	This shows the state of the process (see the table in the *States of the process* section for the possible values).
INFO	Info	This shows the statement that is being executed, if any. Unless SHOW FULL PROCESSLIST is executed (with the FULL option), only the first 100 characters are displayed.
TIME_MS		This is similar to TIME, but is expressed in milliseconds.
STAGE, MAX_STAGE		If the statements support the progress reporting, the job can consist of multiple stages. These columns provide the number of the current stage and final stage.

PROCESSLIST table column	SHOW PROCESSLIST statement column	Description
PROGRESS	Progress	If the statement supports the progress reporting, this is the percentage of the completed job (as FLOAT).
MEMORY_USED		This shows the quantity of memory used by this process. This feature is added in MariaDB 10.0.
EXAMINED_ROWS		This shows the number of rows read by the process and is added in MariaDB 10.0.
QUERY_ID		This shows the ID of the current statement, if any, being executed. This feature is added in MariaDB 10.0.

Querying the threads table causes no locks. However, note that activating the performance_schema database causes an overhead, which affects most server activities. This is the reason why performance_schema is disabled by default in MariaDB 10.0. It stores information about all threads, including internal threads, and not only the connections with the clients. The threads table contains all the columns from SHOW PROCESSLIST, written in uppercase with the PROCESSLIST_ prefix. It also contains the following extra columns:

- THREAD_ID: This is the ID of the thread. It is different from the value of PROCESSLIST_ID, which is the value that is shown by SHOW PROCESSLIST.
- NAME: This indicates the thread types. There are many possible values that reflect the internal MariaDB structures. For example, the value for a thread that is associated to a client connection is thread/sql/one_connection.
- TYPE: This is BACKGROUND for internal threads and FOREGROUND for threads that are visible via SHOW PROCESSLIST.
- PARENT_THREAD_ID: This is the ID of the thread that created it.
- ROLE: This is always NULL. These are currently ignored in the performance_schema database.
- INSTRUMENTED: This indicates whether the thread activities are tracked in the performance_schema database.

The THREAD_ID column can be used to join the threads table with other tables in the performance_schema database. Consider the following example:

```
SELECT *
  FROM performance_schema.events_statements_current s
  LEFT JOIN performance_schema.threads t
  ON s.THREAD_ID = t.THREAD_ID;
```

The following table describes the values of the COMMAND column:

Value	Description
Binlog Dump	This means that the process sends the binary log contents to a slave
Change user	This means that the process changes the current user
Close stmt	This means that the process deallocates a prepared statement
Connect	This means that the process is a slave thread connected to a master
Connect Out	This means that the process is a slave process connected to a master
Creating DB	This means that the process creates a database
Daemon	This means that the process itself is an internal thread
Debug	This means that the process generates the debug information
Delayed insert	This means that the process executes an INSERT DELAYED statement
Drop DB	This means that the process erases a database
Error	This means that a fatal error has occurred in the process
Execute	This means that the process executes a prepared statement
Fetch	This means that the process fetches rows from the result of a prepared statement
Field List	This means that the process retrieves information about table columns
Init DB	This means that the process changes the default database
Kill	This means that the process terminates another process
Long Data	This means that the process retrieves a large amount of data from prepared statement results
Ping	This means that the process replies to a ping
Prepare	This means that the process makes a prepared statement
Processlist	This means that the process gathers information about the existing processes
Query	This means that the process executes a statement
Quit	This means that the process exits
Refresh	This means that the process flushes tables, hosts, or caches; or resets status variables or replication information
Register Slave	This means that the process registers a new slave
Reset stmt	This means that the process resets a prepared statement
Set option	This means that the process changes a connection option
Shutdown	This means that the process stops the server
Sleep	This means that the process waits for a new statement from the client
Statistics	This means that the process gathers information about the server's status
Table dump	This means that the process sends a whole table to a slave

States of the process

The STATE column indicates exactly what the state is doing. It has several possible values. Here, we only list the main values:

Value	Description
After create	This means that the process creates a table, possibly an internal temporary table.
altering table	This means that the process alters a table.
Analyzing	This means that the process calculates the indexes distributions of a table.
checking permissions	This means that the process checks whether the account has the necessary permissions to execute a statement.
Checking table	This means that the process executes a CHECK TABLE command.
cleaning up	This means that the process frees memory after a statement's execution.
closing tables	This means that the process flushes a table's data to a disk. If this operation takes a lot of time, the disk might be full or very busy. On some filesystems, it might also mean that a process is blocked by the journaling block device.
committing alter table to storage engine	This means that the server finishes an ALTER TABLE command and is committing the changes to a storage engine.
converting HEAP to MyISAM	This means that the process converts a MEMORY temporary table to a MyISAM on-disk temporary table (HEAP is the old name of MEMORY).
copy to tmp table	This means that the process executes an ALTER TABLE command, which requires a table copy.
Copying to group table	This means that the process orders the results of a query involving GROUP BY using a temporary table.
Copying to tmp table	This means that the process populates an in-memory temporary table.
Copying to tmp table on disk	This means that the process populates an internal on-disk temporary table.
Creating sort index	This means that the process creates an index for an internal temporary table.
Creating table	This means that the process creates a table, possibly a temporary table.
Creating tmp table	This means that the process creates an internal temporary table.

Value	Description
Creating sort index	This means that the process creates an index for an internal temporary table.
deleting from main table	This means that the process deletes rows from the first table in a DELETE statement.
deleting from reference tables	This means that the process deletes rows from a table (not the first one) in a DELETE statement.
discard_or_import_ tablespace	This means that the process executes ALTER TABLE ... DISCARD/IMPORT TABLESPACE.
end	This means that a statement has just finished its execution but the memory has not been cleaned up.
executing	This means that the process executes a statement.
freeing items	This means that the process cleans up a statement that involves the query cache.
flushing tables	This means that the process waits for other threads to finish their statements, before executing FLUSH TABLES.
init	This means that the process prepares to execute a statement.
Killed	This means that a KILL command (described in the *Aborting connections* section) has been executed against this process. It is waiting for a lock, or executing some actions before disappearing.
logging slow query	This means that the process logs a statement into the slow query log.
login	This means that a user has logged in.
Opening table	This means that the process opens a table. If this operation is not very fast, the table is probably locked.
optimizing	This means that the optimizer determines the statement execution plans.
preparing	This is the stage which precedes optimization; the statement is parser and names are resolved.
preparing alter table	This means that the process performs some preliminary operations before an ALTER TABLE command.
Purging old relay logs	This means that the process removes old relay logfiles.
query end	This means that the process cleans up the memory after a statement, which precedes freeing items.
Removing duplicates	This means that the process removes duplicate rows during a SELECT DISTINCT command.
removing tmp table	This means that the process drops an internal temporary table.

Value	Description
Rolling back	This means that the process executes ROLLBACK.
Updating rows for update	This means that the process executes an UPDATE command which modifies indexed columns. It searches for rows pointed by the index entries that will be modified.
Sending data	This means that the process sends a result set to the client.
setup	This means that the process executes an ALTER TABLE command, which is followed by preparing an alter table.
Sorting for group	This means that the process sorts rows, as requested by an ORDER BY clause.
Sorting result	This means that the process sorts the results of a SELECT query. No internal temporary table is used.
Statistics	This means that the process calculates index statistics.
System lock	This means that the process is on hold because another program (not MariaDB) locked a table file.
update	This means that the process prepares to update a table.
Updating	This means that the process is modifying rows.
Waiting for commit lock	This means that the process waits until a COMMIT command is finished.
Waiting for global read lock	This means that the process waits for a lock that involves all tables (like the one created by the FLUSH TABLES ... WITH READ LOCK statement).
Waiting for tables, Waiting for table flush	This means that the process is similar to Reopen tables, but it has to wait because some threads are using the table.
Waiting for * lock	This means that the process waits for a metadata lock (possibly a metadata lock) to be released and * is replaced by the type of the locked object (for example, table level).
Waiting on cond	This means that the process waits for a condition lock.

Aborting connections

While examining the list of processes, you may notice that one of them is slow and is blocking other processes. Or perhaps, you may notice several sleeping processes. In this case, you may want to terminate them. The KILL statement can be used for this purpose. MariaDB supports more clauses for this command, if compared to the MySQL syntax. The syntax for KILL is as follows:

```
KILL
  [ HARD | SOFT ]
  [ CONNECTION | QUERY [ID] ]
  < id | USER user_name >
```

By default, KILL terminates a connection. The CONNECTION keyword just makes this clear for the one who reads the statement. If the QUERY keyword is specified, only the statement executed by a connection is killed, while the connection itself remains open.

The ID of the connection or statement to be killed must be specified. Even with the QUERY keyword, the thread ID must be specified; MariaDB expects a query ID only if the ID keyword is specified too. Remember that the connection ID becomes visible by querying the PROCESSLIST table, not with SHOW PROCESSLIST.

As an alternative, you can specify the USER clause followed by an account name or a username to destroy all the connections or queries that belong to the specified account or user. To kill all connections or statements that belong to our account, we can also specify CURRENT_USER().

Killing a query or connection with the SOFT option, which is the default option, can be slower but it is also safer. The HARD keyword is a faster but more brutal way to terminate operations, which should only be used if SOFT KILL takes too long. After a HARD KILL, we are likely to experience data corruption. This is how the command works:

1. The KILL command sets a flag for the target connection. If a connection is flagged by KILL, SHOW PROCESSLIST shows 'Killed' in the Info column.

2. Whenever it is safe to interrupt the current operation, the target connection checks whether the flag has been set. If it has, the connection or the statement terminates.

3. Sometimes, even if it is not safe, the connection checks whether a HARD KILL command was requested. If so, the connection or statement is terminated immediately, probably leaving a table in an inconsistent state.

But in the current versions, this difference only concerns the repairing of Aria or MyISAM tables, and the creation of an index on such tables. Remember that, in the first case, the data could be even more corrupted than before, and in the second case the new index will need to be rebuilt.

The following example shows how to kill a statement without closing the connection.

In a mysql command-line client, let's execute this statement:

```
MariaDB [(none)]> DO SLEEP(2000);
```

The preceding statement is not harmful for anyone, but it is good for our example because it makes the thread pause for 2000 seconds.

Next, let's open another client and execute the following statement:

```
MariaDB [(none)]> SHOW PROCESSLIST;
+----+-----------------+-----------+------+---------+-------+-----------
-----------+-----------------+-----------+
| Id | User            | Host      | db   | Command | Time  | State
| Info            | Progress  |
+----+-----------------+-----------+------+---------+-------+-----------
-----------+-----------------+-----------+
...
|  9 | root            | localhost | NULL | Query   |     8 | User sleep
| DO SLEEP(2000)  |   0.000   |
+----+-----------------+-----------+------+---------+-------+-----------
-----------+-----------------+-----------+
3 rows in set (0.00 sec)
```

Many rows are returned, but we only care about the one that shows the previous statement. The thread ID is 9. Let's use this information to terminate the statement:

```
MariaDB [(none)]> KILL QUERY 9;
Query OK, 0 rows affected (0.00 sec)
```

We can verify that the KILL statement worked by using SHOW PROCESSLIST.

An inactive connection is automatically closed by the server when the timeout specified with the wait_timeout server variable expires.

Summary

MariaDB supports SSL connections to gain a better security level. Also, authentication plugins are mainly supported to use external authentication sources instead of MariaDB authentication. We tried the `unix_socket` plugin as an example in order to show how to use the system authentication. PAM authentication is also supported. It is also possible to limit the actions that a user can execute in an hour, preventing them from using too many resources.

It is possible for a user to connect via SSL or use an authentication plugin. This requirement can always be valid or may only apply when the user connects from certain hosts. This is possible because MariaDB permissions are based on accounts, a combination of username and hostname. The `LIKE` operator's wildcards can be used to match a few permissions to multiple usernames or hostnames.

MariaDB supports two thread handling methods: one thread per connection is the one that was historically used in MySQL, and pool of threads is a new method, which collects threads into groups, to improve the connections management with some workloads (typically, OLTP). MariaDB uses two different pool of threads implementations on Unix and Windows systems, which must be configured in different ways.

The `SHOW PROCESSLIST` statement, the `information_schema.PROCESS` table, and the `performance_schema.threads` table allow monitoring the active connections and their activities. If necessary, the `KILL` command (which has a rich syntax in MariaDB) can be used to terminate connections.

The next chapter discusses the caches used by MariaDB and various storage engines.

6
Caches

Table data and indexes are normally written on mass memories, such as disks, SSDs, or flash memories. However, accessing these media is a slow process; if the server has to do it too often, the input or output is probably the bottleneck. To avoid accessing disks, MariaDB and storage engines have several caches that a DBA should know about. The following topics will be covered in this chapter:

- The InnoDB buffer pool and doublewrite buffer
- The MyISAM key cache
- The Aria page cache
- The query and subquery cache
- The table open cache
- The main per-session buffers

Before beginning our discussion on the caches, a warning is needed. Many authoritative resources, such as the *MariaDB Knowledge Base* or the MySQL manual, suggest dedicating a huge amount of memory to the InnoDB buffer pool or to the default storage engine's main cache if most tables are not InnoDB tables. Many articles suggest dedicating about 70 percent or even 80 percent of the memory to the buffer pool. For MyISAM and Aria, much less memory is required by the main cache because only keys are cached by the storage engine. To cache data files, MariaDB relies on the operating system. While this hint may be valid in many cases, the DBA should carefully consider how much memory is needed by other caches. The query cache, if used, is usually not small. And if there are many concurrent connections, the per-session caches can consume a big amount of memory. Also, such suggestions apply to servers that are only dedicated to MariaDB. Any additional running daemon requires some memory.

InnoDB caches

Since InnoDB is the recommended engine for most use cases, configuring it is very important. The InnoDB buffer pool is a cache that should speed up most read and write operations. Thus, every DBA should know how it works. The doublewrite buffer is an important mechanism that guarantees that a row is never half-written to a file. For heavy-write workloads, we may want to disable it to obtain more speed.

InnoDB pages

Tables, data, and indexes are organized in pages, both in the caches and in the files. A page is a package of data that contains one or two rows and usually some empty space. The ratio between the used space and the total size of pages is called the **fill factor**.

By changing the page size, the fill factor changes inevitably. InnoDB tries to keep the pages 15/16 full. If a page's fill factor is lower than 1/2, InnoDB merges it with another page. If the rows are written sequentially, the fill factor should be about 15/16. If the rows are written randomly, the fill factor is between 1/2 and 15/16. A low fill factor represents a memory waste. With a very high fill factor, when pages are updated and their content grows, they often need to be reorganized, which negatively affects the performance.

The columns with a variable length type (TEXT, BLOB, VARCHAR, or VARBIT) are written into separate data structures called **overlow pages**. Such columns are called off-page columns. They are better handled by the DYNAMIC row format, which can be used for most tables when backward compatibility is not a concern. Row formats will be discussed in the next chapter.

A page never changes its size, and the size is the same for all pages. The page size, however, is configurable: it can be 4 KB, 8 KB, or 16 KB. The default size is 16 KB, which is appropriate for many workloads and optimizes full table scans. However, smaller sizes can improve the performance of some OLTP workloads involving many small insertions because of lower memory allocation, or storage devices with smaller blocks (old SSD devices). Another reason to change the page size is that this can greatly affect the InnoDB compression (which will be discussed in *Chapter 7, InnoDB Compressed Tables*).

The page size can be changed by setting the innodb_page_size variable in the configuration file and restarting the server.

The InnoDB buffer pool

On servers that mainly use InnoDB tables (the most common case), the buffer pool is the most important cache to consider. Ideally, it should contain all the InnoDB data and indexes to allow MariaDB to execute queries without accessing the disks. Changes to data are written into the buffer pool first. They are flushed to the disks later to reduce the number of I/O operations. Of course, if the data does not fit the server's memory, only a subset of them can be in the buffer pool. In this case, that subset should be the so-called **working set**: the most frequently accessed data.

The default size of the buffer pool is 128 MB and should always be changed. On production servers, this value is too low. On a developer's computer, usually, there is no need to dedicate so much memory to InnoDB. The minimum size, 5 MB, is usually more than enough when developing a simple application.

Old and new pages

We can think of the buffer pool as a list of data pages that are sorted with a variation of the classic **Last Recently Used** (**LRU**) algorithm. The list is split into two sublists: the new list contains the most used pages, and the old list contains the less used pages.

The first page in each sublist is called the **head**. The head of the old list is called the **midpoint**. When a page is accessed that is not in the buffer pool, it is inserted into the midpoint. The other pages in the old list shift by one position, and the last one is evicted.

When a page from the old list is accessed, it is moved from the old list to the head of the new list.

 A description of this simple algorithm can be found on the site of George Mason University, Department of Computer Science, at the following URL: http://cs.gmu.edu/cne/modules/vm/yellow/lru.html

When a page in the new list is accessed, it goes to the head of the list. The following variables affect the previously described algorithm:

- `innodb_old_blocks_pct`: This variable defines the percentage of the buffer pool reserved to the old list. The allowed range is 5 to 95, and it is 37 (3/5) by default.

- `innodb_old_blocks_time`: If this value is not 0, it represents the minimum age (in milliseconds) the old pages must reach before they can be moved into the new list. If an old page is accessed that did not reach this age, it goes to the head of the old list.

- `innodb_max_dirty_pages_pct`: This variable defines the maximum percentage of pages that were modified in-memory. This mechanism will be discussed in the *Dirty pages* section later in this chapter. This value is not a hard limit, but InnoDB tries not to exceed it. The allowed range is 0 to 100, and the default is 75. Increasing this value can reduce the rate of writes, but the shutdown will take longer (because dirty pages need to be written onto the disk before the server can be stopped in a clean way).

- `innodb_flush_neighbors`: If set to 1, when a dirty page is flushed from memory to a disk, even the contiguous pages are flushed. If set to 2, all dirty pages from the same extent (the portion of memory whose size is 1 MB) are flushed. With 0, only dirty pages are flushed when their number exceeds `innodb_max_dirty_pages_pct` or when they are evicted from the buffer pool. The default is 1. This optimization is only useful for spinning disks. Write-incentive workloads may need an aggressive flushing strategy; however, if the pages are written too often, they degrade the performance.

Buffer pool instances

On MariaDB versions older than 5.5, InnoDB creates only one instance of the buffer pool. However, concurrent threads are blocked by a mutex, and this may become a bottleneck. This is particularly true if the concurrency level is high and the buffer pool is very big. Splitting the buffer pool into multiple instances can solve the problem.

Multiple instances represent an advantage only if the buffer pool size is at least 2 GB. Each instance should be of size 1 GB. InnoDB will ignore the configuration and will maintain only one instance if the buffer pool size is less than 1 GB. Furthermore, this feature is more useful on 64-bit systems.

The following variables control the instances and their size:

- `innodb_buffer_pool_size`: This variable defines the total size of the buffer pool (no single instances). Note that the real size will be about 10 percent bigger than this value. A percentage of this amount of memory is dedicated to the change buffer (discussed in *Chapter 7, InnoDB Compressed Tables*).

- `innodb_buffer_pool_instances`: This variable defines the number of instances. If the value is `-1`, InnoDB will automatically decide the number of instances. The maximum value is `64`. The default value is `8` on Unix and depends on the `innodb_buffer_pool_size` variable on Windows.

Dirty pages

When a user executes a statement that modifies data in the buffer pool, InnoDB initially modifies the data that is only in memory. The pages that are only modified in the buffer pool are called **dirty pages**. Pages that have not been modified or whose changes have been written on the disk are called as **clean pages**.

Note that changes to data are also written to the redo log. If a crash occurs before those changes are applied to data files, InnoDB is usually able to recover the data, including the last modifications, by reading the redo log and the doublewrite buffer. The doublewrite buffer will be discussed later, in the *Explaining the doublewrite buffer* section. More details on the redo log can be found in *Chapter 11, Data Sharding*.

At some point, the data needs to be flushed to the InnoDB data files (the `.ibd` files). In MariaDB 10.0, this is done by a dedicated thread called the **page cleaner**. In older versions, this was done by the master thread, which executes several InnoDB maintenance operations. The flushing is not only concerned with the buffer pool, but also with the InnoDB redo and undo log.

The list of dirty pages is frequently updated when transactions write data at the physical level. It has its own mutex that does not lock the whole buffer pool.

The maximum number of dirty pages is determined by `innodb_max_dirty_pages_pct` as a percentage. When this maximum limit is reached, dirty pages are flushed.

The `innodb_flush_neighbor_pages` value determines how InnoDB selects the pages to flush. If it is set to `none`, only selected pages are written. If it is set to `area`, even the neighboring dirty pages are written. If it is set to `cont`, all contiguous blocks of the dirty pages are flushed.

On shutdown, a complete page flushing is only done if `innodb_fast_shutdown` is 0. Normally, this method should be preferred, because it leaves data in a consistent state. However, if many changes have been requested but still not written to disk, this process could be very slow. It is possible to speed up the shutdown by specifying a higher value for `innodb_fast_shutdown`. In this case, a crash recovery will be performed on the next restart.

The read ahead optimization

The **read ahead** feature is designed to reduce the number of read operations from the disks. It tries to guess which data will be needed in the near future and reads it with one operation.

Two algorithms are available to choose the pages to read in advance:

- linear read ahead
- random read ahead

The linear read ahead is used by default. It counts the pages in the buffer pool that are read sequentially. If their number is greater than or equal to `innodb_read_ahead_threshold`, InnoDB will read all data from the same extent (a portion of data whose size is always 1 MB). The `innodb_read_ahead_threshold` value must be a number from 0 to 64. The value 0 disables the linear read ahead but does not enable the random read ahead. The default value is 56.

The random read ahead is only used if the `innodb_random_read_ahead` server variable is set to ON. By default, it is set to OFF. This algorithm checks whether at least 13 pages in the buffer pool have been read to the same extent. In this case, it does not matter whether they were read sequentially. With this variable enabled, the full extent will be read. The 13-page threshold is not configurable.

If `innodb_read_ahead_threshold` is set to 0 and `innodb_random_read_ahead` is set to OFF, the read ahead optimization is completely turned off.

Diagnosing the buffer pool performance

MariaDB provides some tools to monitor the activities of the buffer pool and the InnoDB main thread. By inspecting these activities, a DBA can tune the relevant server variables to improve the performance.

In this section, we will discuss the SHOW ENGINE INNODB STATUS SQL statement and the INNODB_BUFFER_POOL_STATS table in the `information_schema` database. While the latter provides more information about the buffer pool, the SHOW ENGINE INNODB STATUS output is easier to read.

The `INNODB_BUFFER_POOL_STATS` table contains the following columns:

Column name	Description
POOL_ID	Each InnoDB buffer pool instance has a different ID.
POOL_SIZE	Size (in pages) of the instance.
FREE_BUFFERS	Number of free pages.
DATABASE_PAGES	Total number of data pages.
OLD_DATABASE_PAGES	Pages in the old list.
MODIFIED_DATABASE_PAGES	Dirty pages.
PENDING_DECOMPRESS	Number of pages that need to be decompressed (InnoDB compression will be discussed in *Chapter 7, InnoDB Compressed Tables*).
PENDING_READS	Pending read operations.
PENDING_FLUSH_LRU	Pages in the old or new lists that need to be flushed.
PENDING_FLUSH_LIST	Pages in the flush list that need to flushed.
PAGES_MADE_YOUNG	Number of pages moved into the new list.
PAGES_NOT_MADE_YOUNG	Old pages that did not become young.
PAGES_MADE_YOUNG_RATE	Pages made young per second. This value is reset each time it is shown.
PAGES_MADE_NOT_YOUNG_RATE	Pages read but not made young (this happens because they do not reach the minimum age) per second. This value is reset each time it is shown.
NUMBER_PAGES_READ	Number of pages read from disk.
NUMBER_PAGES_CREATED	Number of pages created in the buffer pool.
NUMBER_PAGES_WRITTEN	Number of pages written to disk.
PAGES_READ_RATE	Pages read from disk per second.
PAGES_CREATE_RATE	Pages created in the buffer pool per second.
PAGES_WRITTEN_RATE	Pages written to disk per second.
NUMBER_PAGES_GET	Requests of pages that are not in the buffer pool.
HIT_RATE	Rate of page hits.
YOUNG_MAKE_PER_THOUSAND_GETS	Pages made young per thousand physical reads.
NOT_YOUNG_MAKE_PER_THOUSAND_GETS	Pages that remain in the old list per thousand reads.

Column name	Description
NUMBER_PAGES_READ_AHEAD	Number of pages read with a read ahead operation.
NUMBER_READ_AHEAD_EVICTED	The number of pages read with a read ahead operation that were never used and then were evicted.
READ_AHEAD_RATE	Similar to NUMBER_PAGES_READ_AHEAD, but this is a per-second rate.
READ_AHEAD_EVICTED_RATE	Similar to NUMBER_READ_AHEAD_EVICTED, but this is a per-second rate.
LRU_IO_TOTAL	Total number of pages read or written to disk.
LRU_IO_CURRENT	Pages read or written to disk within the last second.
UNCOMPRESS_TOTAL	Pages that have been uncompressed.
UNCOMPRESS_CURRENT	Pages that have been uncompressed within the last second.

The per-second values are reset after they are shown.

The PAGES_MADE_YOUNG_RATE and PAGES_NOT_MADE_YOUNG_RATE values show us, respectively, how often old pages become new and to what extent old pages are never accessed in a reasonable amount of time. If the former value is too high, the old list is probably not big enough and vice versa.

Comparing READ_AHEAD_RATE and READ_AHEAD_EVICTED_RATE is useful to tune the read ahead feature. The READ_AHEAD_EVICTED_RATE value should be low, because it indicates which pages read with the read ahead operations were not useful. If their ratio is good but READ_AHEAD_RATE is low, probably the read ahead should be used more often. In this case, if the linear read ahead is used, we can try to increase or decrease innodb_read_ahead_threshold. Or, we can change the used algorithm (linear or random read ahead).

The columns whose names end with _RATE better describe the current server activities. They should be examined several times a day, and during the whole week or month, perhaps with the help of one of more monitoring tools. Good, free software monitoring tools include **Cacti** and **Nagios**. The Percona Monitoring Tools package includes MariaDB (and MySQL) plugins that provide an interface to these tools.

Dumping and loading the buffer pool

In some cases, one may want to save the current contents of the buffer pool and reload them later. The most common case is when the server is stopped. Normally, on startup, the buffer pool is empty, and InnoDB needs to fill it with useful data. This process is called warm-up. Until the warm-up is complete, the InnoDB performance is lower than usual.

Two variables help avoid the warm-up phase: `innodb_buffer_pool_dump_at_shutdown` and `innodb_buffer_pool_load_at_startup`. If their value is ON, InnoDB automatically saves the buffer pool into a file at shut down and restores it at startup. Their default value is OFF.

Turning them ON can be very useful, but remember the caveats:

- The startup and shutdown time might be longer. In some cases, we might prefer MariaDB to start more quickly even if it is slower during warm-up.
- We need the disk space necessary to store the buffer pool.

The user may also want to dump the buffer pool at any moment and restore it without restarting the server. This is advisable when the buffer pool is optimal and some statements are going to heavily change its contents. A common example is when a big InnoDB table is fully scanned. This happens, for example, during logical backups (which will be discussed in *Chapter 8, Backup and Disaster Recovery*). A full table scan will fill the old list with non-frequently accessed data. A good way to solve the problem is to dump the buffer pool before the table scan and reload it later.

This operation can be performed by setting two special variables: `innodb_buffer_pool_dump_now` and `innodb_buffer_pool_load_now`. Reading the values of these variables always returns OFF. Setting the first variable to ON forces InnoDB to immediately dump the buffer pool into a file. Setting the latter variable to ON forces InnoDB to load the buffer pool from that file.

In both cases, the progress of the dump or load operation is indicated by the `Innodb_buffer_pool_dump_status` and `Innodb_buffer_pool_load_status` status variables. If loading the buffer pool takes too long, it is possible to stop it by setting `innodb_buffer_pool_load_abort` to ON. The name and path of the dump file are specified in the `innodb_buffer_pool_filename` server variable. Of course, we should be sure that the chosen directory can contain the file, but it is much smaller than the memory used by the buffer pool.

The InnoDB change buffer

The change buffer is a cache that is a part of the buffer pool. It contains dirty pages related to secondary indexes (not primary keys) that are not stored in the main part of the buffer pool. If the modified data is read later, it will be merged into the buffer pool. In older versions, this buffer was called the insert buffer, but now it is renamed because it can handle deletions.

The change buffer speeds up the following write operations:

* `insertions`: When new rows are written.

* `deletions`: When existing rows are marked for deletion but not yet physically erased for performance reasons.

* `purges`: The physical elimination of previously marked rows and obsolete index values. This is periodically done by a dedicated thread.

In some cases, we may want to disable the change buffer. For example, we may have a working set that only fits the memory if the change buffer is discarded. In this case, even after disabling it, we will still have all the frequently accessed secondary indexes in the buffer pool. Also, DML statements may be rare for our database, or we may have just a few secondary indexes: in these cases, the change buffer does not help.

The change buffer can be configured using the following variables:

* `innodb_change_buffer_max_size`: This is the maximum size of the change buffer, expressed as a percentage of the buffer pool. The allowed range is 0 to 50, and the default value is `25`.

* `innodb_change_buffering`: This determines which types of operations are cached by the change buffer. The allowed values are `none` (to disable the buffer), `all`, `inserts`, `deletes`, `purges`, and `changes` (to cache inserts and deletes, but not purges). The `all` value is the default value.

Explaining the doublewrite buffer

When InnoDB writes a page to disk, at least two events can interrupt the operation after it is started: a hardware failure or an OS failure. In the case of an OS failure, this should not be possible if the pages are not bigger than the blocks written by the system.

In this case, the InnoDB redo and undo logs are not sufficient to recover the half-written page, because they only contain pages ID's, not their data. This improves the performance.

To avoid half-written pages, InnoDB uses the doublewrite buffer. This mechanism involves writing every page twice. A page is valid after the second write is complete. When the server restarts, if a recovery occurs, half-written pages are discarded. The doublewrite buffer has a small impact on performance, because the writes are sequential, and are flushed to disk together.

However, it is still possible to disable the doublewrite buffer by setting the `innodb_doublewrite` variable to `OFF` in the configuration file or by starting the server with the `--skip-innodb-doublewrite` parameter. This can be done if data correctness is not important.

If performance is very important, and we use a fast storage device, we may note the overhead caused by the additional disk writes. But if data correctness is important to us, we do not want to simply disable it. MariaDB provides an alternative mechanism called **atomic writes**. These writes are like a transaction: they completely succeed or they completely fail. Half-written data is not possible. However, MariaDB does not directly implement this mechanism, so it can only be used on FusionIO storage devices using the DirectFS filesystem. FusionIO flash memories are very fast flash memories that can be used as block storage or DRAM memory. To enable this alternative mechanism, we can set `innodb_use_atomic_writes` to `ON`. This automatically disables the doublewrite buffer.

MyISAM key cache

MyISAM indexes are cached in a data structure called the **key cache** or (less frequently) **key buffer**. This cache should greatly reduce access to the physical index files. The cached indexes can also be modified in memory; only later will the changes be flushed to the disk.

The key cache can be disabled. Data does not have a special cache within MariaDB. Thus, the operating system cache mechanisms are used instead. The same happens with data if the key cache is disabled.

If we mainly use MyISAM tables, the key cache should be very big. If we do not use MyISAM, the key cache can be set to the minimum value, which is 8 (for example, to free the memory for the InnoDB buffer pool). It is not possible to completely disable it. However, remember that, if Aria is not used for internal temporary tables (that is, if `aria_used_for_temp_tables` is `OFF`), MyISAM is used for temporary tables, and the key cache should be used.

The size of the key cache is determined by the `key_buffer_size` server variable.

MyISAM key cache, like MyISAM index files, is organized in blocks. A block is the minimum amount of contiguous memory. Index files and the key cache can use different block sizes. To get good performance, one of these sizes should be a multiple of the other, or they should be equal. The index files blocks and the key cache blocks sizes are determined by the `myisam_block_size` and the `key_cache_block_size` server variables. Key cache blocks can be modified in memory. In this case, they are called dirty blocks. Blocks that have not been modified are called clean blocks.

LRU and the midpoint insertion strategy

By default, MyISAM uses the LRU algorithm to determine which blocks are stored in the cache. This strategy is used if the `key_cache_division_limit` variable is set to `100`. The pure LRU algorithm has a problem that is similar to the one that was explained for the InnoDB buffer pool. If a query performs a full index scan, it accesses the infrequent read blocks. Such blocks would then be inserted into the cache, replacing blocks that should remain in the cache.

An alternative method consists in splitting the key cache into two sublists: the warm list and the hot list. The length of these lists is not a variable but is the minimum percentage of the key cache dedicated to the warm list and is determined by the `key_cache_division_limit` variable.

When a block that was not in the cache is accessed, it is inserted at the end of the warm list, and other warm blocks are shifted toward the end of the list. The block that is at the beginning of the warm list is the first candidate for eviction.

If any warm block is accessed three times, it moves to the end of the hot list. When other blocks are inserted in the hot list, other blocks are moved toward the end of the list. If a block remains at the end of the host list for a certain amount of time, it is moved back to the warm list. The amount of time is calculated as *blocks * key_cache_age_threshold / 100*, where `blocks` is the number of blocks in the cache and `key_cache_age_threshold` is a system variable. A high value for `key_cache_age_threshold` causes blocks to remain in the hot list for a longer time.

Key cache instances

During some operations, the key cache is protected by a mutex. This can be a problem when several connections use it at the same time. To reduce contention, two mechanisms exist: the ability to use several instances of the key cache and the key cache segmentation. Each key cache instance has its own locks. Also, each instance can be configured individually. The default cache cannot be erased or disabled.

By default, only the default instance of the key cache exists. To create more instances, simply configure them. Setting the `key_buffer_size` variable for an instance is enough to create it. The syntax is as follows:

```
SET [<instance_name>.]<variable_name> = <value>;
```

For example, to configure three caches, including the default one, run the following:

```
MariaDB [test]> SET @@global.hot_key_cache.key_buffer_size = 20000 *
1024;
Query OK, 0 rows affected (0.01 sec)
MariaDB [test]> SET @@global.key_buffer_size = 60000 * 1024;
Query OK, 0 rows affected (0.02 sec)
MariaDB [test]> SET @@global.cold_key_cache.key_buffer_size = 20000 *
1024;
Query OK, 0 rows affected (0.00 sec)
```

There is no way to see all the variables related to non-default instances (that is, SHOW VARIABLES will not work). Variables related to instances must be queried individually.

Note that these settings are lost on restart. For this reason, the configuration of the key cache instances should be written in the configuration file, as in the following example:

```
hot_key_cache.key_buffer_size = 20480000
key_buffer_size = 61440000
cold_key_cache.key_buffer_size = 20480000
```

Note that arithmetical expressions, such as *20000 * 60000*, are not permitted in configuration files.

To see which key caches exist and get information about them, we can query the KEY_CACHES table in the `information_schema` database, as in the following example:

```
MariaDB [test]> SELECT KEY_CACHE_NAME FROM information_schema.KEY_CACHES;
+----------------+
| KEY_CACHE_NAME |
+----------------+
| default        |
| hot_key_cache  |
| cold_key_cache |
+----------------+
3 rows in set (0.00 sec)
```

To eliminate a cache, we can set its size to 0, shown as follows:

```
MariaDB [test]> SET @@global.cold_key_cache.key_buffer_size = 0;
Query OK, 0 rows affected (0.00 sec)
MariaDB [test]> SELECT KEY_CACHE_NAME FROM information_schema.KEY_CACHES;
+----------------+
| KEY_CACHE_NAME |
+----------------+
| default        |
| hot_key_cache  |
+----------------+
2 rows in set (0.00 sec)
```

The KEY_CACHE table contains the following columns:

Column name	Description
KEY_CACHE_NAME	This gives the name of the key cache instance, default for the default instance.
SEGMENTS	This gives the number of segments in the instance. It gives NULL, if the instance is not segmented or this row refers to the whole instance. This will be explained in the *Segmented key cache* section.
SEGMENT_NUMBER	If an instance is segmented, each row represents a segment. This column contains the segment progressive number. It gives NULL if the instance is not segmented or this row refers to the whole instance.
FULL_SIZE	This gives the total amount of memory used by the instance.
BLOCK_SIZE	This gives the size of the blocks.
USED_BLOCKS	This gives the number of blocks in use.
UNUSED_BLOCKS	This gives the number of free blocks.
DIRTY_BLOCKS	This gives the number of dirty blocks.
READ_REQUESTS	This gives the pending read operations; see next column.
READS	This gives the number of current copying operations from index files to this instance (reading of uncached blocks).
WRITE_REQUESTS	This gives the pending write operations; see next column.
WRITES	This gives the number of current copying operations from this instance to index files (dirty blocks flushing).

If the working set index entries are contained in the key cache, the number of reads and writes, and particularly the number of waiting reads and writes, should be minimal during normal database activity.

A high number of unused blocks may indicate that the instance (or the segment) is fragmented. It is not possible to defragment a single instance or fragment.

Each index can be stored in only one key cache. Indexes in the same table must use the same cache. If the cache to be associated with a table is not specified, the default cache is used. Thus, if there is only one cache instance, there is no need to specify which instance must be used for a table. To specify that a different instance must be associated with a table, the CACHE INDEX statement can be used. The associations are not immutable: it is possible to reassign a table to a different cache later.

The following is a basic example:

```
MariaDB [test]> CACHE INDEX myisam1, myisam2 IN hot_key_cache;
+---------------+--------------------+----------+----------+
| Table         | Op                 | Msg_type | Msg_text |
+---------------+--------------------+----------+----------+
| test.myisam1  | assign_to_keycache | status   | OK       |
| test.myisam2  | assign_to_keycache | status   | OK       |
+---------------+--------------------+----------+----------+
2 rows in set (0.00 sec)
```

In the example, the index in the myisam1 and myisam2 tables are cached in the instance called hot_key_cache.

If a table is partitioned, it is also possible to associate different partitions to different key cache instances. For example:

```
MariaDB [test]> CACHE INDEX myisam1 PARTITION (p0, p1) IN hot_key_cache;
+---------------+--------------------+----------+----------+
| Table         | Op                 | Msg_type | Msg_text |
+---------------+--------------------+----------+----------+
| test.myisam1  | assign_to_keycache | status   | OK       |
+---------------+--------------------+----------+----------+
1 row in set (0.00 sec)
MariaDB [test]> CACHE INDEX myisam1 PARTITION (p2) IN default;
+---------------+--------------------+----------+----------+
| Table         | Op                 | Msg_type | Msg_text |
+---------------+--------------------+----------+----------+
| test.myisam1  | assign_to_keycache | status   | OK       |
+---------------+--------------------+----------+----------+
1 row in set (0.00 sec)
```

```
MariaDB [test]> CACHE INDEX myisam2 PARTITION (ALL) IN default;
+---------------+---------------------+----------+----------+
| Table         | Op                  | Msg_type | Msg_text |
+---------------+---------------------+----------+----------+
| test.myisam2  | assign_to_keycache  | status   | OK       |
+---------------+---------------------+----------+----------+
1 row in set (0.00 sec)
```

The ALL keyword means that all the partitions must be associated to the specified cache. In this case, the PARTITION clause could simply be omitted. The key cache instances referenced by the CACHE INDEX statement must already exist, or an error is produced.

Like the instances configuration, the association between tables and instances is forgotten when the server stops. For this reason, the CACHE INDEX statement should be written in an init file. An init file can be set with the init-file option in the configuration file. It is always executed on server startup.

Segmented key cache

Another way to reduce contention is to use a segmented key cache. Each instance of the key cache can be composed of several segments. To use this feature, we can set the key_cache_segments system variable, which represents the number of segments. The maximum value is 64. The default value is 0, which disables the feature.

As mentioned previously, if the segmented key cache is used, some rows from the KEY_CACHES table in the information_schema database represent an individual segment. Other rows represent a whole instance even if that instance is segmented. The following example demonstrates this:

```
MariaDB [test]> SET @@global.hot_key_cache.key_cache_segments = 0;
Query OK, 0 rows affected (0.00 sec)
MariaDB [test]> SELECT KEY_CACHE_NAME, SEGMENT_NUMBER, SEGMENTS,
UNUSED_BLOCKS FROM information_schema.KEY_CACHES;
+----------------+----------------+----------+---------------+
| KEY_CACHE_NAME | SEGMENT_NUMBER | SEGMENTS | UNUSED_BLOCKS |
+----------------+----------------+----------+---------------+
| default        |           NULL |     NULL |         48981 |
| hot_key_cache  |           NULL |     NULL |         16172 |
+----------------+----------------+----------+---------------+
```

```
6 rows in set (0.00 sec)

MariaDB [test]> SET @@global.hot_key_cache.key_cache_segments = 4;

Query OK, 0 rows affected (0.00 sec)

MariaDB [test]> SELECT KEY_CACHE_NAME, SEGMENT_NUMBER, SEGMENTS,
UNUSED_BLOCKS FROM information_schema.KEY_CACHES;

+----------------+----------------+----------+---------------+
| KEY_CACHE_NAME | SEGMENT_NUMBER | SEGMENTS | UNUSED_BLOCKS |
+----------------+----------------+----------+---------------+
| default        |           NULL |     NULL |         48981 |
| hot_key_cache  |              1 |        4 |          4043 |
| hot_key_cache  |              2 |        4 |          4043 |
| hot_key_cache  |              3 |        4 |          4043 |
| hot_key_cache  |              4 |        4 |          4043 |
| hot_key_cache  |           NULL |        4 |         16172 |
+----------------+----------------+----------+---------------+

6 rows in set (0.00 sec)
```

The preceding example shows that, with cache segmentation disabled, only one row exists for each cache instance. With the segmentation enabled for hot_key_cache, a row still exists for that instance, but there is also a row for each individual segment. We can easily verify this from the UNUSED_BLOCKS values: each segment has 4043 free blocks, and the sum of these numbers is the number of the whole instance UNUSED_BLOCKS.

Preloading indexes into the cache

Waiting until index blocks are read during the normal database activities and then loading them in a cache would not be convenient. Sometimes, we prefer to preload indexes into the cache with some statements executed at server startup. The LOAD INDEX INTO CACHE statement can be used to preload all indexes of a table into their associated cache or the default cache. If the table is partitioned, it is possible to only preload some partition indexes. For example:

```
MariaDB [test]> LOAD INDEX INTO CACHE myisam1 PARTITION (p0, p1);

+---------------+--------------+----------+----------+
| Table         | Op           | Msg_type | Msg_text |
+---------------+--------------+----------+----------+
| test.myisam1  | preload_keys | status   | OK       |
+---------------+--------------+----------+----------+

1 row in set (0.00 sec)
```

With B-tree indexes, the leaf nodes point to specific table rows. If a specific record is not accessed for a long time, the corresponding index blocks do not need to be accessed. Thus, having them in the cache is not beneficial. With the IGNORE LEAVES option, the leaf nodes are not preloaded into the cache and will only be cached when they are accessed. This is useful if the key cache is not big enough to contain whole indexes, and only a subset of the indexed data is frequently accessed. It also has the secondary effect of reducing the duration of the loading operation, which is as follows:

```
MariaDB [test]> LOAD INDEX INTO CACHE myisam2 IGNORE LEAVES;
+---------------+---------------+----------+----------+
| Table         | Op            | Msg_type | Msg_text |
+---------------+---------------+----------+----------+
| test.myisam2  | preload_keys  | status   | OK       |
+---------------+---------------+----------+----------+
1 row in set (0.00 sec)
```

Aria page cache

Aria caches the index pages in a data structure called the **page cache**. It is very similar to the MyISAM key cache but has fewer features.

 All the ideas behind the page cache and the key cache will not be explained in this section, so the reader needs to read the previous section first.

This section explains the differences between the two data structures and how to use the page cache.

Similar to MyISAM, Aria indexes are organized in blocks. The size of the blocks is determined by the aria_block_size server variable. This variable affects both the index files and the page cache, because all blocks must have the same size. If this variable is changed, all Aria tables need to be recreated. The steps to change this value are as follows:

1. Dump existing Aria tables (as explained in *Chapter 8, Backup and Disaster Recovery*).

2. Stop the server.

3. Set the new value in the configuration file.

4. Restart the server.

5. Drop or empty all Aria tables.

6. Restore the dumped data.

The Aria page cache always has only one instance and cannot be segmented. All other MyISAM key cache features are supported in the Aria page cache and are configured using variables that have slightly different names.

The page cache size can be configured using the `aria_pagecache_buffer_size` variable. If no Aria tables are used, this value can be set to `0`. However, remember that, by default, Aria is used for internal temporary tables (as in the `--aria-used-for-temp-tables` startup option).

The LRU mechanism can be configured using the `aria_pagecache_division_limit` and `aria_pagecache_age_threshold` variables that correspond to the MyISAM `key_cache_division_limit` and `key_cache_age_threshold` variables, respectively.

Since the Aria key cache does not support multiple instances or segmentation, there is no need to store usage statistics in a table such as KEY_CACHES (it would have only one row). Instead, statistics are stored in the status variables that are returned using the following query:

```
SHOW STATUS LIKE 'aria_page%';
```

The following table shows which variables are returned and which KEY_CACHES columns they match with. See the description of KEY_CACHES in the previous section that explain the meanings of these values.

Aria status variable	KEY_CACHES column
Aria_pagecache_blocks_not_flushed	DIRTY_BLOCKS
Aria_pagecache_blocks_unused	UNUSED_BLOCKS
Aria_pagecache_blocks_used	USED_BLOCKS
Aria_pagecache_read_requests	READ_REQUESTS
Aria_pagecache_reads	READS
Aria_pagecache_write_requests	WRITE_REQUESTS
Aria_pagecache_writes	WRITES

The query cache explained

The query cache stores the queries that have been executed against the server and their results. If a user issues a query that is in the cache, the results are returned immediately. Of course, the server still checks whether the account has the right to execute the query.

How the query cache affects the performance of a server strictly depends on the workload. In many cases, it may even cause a performance loss. It is enabled by default, but the DBA should carefully benchmark the applications with the query cache enabled and disabled to determine whether it is beneficial for the server. The tests should also be periodically repeated if the applications change. It is also possible to activate it *on demand*, that is, the query cache will normally be disabled, except for the queries that explicitly ask to be cached. This can be very useful if using the query cache affects performance negatively, but a limited set of queries would be boosted greatly by the cache. The query cache is protected by a mutex. Mutex stands for mutual exclusion; it is a type of lock used by MariaDB to make sure that two threads cannot access the same resource at the same time—usually the resource is a cache. This lock can slow down the database if the concurrency is high or the cache is too big. Also, remember that the query cache necessarily reduces the memory available for data or key caches (such as the InnoDB buffer pool), which are generally more useful.

Any change to table structure or data invalidates the cached queries that involve that table. Note that, even if several cached queries contain many results, even the smallest change to one of the underlying tables invalidates all queries that read it. If an invalidated query can be executed by several connections at the same time, then multiple connections might try to re-execute the query and recache it at the same time. This problem is called a **miss storm** or **cache stampede**.

If the data is changed often, the query cache will hardly improve the performance. If the data is seldom changed (for example, only by night or, even better, once a week), it may be a good idea to execute some queries immediately after the changes to cache them.

In a Galera cluster and in servers with the OQGRAPH storage engine enabled, the query cache must be disabled. It should also be avoided in servers containing SPIDER tables, but it can be used on the remote servers. Galera is explained in *Chapter 12, MariaDB Galera Cluster*, and the SPIDER storage engine is explained in *Chapter 11, Data Sharding*.

A query sent by the user matches a query in the cache only if their text is identical. Case differences, spaces, and (by default) comments can make two queries different, just as in the following examples:

```
SELECT * FROM t;
select * from 1;

SELECT *    FROM t;
SELECT * FROM t;

SELECT * FROM t;
SELECT * FROM t/* */;
```

Also, queries only match if they use the same default database, default character set, SQL_MODE, and protocol version. A prepared statement can be cached if it is sent using the API (not the PREPARE SQL statement). Prepared statements can only match other prepared statements, and they must use the same parameters. Subqueries are not cached, but they have a specific cache. Outer queries containing subqueries can be cached.

Queries cannot be cached in the following scenarios:

- If they generate warnings
- If they are executed within a stored program
- If they use temporary tables or user-defined variables
- If they contain non-deterministic functions, stored functions, or UDFs
- If they use system tables
- If they have one of the following clauses: INTO OUTFILE, INTO DUMPFILE, LOCK IN SHARE MODE, and FOR UPDATE
- If they do not use tables (SELECT version();)
- If they reference a table for which the account has column-level privileges
- If the tables involving some special storage engines, such as SPIDER, cannot be cached

If the query cache is enabled, it is still possible to prevent a query from being cached using the following syntax:

```
SELECT SQL_NO_CACHE …
```

If the query cache is only enabled on demand, the following syntax can be used to cache it:

```
SELECT SQL_CACHE …
```

The query cache contents are modified by the server and, after some time, the memory can get fragmented. To defragment it, the following statement can be used:

```
FLUSH QUERY CACHE;
```

If, for some reason, the cache has been populated with queries that are not useful anymore, it can be emptied with the following statement:

```
RESET QUERY CACHE;
```

Configuring the query cache

If we use the query cache, it is important to configure it properly. It is also a good idea to repeat the tests regularly to be sure that the server's performance benefit from the query cache. The query cache configuration is discussed as follows:

- `query_cache_type`: This enables or disables the query cache. The value 0 or OFF disables it; 1 or ON enables it; 2 or DEMAND only enables it on demand as explained previously. If this variable is set as a startup option, numeric values must be used (for example, `--query-cache-type=2`).

- `query_cache_size`: This specifies the size of the query cache. Its default size is 1 MB. The value 0 disables the cache but, in this case, `query_cache_type` should also be specified to prevent the server from checking whether the queries are cacheable and protecting the cache with a mutex. Very small values are not allowed. This value will be rounded off to the nearest multiple of 1,024.

- `query_cache_alloc_block_size`: This is the size of the memory blocks used in the cache. This value can be modified at any moment. A high value may reduce fragmentation, making the cache faster, but may also waste more memory.

- `query_cache_limit`: This determines the maximum size of the results of the cached queries. If a query returns results that are too big, it cannot be cached. This variable is very important, because it prevents a small number of big queries from consuming all the cache.

- `query_cache_strip_comments`: This variable, if set to ON, causes the comments to be erased from the queries before caching. In this way, identical queries with different comments will match. Note that this is not necessary in case of the used clients or if the API's strip the comments. For example, the mysql client does it unless it is started with the `--comments` option.

Information on the status of the query cache

To get generic information about the status of the query cache, the following query can be used:

```
MariaDB [none]> SHOW STATUS LIKE 'qcache%';
+-------------------------+--------+
| Variable_name           | Value  |
+-------------------------+--------+
| Qcache_free_blocks      | 1      |
| Qcache_free_memory      | 974512 |
| Qcache_hits             | 1      |
| Qcache_inserts          | 7      |
| Qcache_lowmem_prunes    | 0      |
| Qcache_not_cached       | 4      |
| Qcache_queries_in_cache | 7      |
| Qcache_total_blocks     | 16     |
+-------------------------+--------+
8 rows in set (0.00 sec)
```

The `Qcache_free_blocks` and `Qcache_free_memory` caches represent the free memory, measured in memory blocks and bytes. If the query cache is highly used and these values are high, the cache is probably fragmented. In this case, `FLUSH QUERY CACHE` can be used to defragment it.

The value of `Qcache_total_blocks` is the total number of memory blocks, both used and unused. The query cache uses variable-sized blocks.

The value of `Qcache_hits` is the number of queries for which a match was found in the cache. Check that this number is high and always keeps increasing.

The value of `Qcache_inserts` is the number of entries added to the cache. The value of `Qcache_lowmem_prunes` is the number of entries deleted from the cache. The query cache is less efficient if these values are high.

The value of `Qcache_not_cached` is the number of queries that could not be cached.

The value of `Qcache_queries_in_cache` is the number of the currently cached queries.

MariaDB also provides the `query_cache_info` plugin. The plugin is not enabled by default and must be enabled with the following statement:

```
INSTALL SONAME 'query_cache_info';
```

Once installed, the `QUERY_CACHE_INFO` table is added to the `information_schema` database. It stores information about the individual entries in the query cache. Its columns are:

- `STATEMENT_SCHEMA`: The database that was selected when the statement was executed

- `STATEMENT_TEXT`: The cached query

- `RESULT_BLOCKS_COUNT`: The number of memory blocks used to store the results

- `RESULT_BLOCKS_SIZE`: The memory block size

- `RESULT_BLOCKS_SIZE_USED`: The amount of memory used to store results (the blocks' total size is usually bigger than used memory)

Now, we'll look at an example. First, we will empty the cache. We will execute SHOW STATUS and will query the `QUERY_CACHE_INFO` table with the empty query cache. Then, we will execute one simple query and again issue the same commands to see the small differences. The query is as follows:

```
MariaDB [test]> RESET QUERY CACHE;
Query OK, 0 rows affected (0.00 sec)
MariaDB [test]> SHOW STATUS LIKE 'Qcache%';
+-------------------------+--------+
| Variable_name           | Value  |
+-------------------------+--------+
| Qcache_free_blocks      | 1      |
| Qcache_free_memory      | 982192 |
| Qcache_hits             | 1      |
| Qcache_inserts          | 12     |
| Qcache_lowmem_prunes    | 0      |
| Qcache_not_cached       | 17     |
| Qcache_queries_in_cache | 0      |
| Qcache_total_blocks     | 1      |
+-------------------------+--------+
```

```
8 rows in set (0.00 sec)
MariaDB [test]> SELECT * FROM information_schema.QUERY_CACHE_INFO \G
Empty set (0.00 sec)
MariaDB [test]> SELECT COUNT(*) FROM test.t;
+----------+
| COUNT(*) |
+----------+
|        1 |
+----------+
1 row in set (0.00 sec)
MariaDB [test]> SHOW STATUS LIKE 'Qcache%';
+-------------------------+--------+
| Variable_name           | Value  |
+-------------------------+--------+
| Qcache_free_blocks      | 1      |
| Qcache_free_memory      | 980656 |
| Qcache_hits             | 1      |
| Qcache_inserts          | 13     |
| Qcache_lowmem_prunes    | 0      |
| Qcache_not_cached       | 18     |
| Qcache_queries_in_cache | 1      |
| Qcache_total_blocks     | 4      |
+-------------------------+--------+
8 rows in set (0.00 sec)
MariaDB [test]> SELECT * FROM information_schema.QUERY_CACHE_INFO \G
*************************** 1. row ***************************
      STATEMENT_SCHEMA: test
        STATEMENT_TEXT: SELECT COUNT(*) FROM test.t
    RESULT_BLOCKS_COUNT: 1
     RESULT_BLOCKS_SIZE: 512
RESULT_BLOCKS_SIZE_USED: 127
1 row in set (0.00 sec)
```

Explaining the subquery cache

As mentioned before, subqueries are cached in a separate cache called the subquery cache. It is useful if some subqueries occur within different outer queries. The subquery cache has been introduced in MariaDB 5.2 and is enabled by default. To disable it, the following statement can be used:

```
SET @@global.optimizer_switch='subquery_cache=off';
```

Two status variables provide information about the efficiency of the subquery cache. The Subquery_cache_hit variable is the number of subqueries for which a match was found in the cache. The Subquery_cache_miss variable is the number of subqueries for which no match was found. The hit rate is defined as follows:

```
Subquery_cache_hit / (Subquery_cache_hit + Subquery_cache_miss)
```

For each subquery that needs to be cached, a temporary MEMORY table is created. This table stores the results of a subquery and its parameters. As with the internal temporary tables created to order or group query results (see *Chapter 3, Optimizing Queries*), the subquery cache tables are affected by the tmp_table_size and max_heap_table_size system variables. When one of these values is exceeded, the behavior of the cache depends on the hit rate. If the hit rate is less than 0.2, the cache is disabled. If the hit rate is less than 0.7, the table is emptied but its structure is preserved, so it can be refilled later. If the hit rate is greater than or equal to 0.7, the table is written onto the disk.

Alternative query caching methods

The problem with the query cache is that frequent changes to the tables invalidate the cached queries, making the performance hard to predict and causing cache stampedes. For such reasons, depending on the workload, we may want to implement different query caching methods.

Sometimes very expensive queries generate small results. A typical example is an aggregation (such as a count, an average, or a geometric mean) of values in a big table. Such queries usually generate statistical data and possibly need not be always perfectly up-to-date. For example, if a query involves all data aggregated by month (like the sales that happened last month), it is not important for the user that the results include data generated today (or even this week, or this month). In such cases, the workload may benefit from summary tables. A summary table is a table that is periodically emptied and repopulated with the results of a query. The query that populates the table might be expensive, but the query that involves the summary table is much faster.

It may be sufficient to aggregate data into a single summary table, with several queries retrieving a subset of its rows. Or, it is possible to store each different result-set in a different table. Or again, a hybrid solution could be the best choice.

In many cases, queries generate HTML reports or XML documents. Some of these reports are not expected to change every hour or every day. Or, if they do, the changes may be irrelevant. If a report is expected to remain the same for some time or is allowed to do so, the whole report could be cached in a table. This may greatly speed up the applications, particularly if updating the report involves expensive queries.

The MEMORY tables are usually the best choice in both cases. Of course, data is lost if the server crashes, but the tables can be repopulated, because the non-aggregated data are written on on-disk tables. Another option to store such summaries or reports is to use a key-value software that is optimized for this kind of request. Memcached is the most common choice. One of its advantages is the ability to set a timeout for each stored value. This allows us to store stale data that is not invalidated when the underlying data changes, but automatically disappears after a given amount of time. However, when data expires, the cache stampede problem can happen. Thus, for many workloads, this solution may be unable to solve the main problem that affects the query cache.

The table open cache

When a thread needs to access a table's physical file, a file descriptor is needed. To speed up the file access, MariaDB caches the file descriptors that are cached into the table open cache. This is even more useful if many MyISAM tables are contained in the same database. However, keep in mind that searching a file descriptor in this cache has a cost. If the cache cannot be big enough to contain all the needed descriptors, it could be better to disable it. A DBA may want to perform some tests to check whether table open cache is useful for a specific workload.

The table_open_cache server variable determines how many file descriptors are cached. This value should not exceed the maximum number of file descriptors allowed by the operating system, or the server may start to refuse new connections. On Unix systems, this number can be obtained with the following command:

```
ulimit -n
```

On other systems, if the `ulimit` command is not available, the system's documentation should be checked.

For the cache to contain all the needed descriptors, `table_open_cache` should be equal to the maximum number of simultaneous connections (the `max_connections` variable) multiplied by the maximum number of tables that can be referenced in a single statement. Also, remember to reserve some descriptors for the temporary tables. MyISAM and Aria tables need a descriptor for the `index` file, but that descriptor is shared among all connections.

If the server produces errors because it cannot open more files, the `mysqld_safe --open-files-limit` startup option should probably be set to a lower value.

Per-session buffers

MariaDB has several per-session buffers that speed up some queries. If these values are too small, some complex queries may start to take too much time. However, if they are too big and many concurrent connections are established, a big amount of memory could be wasted. The DBA should know the main per-session buffers and keep them reasonably small (but still big enough for the workload).

When an application opens a connection, it should approximately know which kinds of statements it will issue. It is possible that the application establishes different connections for different tasks; for example, this is what web applications usually do. So, it is not uncommon that most connections execute simple queries, while others perform more complex tasks, and thus they need more resources.

Per-session buffers can be configured on a per-session basis: a connection can change the size of some buffers without affecting other connections. This allows the allocation of bigger buffers for some sessions and small buffers for connections that will execute simple queries.

To configure a buffer on a per-session basis, connections need to issue a statement similar to the following:

```
MariaDB [(none)]> SET @@session.join_buffer_size = 64000;
Query OK, 0 rows affected (0.00 sec)
```

To set a default value for all sessions, run the following query:

```
MariaDB [(none)]> SET @@global.join_buffer_size = 160000;
Query OK, 0 rows affected (0.00 sec)
```

But, even with well-configured session variables, memory will be wasted if too many connections are not properly closed when they are not required. Application developers should make sure that connections are closed as soon as possible. Also, connections should have a reasonable timeout. When a connection is idle, it is closed after a certain number of seconds. This number is defined by the `wait_timeout` server variable. We can also force the server to reject connections if they exceed a certain number. This number is defined by `max_connections`. Setting a proper value for this variable can save a server from a **Denial-Of-Service** attack. But, before doing this, we must be sure that we are not underestimating our workload, or some users will not be able to connect to the database.

The following server variables determine the main per-session buffers lengths:

- `sort_buffer_size`: This is a buffer used to speed up the ORDER BY operations. We know it is too small if a SHOW SESSION STATUS statement shows a high value for `Sort_merge_passes`.

- `read_buffer_size`: This optimizes the sequential scans of MyISAM tables.

- `read_rnd_buffer_size`: This speeds up the queries executed with a multirange optimization strategy and all random reads from MyISAM tables.

- `join_buffer_size`: This optimizes the joins that use a batched key access strategy.

- `bulk_insert_buffer_size`: This is used to speed up the multirow inserts (including the LOAD DATA INFILE statement) into a MyISAM table.

Summary

In this chapter, we discussed the main MariaDB buffers. The most important ones are the caches used by the storage engine. We dedicated much space to the InnoDB buffer pool, because it is more complex and, usually, InnoDB is the most used storage engine. Also, while the InnoDB buffer pool caches both data and indexes, MyISAM and Aria only cache indexes.

The query cache is sometimes a useful solution, because it allows us to instantly return the results of a query. Similarly, the subquery cache is used to instantly return the results of a subquery. However, on a typical OLTP workload, data is invalidated too often for these caches to be useful. We have learned when this cache is useful and when it is not even though usually a DBA should perform some tests to be sure. We also discussed some alternatives to the query cache.

We also discussed the table open cache, which is used by the server to avoid opening and closing files too often.

In the last section, we discussed how to keep per-session buffers relatively small and examined the main ones.

The next chapter describes InnoDB compressed tables, and how compressed data is handled in the buffer pool.

InnoDB Compressed Tables

7

Most databases have an important characteristic: they constantly grow. Usually, this means that they become more useful for the users. But this also causes problems to the DBA. This chapter covers an important feature that can sometimes be used to reduce the size of physical files: InnoDB table compression.

InnoDB allows the user to compress InnoDB tables using SQL commands. No external tool is needed. InnoDB compressed tables can still be read and written, just like uncompressed tables. As will be explained in this chapter, this may or may not improve the performance of the queries. It is, however, an important feature to focus on if our data needs too much disk space.

The following sections will be covered in this chapter:

- InnoDB compression requirements
- Creating InnoDB compressed tables
- Implementing the InnoDB compression
- Monitoring the InnoDB compression performance
- Other compression solutions

An overview of the InnoDB compression

InnoDB supports the compression of tables. There are two reasons why we may want to use this feature:

- Saving space on disks
- Reducing the I/O

The first reason is more relevant if we use SSD storage devices because many I/O operations reduce their lifetime.

On many workloads, the I/O from and to disks is the bottleneck. Reducing the data size obviously reduces the amount of data that needs to be moved from disks to the buffer pool and vice versa.

However, InnoDB compression has a cost. The pages read from disks need to be uncompressed before being inserted into the buffer pool. Changes to the buffer pool and the change buffer must be compressed before being written onto the disk. This requires additional work by the CPU. For this reason, using compression may result in a slower performance.

Also, if there is enough memory, InnoDB keeps both compressed and uncompressed versions of all the data in the buffer pool. This means that the buffer pool needs more space, or it will contain less data. In this case, useful pages can be evicted from the buffer pool so that it contains compressed pages. For this reason, InnoDB compression performs much better on read-intensive workloads, and should generally be avoided on write-intensive workloads.

It is also important to consider how much of a table's data can be compressed. InnoDB uses the LZ77 algorithm for compression, which replaces repeated long data patterns with shorter strings. This technique suits texts better and usually does not work very well with numbers. Compressed data formats, such as JPEG images or MP3 videos, will not benefit much from a further LZ77 compression.

The TEXT, BLOB, and VARCHAR columns are stored in separate pages when necessary, as explained in *Chapter 6, Caches*. If a row does not fit its page, the largest columns are moved to special pages called **overflow pages**. The clustered index contains a 20-byte pointer for each overflow page used. This slows down all the operations that involve such columns. If a table compression sensibly reduces the number of overflow pages used by a table, it will probably improve the performance.

While knowing the InnoDB compression characteristics is important, the only exact way to determine whether our workload will benefit from compression is by testing it. We need to test it on a compression basis, execute a realistic workload, and monitor some information_schema tables.

InnoDB compression requirements

To use the InnoDB compressed tables, at least two requirements must be met:

- Each compressed table must be stored in a separate file
- The Barracuda file format must be used

Let's discuss how to satisfy these requirements and what they imply.

Explaining the file-per-table mode

InnoDB tables are stored in storage areas called **tablespaces**, which contain both data and indexes. In older MariaDB versions, by default, InnoDB used only one tablespace called the system tablespace. It also contains the change buffer, the doublewrite buffer, and by default, the undo log. This tablespace is physically stored in the `ibdata` file in the `data` directory of MariaDB (`ibdata1`, `ibdata2`, and so on). While the system tablespace still exists on the latest versions of MariaDB and can still contain all the tables, it is now possible to store each new table in a dedicated tablespace. Each tablespace created in this way is a separate file with the `.ibd` extension, which is located in a database subdirectory. This storage method is called the **file-per-table mode**. It is enabled by default since MariaDB 10.0.

The file-per-table mode is enabled by default. To enable or disable it, we can use the `innodb_file_per_table` system variable. When a table is created, InnoDB checks this variable to determine whether the new table should be created in the system tablespace or in a separate tablespace.

Let's see an example of how it works. Let's create some tables in MariaDB:

```
MariaDB [test_innodb]> CREATE TABLE haon (col INT NOT NULL PRIMARY KEY)
ENGINE = InnoDB;
Query OK, 0 rows affected (0.27 sec)
MariaDB [test_innodb]> SET @@global.innodb_file_per_table = ON;
Query OK, 0 rows affected (0.00 sec)
MariaDB [test_innodb]> CREATE TABLE do (col INT NOT NULL PRIMARY KEY)
ENGINE = InnoDB;
Query OK, 0 rows affected (0.46 sec)
MariaDB [test_innodb]> SET @@global.innodb_file_per_table = OFF;
Query OK, 0 rows affected (0.00 sec)
MariaDB [test_innodb]> CREATE TABLE tri (col INT NOT NULL PRIMARY KEY)
ENGINE = InnoDB;
Query OK, 0 rows affected (0.26 sec)
```

Now, let's check the files in the `data` directory and in the `database` subdirectory:

```
root@this:/usr/local/mysql# ls data/ibdata* -1
data/ibdata1
root@this:/usr/local/mysql# ls data/test_innodb -1
db.opt
do.frm
do.ibd
haon.frm
tri.frm
```

Of course, the system tablespace exists (the `ibdata1` file). In the `test_innodb` subdirectory, we can see:

- The database options file (`db.opt`)
- The files containing the tables definitions, which are created by MariaDB disregarding the storage engine (the `.frm` files)
- Only one tablespace, that is, `do.ibd`

When the **haon** and **tri** tables were created, the `innodb_file_per_table` variable was off, and so, no separate tablespace has been created for them: they are stored in the system tablespace. When the **do** table was created, `innodb_file_per_table` was set to `ON`, and so, it is stored in a file called `do.ibd`.

A brief on InnoDB file formats

Older versions of InnoDB use a file format called **Antelope**. This format is still used by default for backward compatibility, and the system tablespace uses it. A new file format called **Barracuda** supports more features. Table compression is only available with the Barracuda file format.

> The Antelope and Barracuda names start with the first two letters in the English alphabet. Other file formats may come in the future. Their names will keep on following this rule: they will be animal names starting with the next letter in the English alphabet.

When the file-per-table mode is enabled and a new table is created, InnoDB checks the value of the `innodb_file_format` server variable. It contains the name of the file format that will be used for the new tablespace. Both the `INNODB_SYS_TABLES` and `INNODB_SYS_TABLESPACES` tables in the `information_schema` database contain a column called `FILE_FORMAT`, which specify the file format used.

Let's see an example by creating two InnoDB tables with two different file formats:

```
MariaDB [test_innodb2]> SET @@global.innodb_file_per_table = ON;
Query OK, 0 rows affected (0.00 sec)
MariaDB [test_innodb2]> SET @@global.innodb_file_format = 'Antelope';
Query OK, 0 rows affected (0.00 sec)
MariaDB [test_innodb2]> CREATE TABLE um (col INT NOT NULL PRIMARY KEY)
ENGINE = InnoDB;
```

```
Query OK, 0 rows affected (0.37 sec)

MariaDB [test_innodb2]> SET @@global.innodb_file_format = 'Barracuda';

Query OK, 0 rows affected (0.00 sec)

MariaDB [test_innodb2]> CREATE TABLE dois (col INT NOT NULL PRIMARY KEY)
ENGINE = InnoDB ROW_FORMAT = DYNAMIC;

Query OK, 0 rows affected (0.39 sec)
```

Remember that different file formats support different row formats. To use Barracuda, we must specify one of its file formats: DYNAMIC or COMPRESSED. The default row format is COMPACT, which is handled by the Antelope file format, so in this case Barracuda will not be used.

 By using the Antelope file format, we can be sure that we are only using features that can be replicated on MariaDB and MySQL versions older than 5.5. Setting the innodb_file_format variable to Antelope is a way to make sure that no table uses Barracuda.

Now, let's check the INNODB_SYS_TABLESPACES table:

```
MariaDB [test_innodb2]> SELECT NAME, FILE_FORMAT, ROW_FORMAT
FROM information_schema.INNODB_SYS_TABLESPACES
WHERE NAME LIKE 'test_innodb2/%';
```

NAME	FILE_FORMAT	ROW_FORMAT
test_innodb2/um	Antelope	Compact or Redundant
test_innodb2/dois	Barracuda	Dynamic

```
2 rows in set (0.00 sec)
```

When the Antelope format is used, the information_schema tables do not tell us which row format is used by the tables, as shown in the previous example. Compressed tables use the COMPRESSED row format.

The innodbfile_per_table and innodb_file_format variables are also used when altering a table with the copy algorithm (described in *Chapter 4, Transactions and Locks*). This means that a table can be moved from the system tablespace to a separate file or vice versa, and the file format may change. Thus, it is necessary to check the values of these variables before issuing ALTER TABLE, which requires a table copy. Also, when we think that the statement does not require a copy, it is a good idea to specify ALGORITHM = INPLACE for extra safety. This clause specifies that no table copy must be created. If the value of innodb_file_per_table or innodb_file_format is changed, InnoDB will try to rebuild the table, but since this operation requires a table copy, the statement will fail with an error.

Note that the file_per_table and innodb_file_format server variables only exist at the global level. This exposes us to a risk, if the current thread is not the only one with the SUPER privilege. In fact, thread 1 could change one of these variables a fraction of a second before thread 2 executes an ALTER TABLE command.

The Barracuda file format has been introduced with MariaDB 5.5 and MySQL 5.5. For this reason, it is not possible to replicate table compression or use a physical backup of the tables that use the Barracuda format on a server earlier than 5.5.

Creating InnoDB compressed tables

Before creating a compressed table, it is usually better to make sure that we are using the InnoDB strict mode. The reason for this is that InnoDB performs more checks on the CREATE TABLE statements when the strict mode is on. If something is wrong with the table definition, the table will not be created and an error will be produced instead. This prevents us from creating tables that are different from what we expect. However, the existing applications rely on the SQL statements they execute, and the strict mode might break them. For this reason, the strict mode is disabled by default, and it is possible to enable it at the session level. To enable the InnoDB strict mode globally, execute the following command:

```
SET @@global.innodb_strict_mode = ON;
```

In the current versions, the checks performed with the strict mode are only useful while creating compressed tables. However, in future versions, it could be useful in other situations; not necessarily related to table creation. Thus, unless it causes an error in one of our applications, we should leave the strict mode enabled all the time.

After checking the `innodb_file_per_table` and `innodb_file_format` server variables as explained previously, we can create an InnoDB compressed table. To do so, we just need to specify the `COMPRESSED` row format:

```
CREATE TABLE comp_table (
    id INT UNSIGNED NOT NULL PRIMARY KEY,
    c1 VARCHAR(255),
    c2 VARCHAR(255)
) ENGINE = InnoDB,
    ROW_FORMAT = COMPRESSED;
```

For the compressed tables, the size of the index blocks (pages) can be configured on a per-table basis. To do this, we can use the `KEY_BLOCK_SIZE` option. Since this option only makes sense for compressed tables, in this case, specifying the row format is not necessary:

```
CREATE TABLE comp_table (
    id INT UNSIGNED NOT NULL PRIMARY KEY,
    c1 VARCHAR(255),
    c2 VARCHAR(255)
) ENGINE = InnoDB,
    KEY_BLOCK_SIZE = 8;
```

The size of the key blocks does not affect the compression level, which cannot be set per table. However, by changing the page size, we determine how many rows a page can contain. The allowed sizes, expressed in KBs, are 16, 8 (the default), 4, 2, and 1. The value 0 specifies the default value, but in this case, table compression is not used. Normally, `KEY_BLOCK_SIZE` is lower than `innodb_page_size` (whose default value is 16). However, if a table contains TEXT or BLOB values, a 16 KB memory size might allow the storage of many values in normal pages, so that they are not stored in the offset pages (as explained in *Chapter 6, Caches*).

Sometimes, the value we try to assign to `KEY_BLOCK_SIZE` is not adequate for the table indexes. In this case, having the InnoDB strict mode enabled is very important, because it forces MariaDB to produce an error. If the strict mode is disabled, the table will be created, but when we try to insert or modify a row, an error might occur.

The best way to determine the optimal value for `KEY_BLOCK_SIZE` is to create several copies of the table, each one using a different size, and then testing their performance on a realistic workload. The performance of a compressed table can be monitored by querying some tables in `information_schema`, as explained later in this chapter.

It is possible to change the key block size for an existing compressed table using an ALTER TABLE statement:

```
ALTER TABLE comp_table KEY_BLOCK_SIZE = 16;
```

It is even possible to compress an existing table:

```
MariaDB [test]> CREATE TABLE non_comp (
    ->    id INT UNSIGNED NOT NULL PRIMARY KEY,
    ->    c1 VARCHAR(255),
    ->    c2 VARCHAR(255)
    -> ) ENGINE = InnoDB;
Query OK, 0 rows affected (0.36 sec)
MariaDB [test]> ALTER TABLE non_comp KEY_BLOCK_SIZE = 8;
Query OK, 0 rows affected (0.48 sec)
Records: 0  Duplicates: 0  Warnings: 0
```

In both cases, ALTER TABLE can take time but will use the in-place algorithm with no locks.

Explaining the implementation of the InnoDB compression

The InnoDB compression supports different compression levels. The innodb_compression_level server variable is an integer value in the range between 0 and 9. A higher value represents a more efficient, but slower, compression level. The default value is 6. This variable is dynamic and can be changed at any time.

As mentioned previously, when an index entry is read from the disk, it is written into the buffer pool in both its compressed and uncompressed forms. InnoDB tries to avoid performing a huge number of compression and uncompression operations in several ways. For example, it can modify a compressed page without compressing the new data until the page needs to be flushed onto the disk. To do this, it keeps a track of such changes in a page area called the **modification log**, which is uncompressed. Updates and small row insertions can often be applied without recreating the page.

Of course, each page's modification log has a limited space. If InnoDB tries to write a change into the log but it runs out of space, the page is uncompressed, logged changes are applied, and the page is compressed again. In some cases, the page becomes too large after the changes take place, and so, the data needs to be reorganized to fit the page size. When the new page results are too large, a **compression failure** happens.

Rebuilding the compressed pages takes time, thus InnoDB tries to avoid compression failures if they happen too often. If the ratio between compression failures and changes applied exceeds the value of the `innodb_compression_failure_threshold_pct` server variable, InnoDB leaves an empty space at the end of each new compressed page. The `innodb_compression_failure_threshold_pct` server variable is a percentage and its default value is 5. The `innodb_compression_pad_pct_max` server variable specifies the maximum percentage of the free space that can be left in each compressed page. The allowed range is between 0 and 75 and the default value is 50. If any of these variables is set to 0, this optimization is disabled.

If compression failures happen too often for a single table, that table's `KEY_BLOCK_SIZE` is probably too low. If the performance of the compressed tables is slow and is caused by compression failures, `innodb_compression_failure_threshold_pct` should probably be increased. If a typical update can dramatically increase the size of a row, `innodb_compression_pad_pct_max` should be set to a high value.

The next section shows how to monitor the compressed table's performance, both globally and on a table basis.

Monitoring the InnoDB compression performance

The `information_schema` database contains some tables that can be used to monitor the performance of the InnoDB compressed tables. All these tables have their names starting with `INNODB_CMP`, so they can be listed with the following query:

```
MariaDB [information_schema]> SHOW TABLES LIKE 'INNODB_CMP%';
+-------------------------------------------+
| Tables_in_information_schema (INNODB_CMP%) |
+-------------------------------------------+
| INNODB_CMP                                |
| INNODB_CMP_RESET                          |
| INNODB_CMP_PER_INDEX                      |
```

```
| INNODB_CMPMEM_RESET                          |
| INNODB_CMP_PER_INDEX_RESET                   |
| INNODB_CMPMEM                                |
+----------------------------------------------+
6 rows in set (0.00 sec)
```

The main InnoDB tables are:

- INNODB_CMPMEM: This table stores statistics about the compressed table pages in the buffer pool
- INNODB_CMP: This table stores information about the compression and uncompression operations on the whole server
- INNODB_CMP_PER_INDEX: This table stores information very similar to the previous table, but the information is grouped per individual tables and indexes

The reset tables (the ones whose names end with _RESET) are identical to the matching non-reset tables. The difference is that when a reset table is queried, most of its contents are reset. It is possible to query the reset tables at regular time intervals to monitor how the compressed table's performance varies in time. Or, they could be used to check the effects of a variable's change.

> Note that gathering the information stored in the INNODB_CMP_PER_INDEX and INNODB_CMP_PER_INDEX_RESET tables can be expensive. For this reason, these tables are always empty, unless the innodb_cmp_per_index_enabled variable is set to ON. Normally, this should not be the case on production servers.

The INNODB_CMPMEM table

This table shows the statistics of compressed pages in the buffer pool. The statistics are grouped by page size. Each row shows information about how the tables with a particular KEY_BLOCK_SIZE behave. In fact, each table is designed for the DBA who needs to determine the key block size for a table. The following table describes the columns present in the INNODB_CMPMEM table:

Column name	Description
PAGE_SIZE	This is the page size in bytes (not KBs).
BUFFER_POOL_INSTANCE	This is the ID of the buffer pool instance.
PAGES_USED	This is the number of the currently used pages.

Column name	Description
PAGES_FREE	This is the number of the currently free pages. In theory, this value should always be 1. In practice, the buffer pool fragmentation cannot be completely avoided. The more it is fragmented, the higher this value.
RELOCATION_OPS	This is the number of times the pages have been moved. These operations are executed to reduce fragmentation.
RELOCATION_TIME	This is the microseconds elapsed while moving pages.

When the INNODB_CMPMEM_RESET table is read, the RELOCATION_OPS and RELOCATION_TIME fields are set to 0.

Suppose we have a customer table. From the original table, we create three compressed tables with different KEY_BLOCK_SIZE values: customers_16, customers_8, and customers_4. As mentioned earlier, a good testing requires that we run a realistic workload on each table for a while. However, in this example, we just want to see how these tables work, so we will just execute a SELECT COUNT(*) query for each table. Then, we will query INNODB_CMPMEM_RESET, shown as follows:

```
MariaDB [information_schema]> CREATE TABLE test.customers_16
ENGINE=InnoDB ROW_FORMAT=COMPRESSED KEY_BLOCK_SIZE=16 SELECT * FROM
test.customers_non_comp;
Query OK, 1474560 rows affected (59.88 sec)
Records: 1474560  Duplicates: 0  Warnings: 0
MariaDB [information_schema]> CREATE TABLE test.customers_8
ENGINE=InnoDB ROW_FORMAT=COMPRESSED KEY_BLOCK_SIZE=8 SELECT * FROM
test.customers_non_comp;
Query OK, 1474560 rows affected (1 min 36.50 sec)
Records: 1474560  Duplicates: 0  Warnings: 0
MariaDB [information_schema]> CREATE TABLE test.customers_4
ENGINE=InnoDB ROW_FORMAT=COMPRESSED KEY_BLOCK_SIZE=4 SELECT * FROM
test.customers_non_comp;
Query OK, 1474560 rows affected (6 min 54.86 sec)
Records: 1474560  Duplicates: 0  Warnings: 0
MariaDB [information_schema]> SELECT COUNT(*) FROM test.customers_16;
+----------+
| COUNT(*) |
+----------+
|  1474560 |
```

```
+-----------+
1 row in set (2.86 sec)
MariaDB [information_schema]> SELECT COUNT(*) FROM test.customers_8;
+-----------+
| COUNT(*) |
+-----------+
|   1474560 |
+-----------+
1 row in set (5.07 sec)
MariaDB [information_schema]> SELECT COUNT(*) FROM test.customers_4;
+-----------+
| COUNT(*) |
+-----------+
|   1474560 |
+-----------+
1 row in set (7.14 sec)
MariaDB [information_schema]> SELECT * FROM INNODB_CMPMEM_RESET;
```

page_size	buffer_pool_instance	pages_used	pages_free	relocation_ops	relocation_time
1024	0	0	0	0	0
2048	0	0	0	0	0
4096	0	5832	16	3864	0
8192	0	2365	557	3244	0
16384	0	5597	0	0	0

```
5 rows in set (0.00 sec)
```

After running a realistic workload and examining the contents of this table, we will try to choose a low-key block size, which does not require too many relocation operations.

The INNODB_CMP_PER_INDEX table

The INNODB_CMP_PER_INDEX table shows information about the performance of the compressed pages, grouped by index. As mentioned earlier, gathering this information is expensive, thus INNODB_CMP_PER_INDEX is always empty, unless the innodb_cmp_per_index_enabled variable is set to ON.

This table contains the following columns:

- DATABASE_NAME: This is the database that contains the index.

- TABLE_NAME: This is the table that contains the index.

- INDEX_NAME: This is the grouping columns. All the remaining values refer to the operations performed on this index page.

- COMPRESS_OPS: This column specifies the number of times modification log changes are applied to a page.

- COMPRESS_OPS_OK: This is the number of times a compression operation succeeded and did not result in a compression failure.

- COMPRESS_TIME: This is the number of seconds elapsed while compressing data.

- UNCOMPRESS_OPS: This is the number of uncompressed operations. Remember that this number is increased, both when a new index entry is copied to the buffer pool, and when a compression operation fails.

- UNCOMPRESS_TIME: This is the number of seconds elapsed during uncompress operations.

When the INNODB_CMP_PER_INDEX_RESET table is queried, all the columns except for DATABASE_NAME, TABLE_NAME, and INDEX_NAME are reset to 0.

This table allows us to understand how much each index performance is negatively affected by the compress and uncompress operations. The number of compression failures is the difference between COMPRESS_OPS and COMPRESS_OPS_OK. If this value is low and the performance is poor, the index is slow because pages are written to the buffer pool and evicted from it too often. If the buffer pool configuration and the index usage cannot be improved, the table should not be compressed.

If there are many compression failures, we should try to reduce them. If compression operations happen for a singular table (or index), we should consider modifying the KEY_BLOCK_SIZE table option; otherwise, we should try to set innodb_compression_failure_threshold_pct and innodb_compression_pad_pct_max to their optimal values.

The INNODB_CMP table

The INNODB_CMP table is identical to INNODB_CMP_PER_INDEX, except that the values are global and not grouped per index or table. This table is generally less useful, but gathering its contents is less expensive. Thus, the table is always populated.

The INNODB_CMP table has the same columns as INNODB_CMP_PER_INDEX, except for DATABASE_NAME, TABLE_NAME, and INDEX_NAME.

If INNODB_CMP_RESET is queried, its contents are reset completely.

Other compression solutions

Other storage engines offer the ability to compress tables. These engines are:

- TokuDB: This engine always compresses tables; there is no way to avoid this. This is a part of its strategy, which aims to reach high performance by reducing the amount of output to disks.

- ARCHIVE: This storage engine is specifically designed for compressed tables with limited functionalities. It is possible to add new data to an ARCHIVE table, but the existing rows cannot be deleted or updated. Index support is very limited.

- MyISAM: While normal MyISAM tables are not compressed, a special tool called myisampack can be used to compress tables. A compressed MyISAM table is read only.

 Note that while Aria aims to be a more robust and modern version of MyISAM, it does not support this feature.

Compression methods other than the InnoDB COMPRESSED row format are beyond the scope of this chapter. They are not widely used because other storage engines, including TokuDB, do not reach the performance of InnoDB on most workloads. Also, the ARCHIVE storage engine and the myisampack tool are documented and easy to use. However, in most cases, their limitations are not acceptable. The TokuDB storage engine is also capable of a very good compression. However, since TokuDB is not a simple topic, and since it is not enabled by default, it is not covered in this book.

However, an advanced user should know that such solutions exist. The following example shows a comparison between the size of the files of a typical customer's tables:

```
root@this:/usr/local/mysql/data/test# ls -l customers*
-rw-rw---- 1 mysql mysql 201326592 mar 31 00:51 customers_non_comp.ibd
-rw-rw---- 1 mysql mysql 100663296 mar 31 01:03 customers_4.ibd
-rw-rw---- 1 mysql mysql  96468992 mar 31 00:56 customers_8.ibd
-rw-rw---- 1 mysql mysql 188743680 mar 31 00:54 customers_16.ibd
-rw-rw---- 1 mysql mysql    955044 mar 31 01:04 customers_arch.ARZ
-rw-rw---- 1 mysql mysql  82379202 mar 31 01:04 customers_myi.MYD
-rw-rw---- 1 mysql mysql  25600000 mar 31 01:13 customers_myi.MYI
```

The preceding output has been edited to make it more readable, but the values are real. Of course, there are cases when we can get completely different results, so proper tests should be executed if they are relevant for our case. But still, this represents a real case with a table containing many short text fields, an auto increment primary key, and an indexed username field.

The `data` files in the example are:

- `customers_non_comp.ibd`: This is a noncompressed InnoDB table
- `customers_*.ibd`: This is a compressed InnoDB table with a key block size of 4, 8, and 16 KB
- `customers_arch.ARZ`: This is an ARCHIVE table
- `customers_myi.MYD` and `customers_myi.MYI`: These are compressed MyISAM `data` and `index` files

In this example, the compressed MyISAM files are a bit bigger than the best compressed InnoDB tablespace, and thus, ARCHIVE wins.

Since the difference between ARCHIVE and InnoDB is so high, we can conclude that ARCHIVE is a better choice for the general case. However, there are several reasons why InnoDB is more useful:

- ARCHIVE does not support transactions, and this is a concern, except for big tables that are only used for statistical data.
- InnoDB performance for inserts is much better, and the performance of XtraDB is even better.
- Geometric data types such as LINESTRING or POLYGON are not supported in ARCHIVE.

- While compressed tables are not likely to be read often, we may want to index them. ARCHIVE does not support indexing, except for the autoincremental primary keys.

- While the development of InnoDB and XtraDB is very intensive, ARCHIVE did not evolve for many years.

If these limitations are not a concern, ARCHIVE is a very good choice. In other cases, if really needed, modifying the `innodb_compression_level` variable is usually a more acceptable solution than using the ARCHIVE storage engine.

Summary

In this chapter, we discussed InnoDB table compression. We discussed the situations in which this feature should be useful, and how to check whether our particular workload can benefit from it. We learned how to create a compressed table and configure InnoDB compression. Then, we discussed how to monitor the performance of the compressed tables.

While discussing these topics, we also examined some InnoDB important features: the file-per-table mode (which causes new tables to be stored into separated tablespaces) and the InnoDB file format (since only the Barracuda format allows compressing tables).

However, MariaDB provides other useful storage engines. For this reason, in the final part, we compared InnoDB compression to the compression provided by other engines.

In the next chapter, we will discuss how to create or restore a backup and, more generally, how to handle data corruption.

8
Backup and Disaster Recovery

Nowadays, most business processes, if not all, are automated. Activities of a company, from sales to management decisions, generally require an application to access a database server and to read or modify records. If data loss occurs, some of the company's normal activities become impossible to continue until the data is restored. If some data is lost forever, the company probably loses some of its opportunities and some of its vital information. In a sense, we can safely state that each relevant data loss diminishes the value of a company. For this reason, such an event is commonly called a disaster. In technical jargon, the task of restoring as much data as possible is called disaster recovering. Since it is not always possible to repair data files, it is necessary to make regular backups of data so that they can be restored after a disaster. This chapter discusses backup and disaster recovering, some of the most vital tasks of a DBA.

The main topics that will be discussed in the chapter are:

- Types of backups
- Logical backups via `mysqldump`
- Physical backups using the filesystem
- Complete and incremental backups via Percona XtraBackup
- How to restore a backup
- How to repair a corrupt table

Types of backups

Several events can corrupt or delete important data. Some technical problems that may cause data loss are:

- A power failure during a disk write
- Hardware failures (such as disks and motherboards)
- Crashing of the operating system
- MariaDB or storage engines bugs (yes, like all programs, MariaDB has bugs)

But even a human being can cause damage. A cracker can use a software vulnerability to destroy some data. Or, we can accidentally issue a DROP DATABASE command on a database that we did not want to erase.

Since there is no way to be sure that these things will not happen, we need to be prepared to restore all critical data by performing regular and automated backups.

A backup can be performed in several ways. No backup method is better than others in all situations. The choice depends on many factors. Before deciding on a backup plan, we should ask ourselves questions such as:

- How critical is our data?
- How often is our data updated?
- Can the server slow down or be temporarily stopped during the backup process?

After defining our needs, we can wisely choose a backup strategy that best fits our workload.

Logical and physical backups

A **logical backup** creates a representation of the relevant data. Take for instance a CSV file containing all the values, or a text file containing the SQL statements that need to be executed to exactly recreate the original data; this is called a **dump** file.

A **physical backup** is a copy of the files that physically contain the data. It is important to know that MariaDB does not write anything on such files until the copying finishes. This is easier with simple storage engines like MyISAM but harder with complex storage engines such as InnoDB. On MariaDB versions older than 10.0, one has to stop the server before taking a physical backup of InnoDB tables. A physical backup copies the whole data directory. By default, this includes the log and configuration files.

Some storage engines, like MyISAM, store each table in a separated data file; others do not. As explained in *Chapter 7, InnoDB Compressed Tables*, InnoDB is able to store some tables in the system tablespace and others in separate files. If tables are stored separately, it is possible to take a backup of the most relevant table instead of copying the data of all tables. This is very important in situations where some tables rarely (or never) change or where the contents of some tables can easily be recreated starting from other tables (such as the summary tables explained in *Chapter 6, Caches*).

In the case of partitioned tables, each partition is stored in a separate file. Sometimes, only the most recent partition contains recent data, while other partitions contain historical data. For example, a partition might contain the sales that took place in the last month, and other partitions might contain older sales. In such cases, usually we have a backup of historical data, so we can copy only one partition. Partitions are discussed in *Chapter 10, Table Partitioning*.

The pros of the logical backups are:

- The servers need not be completely stopped. However, keep in mind that each of the heavy transaction will affect transactional tables, and the non-transactional tables need to be locked. Also, a backup is normally a read-intensive operation that slows down the server.

- A logical backup is very flexible, because modifying it is relatively easy. For example, we can change a database name in a dump file before applying the backup. Or, we can drop some rows.

- A logical backup can be more selective than a physical backup. If it is based on SQL queries, we can exclude some rows or columns from the copy.

- A logical backup can be restored on a newer or an older version of MariaDB. For this reason, a logical backup should be created before upgrading MariaDB in case something goes wrong.

The pros of the physical backups are:

- Physical backups are much faster, because they are done directly using the filesystem. Also, their size is usually much smaller, because they only include data and indexes in a compact format; SQL statements and data are not in a text format.

- A physical backup usually includes log and configuration files. This is not strictly necessary to recover data, but the loss of the server's configuration or an important log should be considered to be a major disaster.

Hot and cold backups

Hot backups are taken while the server is running. Cold backups are taken while the server is stopped.

A logical backup is always hot. There is no way to get a representation of MariaDB data without querying the server.

With MariaDB 10, it is always possible to lock the physical files during a backup process, so there is no reason to stop the server. However, with older versions, cold backups are necessary for InnoDB files. During hot backups, the server accepts commands from the clients. However, a hot backup allows us to perform logical backups.

But maybe we know that the backup will take too much time, and queuing the client's requests for the duration of the backup makes no sense. Or, maybe the server does not work at certain times, for example, when an office is closed. In such cases, if we want to make a physical backup, we may prefer to stop the server. We need not stop lock tables, and the process will be more straightforward.

Complete and incremental backups

If we work with a considerable amount of data, performing a backup can take a long time; during this period, the tables are probably locked. Also, the backup may need a lot of space. To reduce the backup time and the needed space, we can use **incremental backups** (also called **partial backups**). An incremental backup is a copy of the changes that were made to the data since a well-known instant (the time of the previous backup).

Of course, we don't want to restore the data by applying all incremental backups that have been performed since the server was started for the first time! Such an operation is theoretically possible, but would be slow, require a lot of space for backups, and be error prone. Thus, regular complete backups are still necessary.

However, a mix of complete and incremental backups is usually a good strategy. For example, we can take a complete backup once a week and an incremental backup each night. To restore the data after a disaster, we will restore the most recent complete backup and then apply all subsequent incremental backups (if any).

Backups and replication

Backups and replication are correlated topics. They both duplicate data to allow us to recover them if a disaster occurs.

However, it is important to remember that replication does not replace a good backup strategy. In fact, there is an important conceptual difference between these techniques. A backup is a static consistent snapshot of the data; it will never change. A replication slave repeats all the operations performed by the master, so its databases constantly change.

In a replication environment, we have the important opportunity of choosing the server we will use to perform backups. Creating backups from the master is often a bad idea, because that server is used by the applications, and we should avoid slowing it down or even stopping it, if possible. A slave is theoretically a good idea, especially if it does not work as a master for other slaves. However, we must also keep in mind that slaves can lag behind their master by some hours or even by several days. While this can be acceptable for replication, backups should always contain very recent data. So, slaves are only used for backups if they do not sensibly lag behind. Replication will be discussed in *Chapter 9*, *Replication*.

A database cluster is a complex, very reliable, replication setup. In *Chapter 12*, *MariaDB Galera Cluster*, we will discuss the most common clustering solution for MariaDB. Galera guarantees that all data in all the nodes is always up to date. In this case, if one of the nodes does not normally receive queries from the clients, it is a good choice for backups. Otherwise, we can probably choose the server with the most powerful hardware.

Steps to be followed before performing backups

Until this point, we have discussed backup types, and the benefits provided by each type. The coming sections discuss in detail how to perform these backups in practice. But before that detailed discussion, let's ask this important question: what should we do after choosing a backup strategy?

For each involved backup method that we are going to implement, we should take the following steps:

1. **Write the necessary scripts**:

    Backups need to be automatic, so we will create cron jobs and other scripts to make them take place regularly.

2. **Test data backups**:

    We will use development servers for this. We will set up test data, we will perform a backup, and we will check if the backup has been created. Also, we will check if the time required for the backup methods we have chosen is acceptable.

3. **Test data restoring**:

   At this point, we will perform an operation that heavily modifies the database, and we will restore the backup. We will check if everything is in place. This step is useful to check that we know exactly what to do when disasters occur. We must take the correct actions, and we are probably required to do it quickly.

4. **Document all the procedures**:

   Even the best backup and restore methods are useless if we do not remember how to use them. Document all possible problems and how to solve them.

5. **Switch to production**:

   This should be done only when we are really ready!

This book is specifically about MariaDB. It does not cover cron jobs, system shell, programming, or testing methods. In the following sections, we will only discuss the heart of the topic: how to perform backups and restore data. But when putting these techniques in practice, we will need to follow the preceding steps to make sure that backups always work as expected.

Creating a dump file with mysqldump

The **mysqldump** command is the most used tool to perform hot logical backups. It is included in all MariaDB distributions and is located in the bin directory.

Usually, mysqldump is used to create a dump file: it connects to MariaDB, reads the data we want to back up, and creates a file containing the SQL statements that are required to recreate the same data. It has several options that allow us to control which data is included in the backup and modify the SQL statements that are written in the file. The dump file can also be manually edited to fit particular needs. The generated SQL statements use executable comments (mentioned in *Chapter 1, Understanding the Essentials of MariaDB*) so that it is possible to restore the dump in an older version of MariaDB, in a MySQL installation, or possibly even on different DBMSs.

For all these reasons, mysqldump is an amazingly flexible program. This explains why mysqldump is the preferred tool for taking logical backups. It is also used in other situations, such as copying a database or a table from one server to another, or to generate a dump file that is run during an application's installation.

The drawback of dump files is that they take a lot of space. Not only do logical backups represent the data in an uncompressed way, but a dump file can even put that data inside SQL statements. However, mysqldump is also able to create textual backups, as explained in the next section.

The `mysqldump` command supports three syntaxes depending on whether we want to back up all databases in the server, a limited set of databases, or a set or tables within a database, shown as follows:

```
mysqldump [other_options] --all-databases > file_name
mysqldump [other_options] --databases db1 db2 … > file_name
mysqldump [other_options] db_name table1 table2 … > file_name
```

In the third case, no USE command is included in the dump file. The reason is that the user probably wants to recreate the dumped tables into another database.

Even while dumping multiple databases, it is possible to exclude some tables. To ignore one table, we can add an option like this:

```
--ignore-table=db_name.table_name
```

To ignore multiple tables, we must repeat the option multiple times. Specifying a comma-separated list is not correct. For example:

```
--ignore-table=db_name.table_one --ignore-table=db_name.table_two …
```

The options that tell `mysqldump` how to connect to the server are standard. They are the same as the mysql command-line client and all other client programs distributed with MariaDB.

By default, the dump files include a CREATE DATABASE statement. To skip it, we can use the `--no-create-db` option. Usually, we want to have a DROP DATABASE before CREATE DATABASE. So, if a damaged database exists, it is replaced with complete, correct data. We can use `–add-drop-database`. Both the table's definition and data are included in the dump by default. However, it is possible to exclude table definitions with `--no-create-info` or table data with `–no-data`. The table options in CREATE TABLE are not standard (they only work on MariaDB and mostly on MySQL) and are only included if `--table-options` is specified.

Sometimes, we do not want a dump to destroy and replace existing databases, because they contain some tables that we want to preserve. Even in that case, we probably want the dumped tables to completely replace the existing ones (for example, because at least one of them is damaged). To do this we can use the --add-drop-table option, which adds a DROP TABLE statement before each CREATE TABLE. As an alternative, we may want the data to be inserted with the REPLACE statement instead of INSERT: this way, the dumped data will replace the existing data but, if the table also contains rows that are not in the dump file, those rows will be preserved. This can be done using the --replace option. Or, we can use --insert-ignore, which turns INSERT statements into INSERT IGNORE. This is useful if we want dumped data to be inserted only if they do not exist in the table.

> The main difference between REPLACE and INSERT IGNORE is that REPLACE deletes existing data, while INSERT IGNORE leaves them untouched. An important but often forgotten side effect of the REPLACE statement is that the replaced rows will have new AUTO_INCREMENT values even if all other values are identical to the old ones. If foreign keys are not used to preserve cross-table data integrity, this could be a problem. If foreign keys are used, REPLACE will be slower.

Stored programs (triggers, routines, functions, and events) are not included by default. However, a complete logical backup should include them. Also, they usually do not take much space. To dump stored programs, we can use the --triggers, --routines, and --events options.

Usually, we want the dump to consist of a single transaction. This guarantees data integrity across tables. If we specify the --single-transaction option, mysqldump begins a transaction in the REPEATABLE READ isolation level before starting reading data and issues COMMIT after the dumping process. The --no-autocommit option surrounds each table's inserts in the dump file with SET autocommit=0; and COMMIT. This makes the restore faster, but while a table is populated, other tables can be modified by other sessions.

When dumping non-transactional tables, `--single-transaction` does not guarantee data integrity. Thus, in such cases, we will use an option that locks the tables. The `--lock-all-tables` option acquires a global read lock on all databases. This completely blocks all the write operations on the server until the end of the dumping process but is the only way to guarantee consistency across several databases if non-transactional tables are used. However, often we only need to guarantee data integrity on a per-database basis. In this case, we can use the `--lock-tables` option, which locks one database at a time. The `--add-locks` option adds LOCK TABLES before each table's inserts and UNLOCK TABLES after each table's inserts. The `--disable-keys` option makes the restoring of MyISAM tables faster using ALTER TABLE ... DISABLE KEYS.

> Remember that LOCK TABLES and UNLOCK TABLES implicitly commit the current transaction, thus some of the mentioned options are mutually exclusive. Using `--no-autocommit` and `--add-locks` together makes no sense, because table locks will make transactions useless. Whether we use this option or not, we usually want to use multiple-row INSERT statements instead of one statement for each row. To do this, we can use the `--extended-insert` option.

By default, `mysqldump` reads all the rows from the server into a buffer and writes them together into the dump file. While this is performance optimization, when dumping large amounts of data, it may require too much memory. To avoid bufferizing the rows, the `--quick` option can be specified.

The following is an example of the beginning of a typical dump file:

```
-- MySQL dump 10.14  Distrib 10.0.8-MariaDB, for Linux (x86_64)
--
-- Host: localhost    Database:
-- -------------------------------------------------------
-- Server version    10.0.8-MariaDB-log

/*!40101 SET @OLD_CHARACTER_SET_CLIENT=@@CHARACTER_SET_CLIENT */;
/*!40101 SET @OLD_CHARACTER_SET_RESULTS=@@CHARACTER_SET_RESULTS */;
/*!40101 SET @OLD_COLLATION_CONNECTION=@@COLLATION_CONNECTION */;
/*!40101 SET NAMES utf8 */;
```

```
/*!40103 SET @OLD_TIME_ZONE=@@TIME_ZONE */;

/*!40103 SET TIME_ZONE='+00:00' */;

/*!40014 SET @OLD_UNIQUE_CHECKS=@@UNIQUE_CHECKS, UNIQUE_CHECKS=0 */;

/*!40014 SET @OLD_FOREIGN_KEY_CHECKS=@@FOREIGN_KEY_CHECKS, FOREIGN_KEY_
CHECKS=0 */;

/*!40101 SET @OLD_SQL_MODE=@@SQL_MODE, SQL_MODE='NO_AUTO_VALUE_ON_ZERO'
*/;

/*!40111 SET @OLD_SQL_NOTES=@@SQL_NOTES, SQL_NOTES=0 */;
```

Each database dump begins with lines similar to the following:

```
--

-- Current Database: 'flexviews'

--


CREATE DATABASE /*!32312 IF NOT EXISTS*/ 'flexviews' /*!40100 DEFAULT
CHARACTER SET latin1 */;


USE 'flexviews';
```

Restoring a dump file is simple. Basically, we just need to execute the statements contained in it. There are many ways to do this; for example, if you have a small dump file, you could even copy its content and paste it into your favorite GUI. However, the most practical way is invoking the mysql command-line client using the file as input. The following syntax works on all systems, including Windows:

```
mysql [options] < file_name
```

If we already have a mysql instance open, we can use the SOURCE client command:

```
SOURCE 'file_path'path'path';
```

Delimited text backups

A backup of a single table can be a delimited text file: a human-readable text file in which the column values are separated by a specific character. The most common example is the CSV format, where the values are separated by a comma. MariaDB supports the following ways to create text-delimited files:

- The `mysqldump` command with the `--tab` option
- The SELECT ... INTO OUTFILE command
- The CSV storage engine
- The CONNECT storage engine

MariaDB also supports the following methods to restore a text limited backup:

- The `mysqlimport` command
- The `LOAD DATA INFILE` command
- The `CSV` storage engine
- The `CONNECT` storage engine

The --tab option of the mysqldump command

The `mysqldump` command, when invoked with the `--tab` option, produces two files for each dumped table. The name of these files is the name of the original table, followed by an extension. One file has a `.sql` extension, and it contains the `CREATE TABLE` statement that is necessary to recreate the empty table. Of course, this file needs to be executed first to restore a dump unless the table already exists. The other file has a `.txt` extension, and it contains a delimited text backup. By default, a tab character is used to separate values, and a new line character is used to separate lines. But the used characters as well as many file characteristics can be configured using some `mysqldump` options. These options will be discussed later in this section, because they are used by multiple tools and statements.

The `--tab` option specifies the path where the `.sql` and `.txt` files will be located. For example: `--tab=/tmp/backup`.

Loading a dump file with the mysqlimport command

The `mysqlimport` command is a tool that is complementary to `mysqldump` and can be used to import delimited text backups. Like `mysqldump`, it is included in all MariaDB distributions and is located in the `bin` directory. Its syntax is as follows:

```
mysqlimport [options] db_name file [file ...]
```

A database name must be specified so that `mysqlimport` knows where the table is stored. Then, at least one file to import must be specified. The base name of the file must be the same as the table being referred to. The extension, if it exists, is not relevant (it can be `.csv`, `.txt`, or whatever we prefer). This has an interesting consequence: two files with the same base name and different extensions refer to the same table. For very big tables, it could be convenient to split the rows into multiple files. The `mysqlimport` command also has several options that can be used to specify which characters are used to separate columns and rows, and other characteristics of the files to import. These options are described later in this section.

By default, the delimited text file is expected to be in the server. If `mysqlimport` is executed remotely, the file can also be located in the client; in this case, the `--local` option must be specified.

It is possible to skip the first lines in the source file by specifying the `--ignore-lines` option, for example, `--ignore-lines=1`. This is useful when the first line is composed of the columns names, or the file begins with some informative lines (like the timestamp of its creation or the name of the software that produced it).

Another important option is `--delete`, which empties the tables before importing the rows.

In case of duplicate values, the `--replace` option causes the imported rows to replace the existing rows in the tables, while the `--ignore` option leaves the existing rows untouched but avoids producing an error.

When importing many data, it may be useful to do it in parallel. The `--use-threads` option specifies how many threads must be used to import data. For example, if we specify `--use-threads=2`, `mysqlimport` will use two threads.

Creating a text-delimited file with the SELECT ... INTO OUTFILE command

The `SELECT` statement has an `INTO OUTFILE` clause, which causes the result set to be written into a file. By default, the file is saved into the MariaDB install directory (not the `data` directory). However, a path can be specified with the filename. Remember that the MariaDB user needs to have the `FILE` privilege to write or read files. Also, the system user used by MariaDB (which is usually `mysql`) needs to have write access to the directory where the file is saved. On Linux systems, the `/tmp` directory is usually a good candidate. Beware of the fact that, if the file already exists, an error is produced. Note, however, that the file needs to be located on the server. With `SELECT ... INTO OUTFILE`, we cannot create a file on the client or on any other host.

The result set will not be sent to the client, but it will receive the number of found rows (or an error).

Here is a simple example:

```
SELECT *
  ->FROM information_schema.TABLES
  ->ORDER BY TABLE_SCHEMA, TABLE_NAME
  ->INTO OUTFILE '/tmp/tables.txt';
```

By default, a tab character is used to separate columns values, and a new line character is used to separate rows. Several clauses exist to use different separators or other file characteristics. They will be discussed later, in the *Separator options and clauses* section, together with the corresponding options of `mysqldump` and `mysqlimport`.

The SELECT ... INTO OUTFILE command is mostly used to exchange data between servers or between MariaDB and other software. Using it to create a backup is not very common. However, this method proves its flexibility when we want to back up only a subset of tables data, for example, using JOIN operations or WHERE clauses.

Running a SELECT ... INTO DUMPFILE statement with the default separators is the same as running a query directly from the command line using the following syntax:

```
mysql -e "SELECT …" > file_name
```

Consider the following example:

```
mysql -e "SELECT * FROM information_schema.TABLES
ORDER BY TABLE_SCHEMA, TABLE_NAME" > /tmp/tables.txt
```

This syntax is very convenient when we want to save the result sets of the queries into files from a shell script. Also, this allows creating a text delimited file on the client, instead of the server.

Dumping a table definition with the SHOW CREATE TABLE command

Sometimes, we want to obtain the SQL statement, which allows us to recreate a table structure and not only the data. The statement that does this is very simple; here is an example:

```
MariaDB [test]> SHOW CREATE TABLE customer \G
*************************** 1. row ***************************
       Table: customer
Create Table: CREATE TABLE 'customer' (
  'id' int(11) NOT NULL AUTO_INCREMENT,
  'hire_date' date NOT NULL,
  'first_name' varchar(50) DEFAULT NULL,
  'last_name' varchar(50) DEFAULT NULL,
  PRIMARY KEY ('id')
) ENGINE=InnoDB AUTO_INCREMENT=6 DEFAULT CHARSET=utf8
1 row in set (0.00 sec)
```

If we need this dump, we probably want to obtain the statement that allows recreating the database, shown as follows:

```
MariaDB [test]> SHOW CREATE DATABASE test;
+----------+-------------------------------------------------------------
--+
| Database | Create Database
|
+----------+-------------------------------------------------------------
--+
| test     | CREATE DATABASE 'test' /*!40100 DEFAULT CHARACTER SET utf8
*/ |
+----------+-------------------------------------------------------------
--+
1 row in set (0.00 sec)
```

Using both these statements, we will be able to recover data from a SELECT ... INTO OUTFILE statement, if the database has been accidentally destroyed. More commonly, these statements allow the exchange of data between servers.

SHOW CREATE TABLE and SHOW CREATE DATABASE do not support a clause to save the results into a file, such as SELECT. However, we can write a simple script to do this.

Loading a dump file with the LOAD DATA INFILE statement

The LOAD DATA INFILE statement is complementary to SELECT ... INTO OUTFILE. It loads data from a delimited test file into an existing table.

The general syntax is:

```
LOAD DATA [LOW_PRIORITY | CONCURRENT]
  [LOCAL] INFILE 'file'
  [REPLACE | IGNORE]
  INTO TABLE tab_name [PARTITION (p_name, …)]
  [CHARACTER SET charset]
  [other_options]
  [IGNORE n {LINES | ROWS}]
  [(column, …)]
  [SET column = expr, …]
```

In this syntax description, the options that specify the separator characters are grouped in the other_options placeholder. They are identical to the ones used for SELECT ... INTO OUTFILE and will be discussed later in this section.

The LOW_PRIORITY and CONCURRENT clauses are only useful with non-transactional tables. The LOW_PRIORITY clause causes the statement to have a lower priority than the read operations. The CONCURRENT clause means that the MyISAM concurrent inserts should be used. Both these clauses may slow down the statement itself, but they will not block concurrent statements: queries from other sessions will have the priority if LOW_PRIORITY is used, and concurrent inserts will be allowed if CONCURRENT is used.

The LOCAL clause means that the specified file must be sent by the client to the server. If this clause is not specified, the file is supposed to be on the server. In this case, the MariaDB user needs to have the FILE privilege. Also, the system user used by MariaDB needs permissions to read the file. Another difference is that, with the LOCAL keyword, duplicate key errors are turned into warnings and do not abort the whole operation.

The REPLACE and IGNORE clauses are used to handle duplicate values. With REPLACE, the new rows replace the existing rows. With IGNORE, the existing rows are left untouched, and no duplicate key error is produced.

The INTO TABLE clause specifies the target table and, optionally, one or more target partitions.

> The CHARACTER SET clause should always be present, and it indicates the character set used by the file. The default value is read from the character_set_database session variable, which depends on the default database and cannot be reliably modified by the user.

It is possible to skip the first lines in the source file by specifying IGNORE n LINES. This is mainly useful if the first line of the file contains the column headers.

By default, the server assumes that the columns are ordered in the same way both in the file and in the table. The order of a table's columns is the order in which they appeared in the CREATE TABLE statement unless ALTER TABLE explicitly changed their order. The order can be seen with a simple DESC statement (which shows a table's columns).

The order can (and usually should) be explicitly specified between the parentheses in the same way we specify them in the INSERT statements.

It is also possible to populate one or more columns with a calculated value with the SET clause. For example, if a product table has a price column; it could also have a sales_tax column that is 10 percent of price. Since MariaDB supports VIRTUAL and PERSISTENT calculated columns, there is usually no need to insert the calculated value with LOAD DATA INFILE. But we may still want to insert those values for some reason, for example, because the database was designed years ago, when such features did not exist, and we do not want to modify it. This may be for MySQL compatibility or because the expression that calculates the values is not deterministic, due to which the database cannot be used for a VIRTUAL column. The LOAD DATA INFILE clause has a SET clause that can be used to insert calculated values:

```
SET sales_tax = price / 100 * 20
```

Separator options and clauses

The mysqldump and mysqlimport command-line tools, and the SELECT ... INTO OUTFILE and LOAD DATA INFILE SQL statements, have a set of options that can be used to specify the characters used to: separate values, enclose strings, escape special characters in strings, and separate rows.

These options are the same for all these tools, except that the SQL syntax is slightly different, and it is slightly more flexible for line separators.

The following table shows the options' syntax and their meaning:

The mysqldump and mysqlimport options	The SELECT ... INTO OUTFILE and LOAD DATA INFILE clauses	Description
--fields-terminated-by=string	FIELDS TERMINATED BY 'string'	Values are separated by this sequence of characters.
--fields-enclosed-by=string, --fields-optionally-enclosed-by=string	FIELDS [OPTIONALLY] ENCLOSED BY 'string'	String values are quoted using the specified sequence of characters. With the optional keyword, the quotes could be omitted when they are unnecessary.
--fields-escaped-by=char	FIELDS ESCAPED BY 'char'	The specified character is used to escape the special characters defined with other options, the NULL value, and the NUL character (ASCII 0x00), which indicates the end of the file on Windows.

The mysqldump and mysqlimport options	The SELECT ... INTO OUTFILE and LOAD DATA INFILE clauses	Description
	`LINES STARTING BY 'string'`	This is only used by `LOAD DATA INFILE`. The rows begin with the specified string, which will be ignored.
`--lines-terminated-by=string`	`LINES TERMINATED BY 'string'`	Lines are separated by this sequence of characters.

In SQL statements, when using multiple field or line clauses, the `FIELDS` and `LINES` keywords must not be repeated. For example, a correct syntax is `FIELD TERMINATED BY ',' ESCAPED BY '|'`. All the SQL clauses are optional; if they are present, they must appear in the same order that is used in the preceding table. Here, `COLUMNS` is a synonym for `FIELDS`.

An example to create and restore dump files

We discussed how to create a dump file and how to restore it if necessary, using both SQL statements and command-line tools. Now, let's see a simple example. We will see how to create a logical backup of a table using `SELECT INTO OUTFILE`, and then we will restore the data with `LOAD DATA INFILE`.

First, let's create a small table with some example rows:

```
MariaDB [test]> CREATE TABLE customer (
    -> id INT NOT NULL AUTO_INCREMENT PRIMARY KEY,
    -> hire_date DATE NOT NULL,
    -> first_name VARCHAR(50),
    -> last_name VARCHAR(50)
    -> )
    -> ENGINE = InnoDB,
    -> CHARACTER SET = 'utf8';
Query OK, 0 rows affected (0.41 sec)
MariaDB [test]> INSERT INTO customer (hire_date, first_name, last_name)
VALUES
    -> ('2011-05-07', 'David', 'Coverdale'),
    -> ('2010-01-20', 'Ritchie', 'Blackmore'),
    -> ('2012-11-15', 'Ian', 'Paice'),
```

```
-> ('2011-06-01', 'Jon', 'Lord'),
-> ('2010-02-28', 'Roger', 'Glover');
Query OK, 5 rows affected (0.10 sec)
Records: 5  Duplicates: 0  Warnings: 0
```

Now, let's create a delimited text file using `mysqldump` and check that the first rows are correct. The table is very small, so it is not really necessary to check only the first rows; however, in a more realistic case, it would be much better. We will also check that the table file exists, shown as follows:

```
root@this:/usr/local/mysql# mysqldump -uroot -proot test customer
--tab=/tmp --fields-terminated-by=, --fields-enclosed-by="'"
--fields-escaped-by=/
root@this:/usr/local/mysql# ls /tmp
customer.sql
customer.txt
root@this:/usr/local/mysql# tail --lines 3 /tmp/customer.txt
'3','2012-11-15','Ian','Paice'
'4','2011-06-01','Jon','Lord'
'5','2010-02-28','Roger','Glover'
```

Everything seems to be okay. Now, let's back up the same table with `SELECT ... INTO OUTFILE`. The statement that is going to issue is equivalent to the former example, except that it does not generate a table definition file. Consider the following code snippet:

```
MariaDB [test]> SELECT *
    -> FROM customer
    -> INTO OUTFILE '/tmp/customer.2.txt'
    -> FIELDS
    -> TERMINATED BY ','
    -> ENCLOSED BY '\''
    -> ESCAPED BY ',';
Query OK, 5 rows affected (0.00 sec)
```

Now, we want to check that the files produced are identical:

```
root@this:/usr/local/mysql# md5sum /tmp/customer.txt
d6b2c04587f9dc56a82a8b9784abe5fe  /tmp/customer.txt
root@this:/usr/local/mysql# md5sum /tmp/customer.2.txt
d6b2c04587f9dc56a82a8b9784abe5fe  /tmp/customer.2.txt
```

Since the MD5 sums of the two files are identical, we can assume that the files are identical too.

Before trying to restore the file, we need to empty the table:

```
MariaDB [test]> TRUNCATE TABLE customer;
Query OK, 0 rows affected (0.25 sec)
```

Now, let's restore the table from a delimited text file:

```
root@this:/usr/local/mysql# bin/mysqlimport -uroot -proot
--fields-terminated-by=, --fields-enclosed-by="'"
--fields-escaped-by=/ test /tmp/customer.txt
test.customer: Records: 5  Deleted: 0  Skipped: 0  Warnings: 0
```

The equivalent LOAD DATA INFILE statement is the following, but we will need to empty the table again, before issuing it:

```
MariaDB [test]> LOAD DATA INFILE '/tmp/customer.txt'
    -> INTO TABLE test.customer
    -> FIELDS
    -> TERMINATED BY ','
    -> ENCLOSED BY '\''
    -> ESCAPED BY ',';
Query OK, 5 rows affected (0.08 sec)
Records: 5  Deleted: 0  Skipped: 0  Warnings: 0
```

Performing a backup using a CONNECT or CSV engine

The tables created with the CSV engine use normal comma-separated data files, which can be used for backups or data exchange. The CONNECT engine is more complex: it supports several table types. Each table type is in a different data format. Supported formats include CSV, XML, HTML, and data files created by dBASE. The CONNECT engine can even read and write data from or to a remote database server using the native protocol if it is a MariaDB or MySQL server or using the ODBC standards for other DBMS types.

Creating a backup from a table using CSV or CONNECT is very simple. The next example shows how to do this with CSV:

```
MariaDB [test]> CREATE TABLE customer_bkp ENGINE = CSV SELECT * FROM
customer;
ERROR 1178 (42000): The storage engine for the table doesn't support
nullable columns
```

But this did not work! The example shows that CSV cannot be used if a table contains NULL values. This is a very important limitation, and it is not the only one. So, we should usually prefer CONNECT, which is much more advanced and flexible. The only reason why we might use CSV instead is probably that CONNECT has been introduced with MariaDB 10 and cannot be installed on older versions.

Since CONNECT is not installed by default, we may need to install it as follows:

```
MariaDB [test]> INSTALL SONAME 'ha_connect';
Query OK, 0 rows affected (0.00 sec)
```

Then, we can use it to perform the backup. We will use the CONNECT storage engine's CSV table type, because it is a good and efficient way to store data. We may use more structured or exotic formats, but there is no reason in this case. Pay attention to the table options in the following example:

```
MariaDB [test]> CREATE TABLE customer_bkp
    -> ENGINE = CONNECT
    -> TABLE_TYPE = CSV
    -> FILE_NAME = '/tmp/customer.csv'
    -> HUGE = 0
    -> COMPRESS = 1
    -> READONLY = 1
    -> DATA_CHARSET = 'utf8'
    -> SEP_CHAR = ','
    -> ENDING = 1
    -> QUOTED = 1
    -> QCHAR = '"'
    -> HEADER = 1
    -> SELECT * FROM customer;
Query OK, 0 rows affected (0.10 sec)
```

In this example, we used all the options that are relevant for the CSV format. They are:

- TABLE_TYPE: As explained earlier, this indicates the data source type for the table (in this case, a CSV file).

- FILE_NAME: This indicates the name and, optionally, path of the data file.

- HUGE: This indicates the default value, which is 0. If the table is bigger than 2 GB, it makes sense to inform CONNECT by setting it to 1.

- COMPRESS: Since this is a backup, we want the table to be compressed. As with InnoDB, CONNECT uses the zlib library and the LZ77 algorithm.

- READONLY: Since this is a backup, making the table read-only is much safer.

- DATA_CHARSET: This indicates the character set to be used.

- SEP_CHAR: This indicates the columns separator.

- ENDING: This indicates the length of the end of line in characters. It is 1 for Unix systems (lines end with \n) and 2 on Windows (lines end with \n\r).

- QUOTED: Strings are quoted. This could be omitted since QCHAR is specified.

- QCHAR: This indicates the quoting character.

- HEADER: This indicates the first row that contains the column names.

Restoring the backup is really simple: we just need to delete the data file in /tmp and replace it with the backup. No further actions are needed to let CONNECT use the backup. Then, we can copy the backup contents into the original table using a normal INSERT ... SELECT or CREATE TABLE ... SELECT statement.

Physical backups

A physical backup is a copy of all the files in which MariaDB stores the database definitions, the data and index files, the configuration files, and the logs. Since data is usually stored in a compact way, a physical backup is usually the most convenient form of backup. Also, only physical backups include the configuration files and the logs.

However, while performing a physical backup, a lock must be acquired so that the server does not use the files. As an alternative, we can stop the server.

Which files should be copied?

A complete backup consists of all the following groups of files: table files, trigger files, logs, and configuration files.

Table files

Table files are stored in the `data` directory. The storage engine, and sometimes its configuration, determines which files contain the table data and indexes. The `data` directory contains a directory for each database. The name of the directory matches the database name, as long as no special characters are used (which is not a good practice, anyway). The table files are stored in the proper database directories. They have a base name, the same as the table name, as long as no special characters are used. They also have an extension that depends on the file type.

If a table is partitioned, of course, it consists of several data and index files. The names of these files follow this pattern:

```
table_name#P#partition_name.file_extension
```

A `.par` file is also used to store partitions metadata.

The `data` directory's path is defined in the `@@datadir` server variable.

The InnoDB system tablespace can be located in a different path specified in the `@@innodb_data_home_dir` system variable. Other tablespaces are located in the path specified in the `@@innodb_data_file_path` system variable. This can be a relative path starting from the `@@innodb_data_home_dir` path.

Some storage engines (including recent versions of InnoDB) allow using a different path for table files. This path is defined using the `DATA_DIRECTORY` and `INDEX_DIRECTORY` table options. The value of these options can be seen, for example, with a `SHOW CREATE TABLE` statement.

Knowing this, we are able to selectively back up only some tables or even only some partitions.

The server creates a `.frm` file that contains the definition of the table. Some storage engines are able to work if this file is not found for some reason, but the file should always exist regardless of which storage engine is used for the table.

InnoDB has a file-per-table mode that affects the creation of table files. The details have been explained in *Chapter 7, InnoDB Compressed Tables*. A system tablespace always exists and is stored in the files whose names start with `ibdata`. When a table is created and the file-per-table mode is enabled, for each new table, an `.ibd` file exists that contains both data and indexes. When the file-per-table mode is not enabled, new tables are created in the system tablespace.

Many storage engines use separate files for indexes and data. The following table shows their extensions:

Storage engine	Data file	Index file
Aria	.MAD	.MAI
MyISAM	.MYD	.MYI
ARCHIVE	.ARZ	
CONNECT	User-defined	.dnx
CSV	.CSV	

The `MERGE` storage engine does not create data or index files, but it uses a `MRG` file that contains the list of the underlying MyISAM tables. Aria also uses logs, whose base name is `aria_log`, and whose extensions are progressive numbers. A filename `aria_log_control` is also necessary. The `ARCHIVE` storage engine has a very limited index support, while `CSV` does not support indexes at all; thus, these engines do not use index files. For the `CONNECT` engine, the `SEP_INDEX` table option allows us to store each index in a separate file. In this case, their names will be in the following format: `tablename_indexname.dnx`. The index name for the primary key is `PRIMARY`.

For example, a MyISAM table called `myisam1` with three partitions called `p0`, `p1`, and `p2`, will use the following files:

```
myisam1.frm
myisam1.par
myisam1#P#p0.MYD
myisam1#P#p0.MYI
myisam1#P#p1.MYD
myisam1#P#p1.MYI
myisam1#P#p2.MYD
myisam1#P#p2.MYIBackuping stored programs
```

Stored routines, triggers, and events are collectively called **stored programs**. They are meant to implement the logic of the database in simple SQL scripts. These objects are not likely to change often, just like table structures. However, a backup of these programs is still necessary to restore the correct behavior of the server. Their definition is stored in system tables, contained in the `mysql` database. A backup of this database contains all existing stored programs.

However, for each trigger, the following files are created in the `data` directory:

- `trigger_name.TRG`
- `trigger_name.TRN`

To correctly obtain a backup of triggers, it is necessary to include these files.

Logfiles

The server's log paths and filenames are defined in some server variables. This has been discussed in *Chapter 2, Debugging*, and *Chapter 3, Optimizing Queries*. However, a summary table with the server logs and the variables that control their path is probably useful and is shown as follows:

Log	Server variable
Error log	`@@log_error`
General query log	`@@general_log`
Slow query log	`@@slow_query_log`
Binary log	`@@log_bin`

Keeping the logfiles in the `data` directory should simplify the backup procedure.

Configuration files

If there is only one MariaDB version on the machine, only one instance is executed. It is always executed using the same system user, and only one configuration file is used. It is generally located in the MariaDB installation directory and called `my.cnf`. On Windows, `my.ini` is also a valid name.

If several MariaDB versions exist on the same machine, or if more than one instance can be executed at the same time, the user can take advantage of the MariaDB modular configuration, with some configuration files containing general settings and more specific files that override certain settings for one or more instances. This usually happens on machines used to test; however, a DBA should be aware that, on any machine, multiple configuration files could exist.

On Linux systems, configuration files can be placed in any of the following paths:

- The `/etc` path
- The `/etc/mysql` path
- The `SYSCONFDIR` path
- The `$MYSQL_HOME` path
- The file indicated with the `--defaults-extra-file` option
- The `~/` path

On Windows systems, the paths are different:

- The `%PROGRAMDATA%\MariaDB\MariaDB Server 10.0` path
- The `%WINDIR%` path
- The `C:\` path
- The installation directory
- The file indicated with the `--defaults-extra-file` option

Hot physical backups

When the server is stopped, copying the files is easy. But when the server is running, we have a problem: we must be sure that the server does not try to modify the files until the backup process is finished.

To do this, we flush the last changes to disks and lock the tables. This can be done with the `FLUSH TABLES ... FOR EXPORT` statement or with the `FLUSH TABLES ... WITH READ LOCK` statement.

Their syntaxes are:

```
FLUSH TABLES <table_list> FOR EXPORT
FLUSH TABLES [table_list] WITH READ LOCK
```

The table list is mandatory with `FOR EXPORT` but is optional with `WITH READ LOCK`. If omitted, `FLUSH TABLES WITH READ LOCK` locks all tables. This is called a global read lock. A table-shared lock is acquired on all named tables.

 Each table locked with one of these statements is removed from the query cache. The reason is that the server knows that the data will probably be replaced, and it will need to read the new contents from files.

The most convenient procedure is as follows:

1. We open a mysql client.
2. We execute FLUSH TABLES ... FOR EXPORT or FLUSH TABLES ... WITH READ LOCK and leave the client open.
3. We copy the file using the system console or any other program we like.
4. In the client, we execute UNLOCK TABLES to release the lock.

The FLUSH TABLES ... FOR EXPORT locks the tables and asks the storage engines to flush all changes to disks. This is the only safe way to back up InnoDB tables on a running server. However, the FOR EXPORT clause is not available on MariaDB versions older than 10.0. Also, some storage engines may not support it.

With FLUSH TABLES ... WITH READ, the flush is done by the server. This means that it works even with storage engines that do not support this statement. However, as mentioned earlier, this method is not safe to back up InnoDB tables on a running server.

For most storage engines, there is no practical difference between these two statements. But, since InnoDB backups require FOR EXPORT, this command is more convenient.

Filesystem snapshots

Some filesystems or volume managers support snapshots. For example, the Veritas filesystem support them; other filesystems, like XFS, can create snapshots via a volume manager like LVM. Snapshots are a very fast way to take physical backups.

Stopping the server is not usually required to create a snapshot. Instead, it is necessary to acquire a global read lock with FLUSH TABLES ... WITH READ LOCK. The procedure is as follows:

1. We open a mysql client.
2. We execute FLUSH TABLES ... WITH READ LOCK and leave the client open.
3. In a system console, we execute a command similar to the following:
   mount vxfs snapshot.
4. In the client, we execute UNLOCK TABLES to release the lock.

The mylvmbackup utility, included in most Linux distribution repositories, automates this procedure.

Incremental physical backups with the rsync command

The `rsync` command is a Linux command that copies files in an incremental way. When it is invoked on a file that it has never copied before, it copies it. But when it is called again on that file, it checks whether the file has been modified since the time of the last copy. If so, `rsync` copies the modified part of the file, which makes it very fast to copy these backups over a network. When called on a directory, `rsync` performs this check for each individual file contained in the directory. The `rsync` command can also delete a file from the target directory if it has been deleted from the source directory. However, for backups this is not a good idea: if a file is missing, maybe we will need to restore it.

The `rsync` command is usually not helpful for OLTP databases. However, OLAP databases typically contain very large tables that are not often updated. When performing a backup of those databases, we may want to save time by only copying the tables that have been modified. If later we need to restore a table, we will use the most recent backup we have for that table.

The following is a typical `rsync` invocation to take a backup:

```
root@this:/usr/local/mysql# rsync --progress --stats --compress -rtl
data /tmp/rsync_bkp
...
data/mysql/db.MYD
        1264 100%    2.07kB/s    0:00:00 (xfer#133, to-check=238/379)
data/mysql/db.MYI
        9216 100%   14.63kB/s    0:00:00 (xfer#134, to-check=237/379)
data/mysql/db.frm
        2677 100%    4.13kB/s    0:00:00 (xfer#135, to-check=236/379)
...
Number of files: 379
Number of files transferred: 371
Total file size: 946950619 bytes
Total transferred file size: 946950619 bytes
Literal data: 946950619 bytes
Matched data: 0 bytes
File list size: 8498
```

```
File list generation time: 0.001 seconds
File list transfer time: 0.000 seconds
Total bytes sent: 103777427
Total bytes received: 7093

sent 103777427 bytes   received 7093 bytes   1356660.39 bytes/sec
total size is 946950619   speedup is 9.12
```

The output of this invocation is usually very long; in this case, it has been manually edited to make it short.

We use the following options:

- `--progress`: This option show progress information. This makes the output very long but is useful if a problem occurs.

- `--stats`: This option prints the final statistics on transferred files.

- `--compress`: This option compresses a copy with zlib. This is usually a good idea, because `rsync` is most useful for copying big files. However, we may want to make the lock time as short as possible. To do this, we may prefer to compress the files after releasing the locks, probably with gzip or similar tools.

- `-r`: This option copies recursively.

- `-t`: This option transfers the information of the file's most recent modifications so that an incremental backup will be possible next time.

- `-l`: This option follows the symbolic links, if any. We generally do not want `rsync` to delete files in the target directory that have been deleted from the source directory. For this reason, we did not use the `--delete` option.

Copying files when the server is running

To restore a backup, most storage engines only require that the tables are locked with FLUSH TABLES WITH READ LOCK before copying the backup files into the data directory. However, this was not possible with InnoDB before MariaDB 10.0. Since MariaDB 10.0, InnoDB supports a feature called **transportable tablespaces**. This means that it is possible to copy the .ibd files from a running server and restore those files into the same (or another) running server later using a special SQL statement. This feature can be used for backups or to copy data between running servers.

This feature has some important limitations:

- The InnoDB file-per-table mode must be on. The system tablespace is not transportable.

- A table cannot be copied this way if it has foreign keys and the `foreign_key_checks` server variable is set to ON. If the table contains a foreign key, the checks must be temporarily disabled by setting it to OFF before the copy. If the file is later restored, the foreign key constraint will not be applied during the restore.

- This feature cannot be used to move tablespaces between different versions of MariaDB. A minor server upgrade (that is, when only the third version number changes) should not invalidate the backup tablespaces, as long as the server version is stable.

- When copying data between servers, the table must exist on the destination server.

To create a backup copy of a tablespace, follow the given steps:

1. Run `FLUSH TABLES table_list FOR EXPORT;`. A table-shared lock is acquired.

2. This creates a `.cfg` file for each InnoDB table. We did not mention those files before. They are only created for InnoDB tables and are only useful when copying a table into a running server.

3. The tables are now consistent and locked. Set the `foreign_key_checks` server variable to OFF if necessary.

4. Copy the `.ibd` and `.cfg` files into a backup directory.

5. Set the `foreign_key_checks` server variable to ON if it was previously disabled.

6. Run `UNLOCK TABLES` to release the lock.

To restore a backup tablespace on a running server:

1. Run `ALTER TABLE table_name DISCARD TABLESPACE;`. An exclusive table lock is acquired.

2. Copy the `.ibd` and `.cfg` files into the `data` directory.

3. Run `ALTER TABLE table_name IMPORT TABLESPACE;`.

Using the binary log for incremental backups

The binary log is a series of files that store the events that modify the data. It is used for incremental backups and for replication. The purpose of the binary log is being able to apply the changes again to a database. In the case of replication, its use is intuitive: the binary log events are sent by the master to the slaves, so that they can apply the same changes and always mirror the master's data (not necessarily immediately). Replication cannot work if the binary log is not enabled.

In the case of backups, the binary logs files are used as incremental backups. If a disaster happens, the data can be restored to the most recent and complete backup. It can be a physical or a logical backup. After that, the data will probably be a bit old. However, if the binary log is used, more recent incremental backups could exist. They contain changes that can be sent to the server, so that they are applied to the complete backup.

An example will make the procedure clearer. We have an online shop that uses MariaDB. Every day, the data changes: new products are sold or bought, new users register, the website traffic statistics are collected, and so on. We obviously need to back up the data frequently. But maybe the database is quite big and the website's traffic is high, so we do not want to slow down the website and use a great quantity of disks performing frequent and complete backups. We choose to perform a complete backup once a week, at the day and time when the traffic is statistically lower. But if the complete backup is taken on Sunday and the database gets corrupted on Saturday night, we do not want to lose all data changes that were made during the last week! So, we also want to take incremental backups every day when the traffic is lower. The most convenient way to do this is by rotating the binary log. Rotating the log means that a new logfile is created, and the currently used file remains in the same directory for archive purposes. For extra security, we generally also want to backup that file on a removable storage device. An old logfile that remains in the same directory will most probably be useful if the data gets corrupted. But what if the disk gets damaged? The old logs should be stored on more than one disk. Also, when a new, complete backup is performed, we will also delete archived logfiles from the disk to save space.

The binary logs events can be stored in three formats:

- Statement-based
- Row-based
- Mixed

With the statement-based format, SQL statements are logged. This format has many limitations: if it used, some SQL statements or functions should be avoided because they can produce different results when reapplied. For example, the result of NOW() depends on the current date and time. With the row-based format, modifications to data are logged. The mixed format logs statements when they are safe; when they are not safe, the mixed format logs data modifications. Choosing the proper format is very important to implement an efficient replication, so the formats will be more thoroughly discussed in *Chapter 9, Replication*.

The binary log will also be more thoroughly described in *Chapter 9, Replication*. However, in this chapter we will discuss the most important concepts about the binary log.

To enable the binary log, we can start the server with the --log-bin startup option or by specifying log-bin in the configuration file. In both cases, it is possible to specify a file base name instead of simply setting the option to ON. The default base name is the server's hostname followed by -bin. The logfiles also have numerical extensions that can be used to order them.

> If the binary log is enabled, the @@log_bin server variable is ON. The @@log_bin_basename variable contains the current logfile's basename.

The SHOW MASTER STATUS statement shows the complete name of the current logfile. It works even if replication is not used. For example:

```
MariaDB [(none)]> SHOW MASTER STATUS;
+---------------+----------+--------------+------------------+
| File          | Position | Binlog_Do_DB | Binlog_Ignore_DB |
+---------------+----------+--------------+------------------+
| binlog.000114 |      323 |              |                  |
+---------------+----------+--------------+------------------+
1 row in set (0.00 sec)
```

The SHOW BINARY LOGS statement shows the current and the old binary logfiles:

```
MariaDB [(none)]> SHOW BINARY LOGS;
+---------------+-----------+
| Log_name      | File_size |
+---------------+-----------+
| binlog.000001 |       849 |
| binlog.000002 |       342 |
```

```
...
| binlog.000113 |        342 |
| binlog.000114 |        323 |
+---------------+-----------+
114 rows in set (0.01 sec)
```

The binary logfiles are written in a compact format that cannot be read by a human or by MariaDB. To examine the files, or apply the changes, we can use `mysqlbinlog`. This utility is included in all MariaDB distributions, and it translates a logfile into readable SQL statements.

The `mysqlbinlog` command can be used to send these statements to the mysql client so that it executes them:

```
../bin/mysqlbinlog binlog.000113 binlog.000114 | mysql -uroot -proot
```

Note that it is possible to translate multiple files with one invocation, just as in the previous example. The files must be specified in the correct order. Also, we should never send files to the server with multiple calls. This is because a file could try to use a temporary table that has been created in another file. If we use separate invocations, the temporary tables are lost at the end of the file execution and will not be available for the next file.

Sometimes, we may want to recover data that has been destroyed with a wrong statement, such as DELETE, DROP TABLE, or DROP DATABASE. In that case, we need to restore the last complete backup and apply the changes from the recent binary logfiles. But, we also need to avoid executing again the statement that destroyed important data. To do so, we can write the output of `mysqlbinlog` into a file, manually edit the file, and then send the statements to the server. For example:

```
root@this:/usr/local/mysql/data# ../bin/mysqlbinlog binlog.000113 > apply
root@this:/usr/local/mysql/data# ../bin/mysqlbinlog binlog.000114 >>
apply
root@this:/usr/local/mysql/data# gedit apply
root@this:/usr/local/mysql/data# mysql -uroot -proot < apply
```

We can also select the events to be applied based on their datetimes. We can specify a start datetime, an end datetime, or both. For example:

```
../bin/mysqlbinlog binlog.000114 --start-datetime="2014-04-08 14:10:00"
--stop-datetime="2014-04-08 15:01:30" | mysql -uroot -proot
```

This technique can be used to avoid executing a set of statements that delete important data. Generally, we need to examine the output of `mysqlbinlog` (perhaps written in a file) to be sure about the datetimes of the statements that we do not want to execute.

For many workloads, the datetimes are not precise enough. Since these timestamps do not have a sub-second precision, several events will probably occur at the same datetime, and we generally do not want to exclude all of them. Fortunately, each event has a number indicating its position in the binary log. By examining the output of mysqlbinlog, we can find the positions of the events that we do not want to execute. They are written as comments along with other metainformation:

```
#140408 15:26:14 server id 1  end_log_pos 694      Query      thread_id=4
exec_time=0    error_code=0
SET TIMESTAMP=1396963574/*!*/;
INSERT INTO myisam1 VALUES (3,3)
/*!*/;
# at 694
```

In this example, the INSERT statement is at position 694.

Adding the --start-datetime and --stop-datetime options to mysqlbinlog can help us find the exact positions of those statements. Then, we can specify the exact positions of the statements to skip, just as in the following example:

```
../bin/mysqlbinlog binlog.000114 --start-position= 25392 --stop-
position=25399 | mysql -uroot -proot
```

Percona XtraBackup

Percona XtraBackup is a tool from Percona that can be used to create physical backups. Its most important feature is that it operates while the server is running and requires no lock at all for InnoDB tables. Tables that use other storage engines only require a lock at the end of the copy. Percona XtraBackup supports incremental backups. Percona XtraBackup is available on the Percona website.

Percona XtraBackup consists of several components. The core component is the **xtrabackup** program. It embeds a modified version of InnoDB that is used to access the InnoDB tablespaces. The user usually does not invoke it directly. A Perl script called innobackupex performs the backup of other storage engines, table definition files, and triggers, and calls xtrabackup to back up the .ibd files. Percona XtraBackup is a complex tool. The xbcrypt command is a standalone tool that encrypts or decrypts backup files. In this book, we will only cover a general explanation of how to use innobackupex to create or restore complete and incremental backups. It is recommended that you read the documentation for more details on the XtraBackup features. The documentation is available on the Percona website at the following URL http://www.percona.com/doc/percona-xtrabackup/.

Performing backups

Percona XtraBackup is able to perform complete backups and partial backups. A partial backup is a copy that does not include all tables from all databases. After a first complete or partial backup is made, Percona XtraBackup can perform incremental backups. This section explains how to perform all the backup types.

Complete backups

To create a complete backup, we do not need any particular option. The following is a typical `innobackupex` invocation:

```
innobackupex --user=root --password=root /tmp/backup
```

Of course, the `--user` and `--password` options specify, respectively, the MariaDB user and password. The last argument is the directory that contains backup.

By default, a subdirectory is created within the `backup` directory, which contains the current backup. The directory's name will be the current datetime in the following format: `2014-04-10_16-30-18`. This is generally a very practical way to archive backups. However, we may want to specify a path for this particular backup and not a general backup directory with an automatically named subdirectory. In this case, we can just add the `--no-timestamp` option.

Partial backups

By default, a backup is complete; that is, it includes all tables from all databases. However, it is also possible to specify which tables and databases must be included in the copy.

The `--databases` option can be used to specify databases and optionally, tables to be included. The value for this option is a space-separated list. Each argument can be a database or a table. When only the database is specified, all tables from that database are included. For example, to include all tables from `db_1` and the table user from `db_2`, we can use this syntax:

```
innobackupex --user=root --password=root --databases="db_1 db_2.user"
/tmp/backup
```

The list of databases and tables to be included can also be specified in a text file. The syntax for the list is the same, except that each database or table must be specified in a different line. The name and path of the file need to be passed to `innobackupex` using the `--tables-file` option, shown as follows:

```
innobackupex --user=root --password=root
--tables-file="tmp/backup/t_list" /tmp/backup
```

The `--include` option allows us to specify the table names as a regular expression, to be evaluated against fully specified table names:

```
innobackupex --user=root --password=root
--include=^db1[.]tab[0-9]
 /tmp/backup
```

Preparing backups

Percona XtraBackup copies the InnoDB files at different times with no locking at all. This means that, while a table was being copied, users could modify another table. As a result, the copied tables are probably not consistent with each other. Trying to restore an inconsistent backup would crash the server. To make the backup consistent, it needs to be prepared. The preparation is performed after the copy and does not require a connection to the server or access to any file stored in the server. The only limitation is that the version of `xtrabackupex` that performed a backup must be the same as the version of `xtrabackupex` that prepares that backup.

InnoDB has some transaction logs that can be used to retry or undo a transaction. Such logs are copied by Percona XtraBackup as part of the backup. During the preparation stage, the `xtrabackup` binary undoes some transactions and repeats other transactions. It can do this safely because it embeds a slightly modified InnoDB version. At the end of the process, all the `.ibd` files and the logs are perfectly consistent and ready to be imported into the server's `data` directory, if necessary.

Preparing complete backups

To prepare a backup, we need to apply InnoDB logs. In fact, to prepare a backup, we just need to call `innobackupex` again with the `--apply-logs` option and the backup path:

```
xtrabackup --prepare /media/ext1/backup/2014-04-10_16-30-18
```

The preparation process may be slow for backups that include big InnoDB tables. Percona XtraBackup can prepare a backup more quickly if it uses a big amount of memory. The default amount of memory it uses is 100 MB, which is very low, because it could be used on the same server that runs MariaDB. To allow it to use more memory, we can specify the `--use-memory` option: `--use-memory=2G`.

If the preparation succeeds, the last line of the `innobackupex` output tells us the sequence number of the last log entry. If we plan to perform an incremental backup and Percona XtraBackup does not have access to this particular backup, we need to save that sequence number somewhere. This could happen, for example, because we are going to copy the backup on a removable device and delete it from the server.

Preparing partial backups

The syntax to prepare a partial backup is slightly different. The following is a typical invocation:

```
xtrabackup --prepare --export /media/ext1/backup/2014-04-10_16-30-18
```

For each table not included in the backup, a warning might appear that informs us that the table is missing. This happens because the `.frm` files contain the definitions for those tables. We can safely ignore such warnings.

For each included table, a `.exp` file is created in the `backup` directory. Such files are required to restore partial backups.

Restoring backups

To restore a backup, we can simply copy the needed files into the `data` directory. However, the `xtrabackupex` script provides an easier way to do this.

Restoring complete backups

Percona XtraBackup cannot restore a complete backup into a running server. To restore a complete backup, we need to stop the server first. Then, we can call `innobackupex` with the `--copy-back` option and pass it the `backup` directory path. The `innobackupex` command automatically reads the path of the `data` directory from the configuration file, shown as follows:

```
innobackupex --copy-back /path/to/BACKUP-DIR
```

Restoring partial backups

It is possible to restore individual tables, even on a running server, using the methods already explained in this chapter.

Securing backups

If a database contains sensible data, its backups will contain sensible data too. This is something we must never forget. There are several good practices that companies should follow to keep backups safe:

- **Setting proper permissions**: Only the user who performed the backups, probably a DBA, should have the permissions to read or write them.
- **Transfer backups in a secure way**: If backups are performed on the database server and then copied into another machine, the transfer must be done in a safe way. For example, the scp command can be used to copy the files with an SSH connection.
- **Encrypt backups**: After all, in theory, stealing a backup is always possible.
- **Physically store backups in a safe place**: A safe place is a place that unauthorized persons cannot access. A safe place should also be equipped with antitheft and antifire devices.

If necessary, SELinux or firewalls can be used to improve security.

Repairing tables

When a table is damaged, sometimes replacing it with a backup is not necessary. It is certainly a solution, but it implies some data loss unless the table is unchanged since the last backup. When possible, repairing the damaged table is a better solution.

The procedure we must follow to repair the table depends on the storage engine.

InnoDB has a recovery process that is launched on server startup. While this process is automatic, it must be configured by the DBA.

MyISAM and Aria also have an automatic recovery process on startup. But they also support recovery via the REPAIR TABLE SQL statement or when the server is stopped, via specific tools distributed with MariaDB.

Other storage engines also support REPAIR TABLE.

Some repairing techniques are considered less safe than others. However, even when the safest method is used, it might still fail to recover the table and cause more corruption. The possibility is usually very small, but it exists. For this reason, it is always recommended to make a physical backup of all corrupted tables before trying to repair them.

Recovering InnoDB tables

Usually, an InnoDB table does not need to be repaired. The SELECT ... INTO OUTFILE statement should create a file with the correct data, even when a table is damaged. As explained earlier, this creates a backup that can be restored later. However, if a certain type of corruption occurs, SELECT might crash InnoDB. In that case, we will need to repair the damaged tables or restore the most recent backup.

Checking tables

InnoDB supports the CHECK TABLE statement. If a table is corrupted, usually that statement returns a result set whose last row has a value error for the Msg_type column and a value Corrupt for the Msg_text column. In this case, the damaged table or index is marked as corrupted, and it will not be used until the problem is fixed. If some types of corruption are detected during a CHECK TABLE statement, InnoDB might crash the server to immediately stop the problem from spreading. The CHECK TABLE statement is discussed later in this chapter in the *Repairing tables* section.

Transaction logs

InnoDB uses two logs for transactions: the redo log and the undo log. They are used to repeat transactions and to cancel uncommitted transactions, respectively. They both are used during crash recovery.

Before modifying the data in a table, InnoDB records the needed modifications into the redo log. If the server crashes before modifications are complete, InnoDB should still be able to use the information in the redo log to repeat the whole transaction on restart.

The redo log is physically stored in dedicated files. A buffer allows InnoDB to safely reduce the writes on those files ideally until a transaction is committed. The undo log is physically stored in the system tablespace and, optionally, in other tablespaces. Configuring the physical storage of these logs can be important for performance tuning if the disks are the bottleneck of the server. The configuration of transaction logs will be explained in *Chapter 11, Data Sharding*.

Forcing data recovery

Even if data corruption is detected, InnoDB data recovery is not performed by default. InnoDB starts the recovery process only if the `@@innodb_force_recovery` is set to a value higher than 0. This variable is not dynamic, so it must be set using the `--innodb_force_recovery` startup option or the `innodb_force_recovery` option in the configuration file.

Only values higher than 0 must be used to recover the data. After a successful recovery, the server must be restarted with `@@innodb_force_recovery` set to 0.

The `@@innodb_force_recovery` command determines which actions are taken by InnoDB to perform the recovery. Each value includes all the actions that are taken with lower values. Low values are safer; thus they should be tried first. However, if the recovery fails with a low value, it will be necessary to try a higher value. Values from 1 to 3 are considered safe. The value 4 might corrupt secondary indexes. If the data is fixed, the secondary indexes can be rebuilt later. The value 5 might also cause inconsistent results. The value 6 causes pages to be left in an obsolete state. This might propagate corruption. This value should not be used if not definitely necessary.

With values higher than 3, InnoDB rejects DML statements that try to modify data. With a value 6, InnoDB also rejects CREATE TABLE and DROP TABLE.

The following table explains what the different `@@innodb_force_recovery` values do:

@innodb_force_recovery value	InnoDB behavior
0	Normal execution (no recovery).
1	Tries to simply skip corrupted pages. The SELECT statements should not crash InnoDB; corrupted data will not be returned.
2	Does not start the master thread and the purge threads.
3	Skips the rollback of transactions.
4	The change buffer will not merge pages. InnoDB table statistics are not calculated (this does not affect engine-independent statistics).
5	Ignores the undo log. Rollback of half-executed transactions does not occur.
6	Ignores the redo log. Since MariaDB 10.0, InnoDB is made read-only until the server restarts.

With a value 6, SELECT containing clauses such as WHERE or ORDER BY could fail. Simple queries that read the whole table might allow us to create a backup. However, they might fail when they encounter corrupted pages. If a query fails at some point, we can still try to skip corrupted pages using WHERE and ORDER BY.

Repairing non-InnoDB tables

As mentioned earlier, the procedure to repair a corrupted table depends on the storage engine. Fortunately, most storage engines support SQL statements that allow one to check file integrity and repair them without restarting the server, In addition to this, MyISAM and Aria also support other recovery methods. The SQL statements that allow us to deal with data corruption are:

* The CHECK TABLE command that checks whether a table is corrupted
* The REPAIR TABLE command that tries to fix the data corruption

MyISAM and Aria also support:

* Automatic recovery on startup
* The myisamchk and aria_chk tools that try to repair MyISAM and Aria tables

The CHECK TABLE statement

Sometimes, when running a SQL statement, we receive an error that informs us that a table we are using is damaged. Here is an example:

```
MariaDB [test]> SELECT * FROM product;
ERROR 130 (HY000): Incorrect file format 'product'
```

In other cases, MariaDB does not realize that a table is corrupted. We might realize it because we receive incomplete result sets. In the worst case, the server crashes. If we periodically scan the error log for crashes, we will notice this. Just before the crash, we might see InnoDB errors informing us that a table is corrupted.

If we suspect that a table is corrupted but we are not sure, the CHECK TABLE statement allows us to verify table integrity without stopping the server. The following storage engines are known to support this statement: InnoDB, MyISAM, Aria, Archive, and CSV. The syntax is as follows:

```
CHECK TABLE <table_list> [option...];
```

While this statement works on partitioned tables, the following syntax allows the checking of only one particular partition instead of the whole table:

```
ALTER TABLE <table_name> CHECK PARTITION <partition_list> [option...];
```

The `table_name` and `partition_list` parameters are the comma-separated list of tables, or partitions, that we want to check. It is possible to specify zero or more options. The options allowed are as follows:

- `FOR UPGRADE`: This is useful when importing table files created with an older version of MariaDB. The `mysql_upgrade` script should always be used before using data files with a new version of the server. However, this option can also upgrade table files.

- `CHANGED`: Only tables that were modified since the last `CHECK TABLE` command are checked. The last update time and last check time can be seen by querying the `TABLES` table in the `information_schema` database. This option only takes effect for MyISAM and Aria tables.

- `FAST`: This option checks whether tables have been closed properly or not, or whether tables or indexes are marked as corrupted. After a server crash, this option should be sufficient to detect table corruptions. It only takes effect with MyISAM and Aria tables.

- `QUICK`: The delete link chain is not checked. Such operations can be quite long, but this option detects most types of corruption. This option only takes effect with MyISAM and Aria tables. When `CHANGES` is specified, this option is also used by default.

- `MEDIUM`: The integrity of data and indexes is checked by comparing their checksums. It rarely happens that an anomaly is not detected with this option. This is the default mode.

- `EXTENDED`: This option performs a complete integrity check. On big tables, this takes a long time.

If `CHECK TABLE` does not detect any problem, it generates a result set with only one row, similar to the following:

```
MariaDB [test]> CHECK TABLE user;
+-----------+-------+----------+----------+
| Table     | Op    | Msg_type | Msg_text |
+-----------+-------+----------+----------+
| test.user | check | status   | OK       |
+-----------+-------+----------+----------+
1 row in set (0.00 sec)
```

If CHECK TABLE cannot correct the problems, it generates a result set similar to the following:

```
MariaDB [test]> CHECK TABLE product;
+--------------+-------+----------+----------------------------------+
| Table        | Op    | Msg_type | Msg_text                         |
+--------------+-------+----------+----------------------------------+
| test.product | check | Error    | Incorrect file format 'product'  |
| test.product | check | error    | Corrupt                          |
+--------------+-------+----------+----------------------------------+
2 rows in set (0.00 sec)
```

What we should notice is that the last line has the Msg_type error column set to error and the Msg_text column set to Corrupt.

As explained previously, when CHECK TABLE is used against a corrupted InnoDB table, it could deliberately crash the server to immediately stop the anomaly propagation. If this happens, we will need to force InnoDB to try to repair the damaged tables on startup.

The REPAIR TABLE statement

If a table is corrupted, we can try repairing it without stopping the server. The REPAIR TABLE statement can be used to do this. The following storage engines are known to support this statement: MyISAM, Aria, Archive, and CSV.

 InnoDB does not support REPAIR TABLE.

The syntax is shown as follows:

```
REPAIR NO_WRITE_TO_BINLOG TABLE <table_list>
[QUICK] [EXTENDED] [USE_FRM]
```

Similar to CHECK TABLE, while this statement can be used with partitioned tables, it is possible to repair a specific partition with the following syntax:

```
ALTER TABLE <table_list> REPAIR PARTITION <partition_list> [QUICK]
[EXTENDED];
```

Note that, however, USE_FRM is not supported with the latter syntax.

The table_list and the partition_list are the comma-separated lists of tables, or partitions, that we want to repair.

With QUICK, this statement only repairs the index file. This option is useful because indexes get corrupted more often than data.

With EXTENDED, indexes are recreated in a slower but safer way. However, many garbage rows could be generated. For this reason, EXTENDED should not be used unless really necessary.

The USE_FRM command can be used with MyISAM tables if the index file (.MYI) is missing. This can happen, for example, if a failed REPAIR TABLE statement crashes the server and leaves an empty index file. This is a very unlikely situation. However, as mentioned earlier, we should always make a backup of the corrupted tables before trying to repair them.

Note that, with USE_FRM, the links to the deleted blocks are deleted; this means that it will not be possible to reclaim the unused space with an OPTIMIZE TABLE statement. Also, the table's AUTO_INCREMENT value, if any, is lost. For these reasons, USE_FRM should never be used if there is an alternative. Also, it should never be used against compressed tables, because it would only damage them. The myisamchk or aria_chk commands can be used instead.

With NO_WRITE_TO_BINLOG, the statement is not written into the binary log. This is useful in a replication environment to avoid the statement to be replicated by the slaves. Here LOCAL is a synonym for NO_WRITE_TO_BINLOG.

Repairing CSV tables

The CSV storage engine supports the CHECK TABLE and REPAIR TABLE commands. However, REPAIR TABLE has an important limitation for the CSV engine: it only recovers the rows that are physically stored before the first corrupted row.

For example, if a table has 1,000 rows and the tenth row is corrupted, REPAIR TABLE will only recover the first nine rows. We can then restore a backup of the damaged table, open it with a text editor, delete the tenth row, and repeat the process until all the non-corrupted rows are restored. But this method is error-prone, slow, and frustrating.

Repairing tables with the myisamchk and aria_chk tools

The myisamchk and aria_chk tools are included in all distributions of MariaDB and are located in the bin directory. They can be used to check or repair MyISAM or Aria tables, respectively. The myisamchk tool requires that no other programs access the tables until they are running. Thus, before running myisamchk, it is necessary to lock the relevant tables or stop the server.

 The myisamchk and aria_chk tools do not work with partitioned tables.

The correct syntax to invoke them is as follows:

```
myisamchk [options] table_list …
aria_chk [options] table_list …
```

The table_list parameter can be specified in several ways:

- As a table name
- As the name of a table's index file; the data will still be checked
- As a pattern using wildcard characters

This allows the specifying of table names with powerful patterns. For example, the following expression selects all MyISAM tables in the joomla database:

```
/usr/local/mysql/data/joomla/*.MYI
```

To specify all MyISAM tables in all databases, use the following command:

```
/usr/local/mysql/data/*/*.MYI
```

To specify two tables, called customer and user, located in a database called db_1, use:

```
/usr/local/mysql/data/db_1/customer /usr/local/mysql/data/db_1/user
```

 Note that the path must always be specified unless the files to be checked are located in the same directory as myisamchk or aria_chk. These tools do not know the MariaDB directory tree.

The following `myisamchk` and `aria_chk` options control which action is performed by the tool we are invoking. All other options control the way this action is executed. Have a look at the following list of options:

- `--check`: This option checks the selected tables for corruption. This is the default action.

- `--force`: This option is used along with `--check`; if a table is corrupted, it tries to repair the table.

- `--repair`: This option tries to repair the selected tables if they are corrupted.

- `--analyze`: This option analyzes indexes such as the ANALYZE TABLE statement.

The following table shows other important `myisamchk` and `aria_chk` options that are useful while checking tables:

Option	Description
`--check-only-changed`	Like CHECK TABLE ... CHANGED
`--update-state`	Checks tables that were not properly closed
`--fast`	Like CHECK TABLE ... FAST
`--medium-check`	Like CHECK TABLE ... MEDIUM
`--extend-check`	Like CHECK TABLE ... EXTENDED
`--read-only`	The tables will not be marked as checked

When repairing tables, the following options are used:

Option	Description
`--backup`	Before attempting to repair tables, it creates backups. A backup is a file with a .BAK extension.
`--correct-checksum`	It corrects the tables' checksum values.
`--quick or -q`	It performs a quick repair; it does not modify the data files unless -q is specified twice.
`--extend-check`	Like REPAIR TABLE ... EXTENDED.
`--recover`	It should find any error except for duplicate key values.
`--sort-recover`	Like `--recover`, but forces the repair in case it requires a very big data file.
`--safe-recover`	Like `--recover` but uses an old (slower) algorithm. In rare cases, this algorithm works better.

Aria uses the logfiles (the files with names like `aria_log.00000001`) and the log control file (`aria_log_control`) to repair corrupted tables. The `aria_chk` command has some specific options that control the way these files are used:

The aria_chk option	Description
`--datadir=path`	The path of the `aria_log_control` file.
`--ignore-control-file`	Ignores the `aria_log_control` file. This option is unsafe if another program accesses the file.
`--require-control-file`	The repair is aborted if `aria_log_control` is not found.
`--logdir=path`	The path of the logfiles.

MyISAM and Aria autorecovery

The MyISAM and Aria storage engines support the autorecovery functionality. When the server opens a MyISAM table and MyISAM recovery is enabled, the server checks whether the table is marked as crashed or was not properly closed because of a crash. If so, the server checks the table; if an error is found, the server tries to repair it. The same happens when an Aria table is opened and the Aria autorecovery is enabled.

Since the system tables in the `mysql` database use the MyISAM storage engine, enabling the MyISAM autorecovery is very important. All production servers should have this functionality enabled. The repairing of a MyISAM table is more likely to succeed if the table uses the **FIXED** row format. The reason is that, with this format, MyISAM always knows in which positions fields and rows begin or end.

The *MariaDB Knowledge Base* claims that Aria is a crash-safe storage engine. This does not mean that an Aria table cannot be corrupted; however, each statement that modifies data is atomic. It should completely succeed or completely fail.

The MyISAM recovery is configured by setting the `myisam_recover_options` option in the configuration file or the `--myisam-recover` startup option. They accept multiple values separated with a comma. The valid values are:

- `OFF`: Autorecovery is disabled.
- `QUICK`: A quick check is performed
- `FORCE`: A better, slower check is performed
- `BACKUP`: A backup of the `data` files is kept
- `BACKUP_ALL`: A backup of the `data` and `index` files is kept
- `DEFAULT`: Same as `OFF` or not specifying the option

Similarly, Aria recovery can be enabled by setting the `aria_recover` option in the configuration file or the `--aria-recover` startup option. The list of valid values is slightly different:

- `OFF`: Autorecovery is disabled. This is the default value.
- `QUICK`: A quick check is performed.
- `NORMAL`: A check is performed.
- `FORCE`: An extensive check is performed.
- `BACKUP`: A backup of the data files is kept.

The safest configuration for these options, in the configuration file, is the following:

```
myisam_recover_options=FORCE,BACKUP_ALL
aria_recover=FORCE,BACKUP
```

Summary

In this chapter, we discussed the various backup techniques and tools that can be used with a MariaDB server. A DBA should know all the backup methods, because each one can be the best choice for some types of workloads.

We discussed how to perform a physical or logical complete backup. When we have a complete backup, we can then perform incremental backups, which are always smaller than complete backups and take less time. Then, we discussed how to take partial backups that do not include all tables from all databases. The restoring of all types of backups has also been explained.

Backups of InnoDB tables are slightly more complicated and, before MariaDB 10.0, required the server to be stopped. We discussed how to back up and restore InnoDB tables. Special attention has been paid to Percona XtraBackup, which is optimized for InnoDB and allows taking fast, physical backups without stopping the server.

When a table is corrupted, restoring an old backup is not always the only solution. We discussed how to repair a table. The procedure strictly depends on the storage engines. The InnoDB recovery process is used at server startup. Some other storage engines support table repairs using SQL statements. Two special tools allow us to repair Aria and MyISAM tables.

In the next chapter, we will discuss how to set up and manage a replication environment.

9
Replication

MariaDB supports built-in replication; it can be used for several purposes. The most common reason to build a replication environment is to increase data redundancy for improving the fault tolerance. Also, while replication does not replace a good backup plan, a slave data can sometimes be used as a backup for the master in case of data loss. Another use of replication is writing data into the master and spreading the queries through two or more slaves, to improve performance.

In the previous chapter, we discussed backups. Knowing this topic is very important now, because replication, just as with some backup types, is based on the binary log.

In this chapter we will learn:

- How replication works in MariaDB
- Setting up a master and a slave
- Loading data into a slave or a new master
- Configuring masters and slaves
- Rotating replication logs
- Checking the slaves' data integrity
- Solving the most common replication problems

An overview of replication

MariaDB supports built-in replication. This feature is one of the most ancient and an advanced MariaDB feature. The first version of the code saw the light in MySQL 3.23.15, in May 2000. At that time, MySQL did not even include InnoDB, and did not support important features such as views or the UNION statement. Of course, the first version of replication was quite poor. Basically, a master just logged SQL statements and sent the log entries to the slaves. However, the age of this feature reveals how stable it is nowadays.

MariaDB replication is based on the binary log. The binary log keeps track of the events that modify the databases. The binary log supports three formats:

- STATEMENT
- ROW
- MIXED

With the STATEMENT format, events are all SQL statements that do or could modify some data. With the ROW format, events are all modifications that occur as a consequence of such statements. The MIXED format records the statements when possible, but it can also record the modifications. Depending on the format, we commonly define the replication as **statement-based** or **row-based**. The binary log will be explained in detail in this chapter. It has already been mentioned in *Chapter 8, Backup and Disaster Recovery*.

MariaDB's built-in replication is called **asynchronous** replication. This means that there is no need for a permanent connection between the slaves and the master.

> It is possible to stop the replication at any moment to obtain a snapshot of the master's data. This can be done, for example, to perform a fast backup. When the slave is started again, it will receive all the events that occurred while the replication was not working. The same happens if the slave had crashed for some reason.

The slave can be queried by clients. Read-heavy workloads can greatly benefit from this feature. Connecting several slaves to one master allows us to distribute queries on the slaves.

Each slave can also be a master. For example, server A can be the master for server B, while B can also be the master for server C. If B crashes, replication to C will be temporarily stopped; however, if B loses data, C can be used as a backup. Also, in our example, C could be a master of A. This kind of configuration forms a ring, and it is called **circular replication**. It allows modifying or reading data on any server. Data consistency is guaranteed, because each modification will eventually be replicated by all servers in the ring. The main disadvantage is that none of the servers contain a version of the data that is always up-to-date.

MariaDB 10.0 supports **multisource replication**. This feature allows each slave to replicate data from multiple masters. There is no conflict handling in MariaDB. Thus, the master must contain different data. It is not possible to replicate the same database from two or more masters. Multisource replication allows you to use one machine, or a limited number of machines, to replicate data from several masters. The cost of the hardware can be reduced with this technique.

Ideally, in a replication environment all the masters and slaves should use the same MariaDB version. Replication from an older master to a newer slave does not work. For example, a 5.5 master cannot replicate to a 10.0 slave. Replication from a newer master to an older slave is generally supported, but it may cause problems. MySQL servers can be present in the replication topology.

How replication works

In this section, we will be provided with information on how replication is implemented in MariaDB. In particular, the read operation will learn which threads are used and which logs are kept. This is necessary before proceeding with the following section, which explains how to set up the master and slave servers in a replication environment, and how to maintain them.

Replication threads

In MariaDB replication, three kinds of threads are used, as shown in the following table:

Where it runs	Thread name
master	Binlog dump thread
slave	SQL I/O thread
slave	Slave SQL thread

The connections between each slave and a master are requested by the slaves. When a slave is started, it creates the SQL I/O thread. This thread connects to the master and requests events that must be replicated.

On the master, a Binlog dump thread runs. This thread is a daemon that accepts requests from the slave's SQL I/O threads and sends them the binary log events. In the output of SHOW SLAVE STATUS, this thread is called Slave_IO_running. The output of SHOW PROCESSLIST shows this thread as Binlog Dump.

The SQL I/O thread does not execute events directly. It just writes them in a log on the slave called the **slave relay** log.

The Slave SQL thread reads the relay log and executes the events in the database.

Parallel replication

Before MariaDB 10.0, only one slave SQL thread was started for each slave server. This could lead to poor performance, because normally a master executes the same write operations using several parallel threads. Sometimes a single thread is not sufficient to replicate the master's workload with acceptable performance.

In MariaDB 10.0, a feature called **parallel replication** has been introduced. Oracle introduced a similar feature in MySQL 5.6. However, MySQL users should note that MariaDB and MySQL use different implementations of parallel replication, configured in different ways. For example, the most important server variable for MariaDB parallel replication is `@@slave_parallel_threads`, that is not present in MySQL; and the most important server startup option for MySQL parallel replication is `--slave-parallel-workers`, which is not present in MariaDB.

Parallel replication consists of starting a pool of threads that is able to apply many events in a parallel way. Each thread in this pool is called a **worker** thread. Note that not all the events can be applied by parallel threads. MariaDB will still execute some operations sequentially, when this is necessary to correctly replicate the data.

This feature is optional and is not enabled by default. To use it, it is necessary to configure it on the master, by setting the `@@slave_parallel_threads` server variable. This value is the number of worker threads that will be started on each slave. As a consequence, all the slaves replicating data from the same master will have the same number of worker threads. Also, if a slave replicates multiple masters, the same number of worker threads must be configured on all the masters.

Slave logs

Slaves need to record information about the replication configuration and current progress. This information must not be lost, even in the event of a crash. So, each slave maintains three logs:

- The `relay` log contains the events that were received by the master's binary logs. As explained previously, this log is written by the slave I/O thread and read by the slave SQL thread, or by pool worker threads if parallel replication is used.

- The `master` log stores the information that is necessary to connect to the master, as well as the master's binary logs coordinates. The coordinates consist of a logfile name and the position of the last binary log event that has been received.

- The `relay` log info log stores information about the last relay log event that has been applied by the slave SQL thread or the worker threads.

The `relay` log is always written into files. The `master` log information and the `relay` log information can be written in files or into system tables in the `mysql` database.

Even in multisource replication, each slave has only one log for each type.

Choosing a binary log format

Choosing a binary log format is very important. The replication format can greatly be affected by this choice. Also, if the STATEMENT format is used, the developers should be aware of its important limitations.

To choose the binary log format, we can set the `binlog_format` variable in the configuration file or the `--binlog-format` startup option. If not specified, the format defaults to STATEMENT. We can also obtain the currently used format by querying the `@@binlog_format` server variable.

> The `@@binlog_format` variable is a dynamic variable that exists at both the global and session level. This means that it is possible to change the binary log format on the master while it is running, for all connections or only for the current connection. However, this should never be done. Changing the binary logging format on the master might cause the replication to fail, or it may cause an unexpected behavior. For this reason, changing the value of `@@binlog_format`, even at session level, requires the SUPER privilege. However, changing this variable on a slave is always safe.
>
> Note that it is not possible to change the value of `@@binlog_format` within a stored program.
>
> The master and the slaves do not need to use the same binary log format.

Statement-based binary logging

The STATEMENT format is the most ancient binary log format. When this format is used, the log contains the queries that could modify data. Statements such as UPDATE, DELETE, or REPLACE with a WHERE clause sometimes do not modify any row. However, these statements will still be written to the log. Statements such as SELECT are never written to the log, because they cannot modify any data.

The STATEMENT format has an important limitation: only deterministic statements should be sent to the server. Deterministic means that, if they are executed twice on identical databases, they must necessarily have the same effects. Of course this limitation does not apply to the statements that do not modify data, such as SELECT queries, because they are not logged and do not affect the replicated data. If a statement uses the current timestamp, the current user, or random data, they will produce different results on the slaves.

If the STATEMENT format is in use, MariaDB tries to detect the unsafe statements and produces the following warnings:

```
Note (Code 1592): Unsafe statement written to the binary log using
statement format since BINLOG_FORMAT = STATEMENT. Statement is unsafe
because it uses a system function that may return a different value on
the slave.
```

However, MariaDB does not check if the values assigned to user variables are deterministic or not. Thus, when using variables, it is easy to insert the non-deterministic data without getting any warning:

```
MariaDB [test]> SET @a = RAND();
Query OK, 0 rows affected (0.00 sec)
MariaDB [test]> CREATE TABLE example ENGINE = InnoDB SELECT @a;
Query OK, 1 row affected (0.50 sec)
Records: 1  Duplicates: 0  Warnings: 0
```

If stored programs are used, special attention should be paid to these kinds of mistakes.

On the other hand, the heuristics used by MariaDB to detect non-deterministic statements are a bit too pessimistic. In other words, since the algorithms used here do not properly analyze some statements, the 1592 warning is produced for some deterministic statements. This is a well-known problem that can cause the error log to grow too quickly. In extreme cases, this could be a good reason to switch to the MIXED format.

Here is a list of the possible causes why a statement is not deterministic:

- Non-deterministic functions, such as RAND() or USER(). Note that FOUND_ROWS(), ROW_COUNT(), and LOAD_FILE() are considered non-deterministic.

- User-defined functions (functions written in the C language and installed in the server).

- References to server variables. Their value can differ on slaves. There are some exceptions but, since they are currently not documented, we must rely on our logic to find them, or simply avoid referencing server variables at all.

- An UPDATE statement with a LIMIT clause (even if a deterministic ORDER BY is specified; this is a known bug).

- An AUTO_INCREMENT column is modified, and the statement causes a trigger to be executed or calls a stored function.

- An `AUTO_INCREMENT` value is automatically generated, and it is not the first column in the primary key (this is rare and probably not efficient).

- The `LOAD DATA INFILE` statement was not considered safe before Version 10.0.

- The `INSERT DELAYED` command against a MyISAM table (other storage engines ignore the `DELAYED` clause).

- A system table is involved in a statement. Tables in any system database (`mysql`, `information_schema`, or `performance_schema`) can store different data on different servers, even if the servers received the same statements.

Only `READ COMMITTED` and `READ UNCOMMITTED` can be used with the `STATEMENT` format. The reason is that, with `REPEATABLE READ` and `SERIALIZABLE`, the order of statement execution can sometimes depend on the statement's execution time. This happens because a statement that uses locks can delay the execution of other statements.

Note that some non-deterministic functions are safe. The reason is that the binary log contains the information necessary to replicate them exactly. For example, date or time functions are safe because the binary log stores a timestamp for each statement. The safe non-deterministic functions are:

- `DATABASE()`, `SCHEMA()`
- `CONNECTION_ID()`
- `LAST_INSERT_ID()`
- `CURDATE()`, `CURRENT_DATE()`
- `CURTIME()`, `CURRENT_TIME()`
- `CURRENT_TIMESTAMP()`, `UNIX_TIMESTAMP()`, `NOW()`
- `UTC_DATE()`, `UTC_TIME()`, `UTC_TIMESTAMP()`
- `LOCALTIME()`, `LOCALTIMESTAMP()`

> The `SYSDATE()` function is the only unsafe time function. The reason is that it returns the exact time of the function call, not the time of the statement execution. Multiple `SYSDATE()` calls in the same query can return multiple different values. It is thus impossible to replicate it obtaining the same return value.
>
> Note that these limitations apply to the statement-based binary logging itself. Even if replication is not used, the binary log should never contain non-deterministic statements using this format. This would make backups unreliable.

Row-based binary logging

As mentioned previously, if the ROW format is used, the binary log contains the changes to the data. There are, however, some exceptions: some operations are written to the log in a different way. These exceptions are the following:

- DDL statements, such as CREATE TABLE and DROP TABLE.

- Statements that implicitly modify tables in the mysql database. This includes statements such as CREATE USER or GRANT, but not statements that explicitly modify system tables, such as INSERT or UPDATE.

- Statements that involve temporary tables.

These exceptions are logged as statements, as if the STATEMENT format was in use. The CREATE ... SELECT clause is logged in a different way: the CREATE TABLE part of the command is written as a statement and is logged as a statement, but the selected data is logged as rows.

The main advantage of this format is that it does not have the limitations of the STATEMENT format: all statements are safe with the ROW format. Since data modifications are logged, it is irrelevant if the statements that produced the changes were deterministic or not. Any isolation level can be used with the ROW format, including READ COMMITTED and READ UNCOMMITTED.

Also, the slaves do not need to execute the SQL statements. Executing statements can include extra work such as the grouping or ordering of the rows, the execution of functions, and so on. Applying changes to the rows is a simple operation for the slaves. If complex statements are executed on the master, this is an important advantage.

However, there is also an important disadvantage: if a statement modifies many rows, the ROW format requires much more data to be written into the log. This can make the binary log too large. If replication is used, the master will need to send much more data to the clients.

However, the ROW format is more compact for data itself. Usually, the data that need to be written into a database are written in an INSERT or UPDATE statement. If many data are inserted this way, the STATEMENT format could result in a bigger binary log. Also, the STATEMENT format is not efficient for workloads consisting of many statements that only modify a single row.

The MIXED binary logging format

While the STATEMENT format has many limitations, the ROW format is less efficient for the majority of workloads. For this reason we may want to use the MIXED format, in most cases. When it is used, most statements are logged with the STATEMENT format. When a non-deterministic statement is detected, it is logged using the ROW format. The logging of binary data performed by the MIXED format is called **binary injection**. Note that only the READ COMMITTED and READ UNCOMMITTED isolation levels can be used with the STATEMENT or MIXED format. This is because, with the REPEATABLE READ format, the duration of locking transactions can affect the order of execution of other statements. This can cause discrepancies between the slaves and the master.

The binary logging of stored programs

Stored routines (procedures and functions) are only safe if they are deterministic and do not modify any data. Thus, when the binary log is enabled, MariaDB prevents the creation of stored functions if they are not declared with the NOT DETERMINISTIC clause, or one of the READS SQL DATA, CONTAINS SQL, or NO SQL clauses. To force their creation, it is possible to set the @@log_bin_trust_function_creators variable. However, such statements will not be safe with the STATEMENT format.

Triggers cannot be declared as DETERMINISTIC or NOT DETERMINISTIC. However, if they contain non-deterministic statements, they are not safe.

Also, we must remember that SQL statements can behave differently if permissions are different. The slave executes all the statements with a user who has all the privileges. If we are not definitely sure that the stored programs always have the rights to perform all the operations they attempt on the master, we should not log them with the STATEMENT format.

Configuring replication

In this section we will see which configuration parameters are required on the master and slave servers.

All the following explanations also apply to the multisource replication environments. However, there are some differences that will be explained after the common tasks.

Setting up a replication environment requires at least the following steps:

1. Configuring a new replication master
2. Configuring one or more replication slave
3. Loading data from the master
4. Starting the slave
5. Checking if the slaves are running

These tasks, along with other useful topics, will be explained in this section.

Configuring a new replication master

When setting up a replication environment, the first thing to do is of course to set up at least one master. This is an easy task, as the master is just a normal MariaDB server that has a unique ID and maintains a binary log.

First, a server ID needs to be set on all masters and slaves. The server ID needs to be unique. It must be an integer value of 4 bytes with the minimum value 1. If the server ID is not set, or it is set to 0, the replication is disabled.

Also, as explained previously, the binary log must be enabled on the master server. This is needed to record the events that will be sent to the slaves.

A master's configuration file needs to contain lines similar to the following:

```
server-id=1
log_bin="binlog"
binlog_format=STATEMENT
```

The `@@server_id` and `@@binlog_format` variables are dynamic; thus they can simply be changed at runtime without stopping the server:

```
MariaDB [(none)]> SET @@server_id = 1;
Query OK, 0 rows affected (0.00 sec)
MariaDB [(none)]> SET @@binlog_format = 'MIXED';
Query OK, 0 rows affected (0.03 sec)
```

The `@@log_bin` variable is not dynamic, so enabling the binary log requires a restart.

Note that it is always necessary to modify the configuration file. In this way, if the server is restarted these settings are not lost. A restart can be automatically made by `mysqld_safe`, if the server crashes.

Then, we need to create at least one account for replication slaves. Strictly speaking, a slave only needs the REPLICATION SLAVE privilege to work properly. If some databases must not be replicated, this permission should not be granted on them. It is possible for all the slaves to use the same user; they could even use an account that is shared with other clients. However, since the password is stored in clear text in a file called `master.info`, it is generally better for them to use different passwords. Also, to improve the security of data, each slave user should only be able to connect from a specific hostname. It could also be a good idea to force the slaves to connect using SSL.

Here is an example that shows how to create a secure replication account:

```
MariaDB [test]> CREATE USER 'mslave1'@'host10' IDENTIFIED BY 'somepwd';
Query OK, 0 rows affected (0.00 sec)
MariaDB [test]> GRANT REPLICATION SLAVE ON *.* TO 'mslave1'@'host10'
REQUIRE SSL;
Query OK, 0 rows affected (0.00 sec)
```

Note that the REPLICATION SLAVE permission must not be confused with REPLICATION CLIENT. This permission should be granted to the user who performs replication configuration and diagnostics, because it allows you to execute the SHOW MASTER STATUS and SHOW SLAVE STATUS statements. On production servers, root should not be used unless we really need all the permissions for the current session.

For details about security and user management, see *Chapter 5, Users and Connections*.

Configuring a new replication slave

After setting up one or more master, we need to properly configure the slaves. This step is required when setting up a replication environment, and every time we want to add a new slave.

Similarly to the masters, each slave needs to have a unique server ID.

It is not necessary to enable the binary logging on the slaves, unless a slave should also act as a master of another slave. If this is not the case, the binary log can still be useful for taking backups, but it affects the performance.

The following example shows the most minimalist configuration settings required for a slave to work, in the configuration file:

```
server-id=2
```

The slave might also act as a master of one or more slaves. In this case, the slave needs to log into the binary log the events that it receives from its masters, so that its slaves will be able to retrieve them. However, the replicated events are not logged by default. To replicate them, we must enable the binary log and set the `@@log_slave_updates` server variable to ON. This variable is not dynamic, so changing its value requires a server restart.

The following example shows a minimalist configuration for a slave that also acts as a server:

```
server-id=2
log_bin="binlog"
binlog_format=STATEMENT
log_slave_updates=ON
```

Starting a slave

If a master has no data yet, setting up a replication between the master and a slave is very straightforward. After starting the master and the slave as explained previously, we will follow this procedure:

1. Lock the master with a global lock. We want to be sure that it does not start to work before we set up the slaves.
2. Obtain the binary log coordinates. The coordinates are the name of the binary logfile currently in use, and the position of the last written event.
3. Unlock the master.
4. Provide the slave with the information that is necessary to access the master. We will do this using the CHANGE MASTER TO statement.
5. Repeat these operations for each slave.

The following example shows how to obtain the master's binary log coordinates:

```
MariaDB [(none)]> FLUSH TABLES WITH READ LOCK;
Query OK, 0 rows affected (0.04 sec)
```

```
MariaDB [(none)]> SHOW MASTER STATUS;
+----------------+----------+--------------+------------------+
| File           | Position | Binlog_Do_DB | Binlog_Ignore_DB |
+----------------+----------+--------------+------------------+
| binlog.000031  |      323 |              |                  |
+----------------+----------+--------------+------------------+
1 row in set (0.02 sec)
MariaDB [(none)]> UNLOCK TABLES;
Query OK, 0 rows affected (0.00 sec)
```

In this case, the coordinates are the `binlog.000031` logfile and the position `323`. The slave will start to replicate the data from these coordinates.

The `CHANGE MASTER TO` statement can be used to tell the slave which master it has to replicate. The following basic example shows how to do this:

```
MariaDB [(none)]> CHANGE MASTER TO
    -> MASTER_HOST = '162.100.100.100',
    -> MASTER_USER = 'slave01',
    -> MASTER_PASSWORD='somepwd',
    -> MASTER_PORT = 5000,
    -> MASTER_LOG_FILE = 'binlog.000031',
    -> MASTER_LOG_POS = 3234;
Query OK, 0 rows affected (0.23 sec)
```

At this point, the slave knows all it has to know about replication, the necessary permissions on the master are set, and both are running. To start replication, we will just use the `START SLAVE` statement:

```
MariaDB [(none)]> START SLAVE;
Query OK, 0 rows affected (0.02 sec)
```

The parameters of the connection between the slave and the server can be changed in the future. However, while this is done, the slave must be temporarily stopped. For example:

```
MariaDB [(none)]> STOP SLAVE;
Query OK, 0 rows affected, 1 warning (0.00 sec)
MariaDB [(none)]> CHANGE MASTER TO MASTER_PASSWORD = 'my_new_pwd';
Query OK, 0 rows affected (0.22 sec)
MariaDB [(none)]> START SLAVE;
Query OK, 0 rows affected (0.00 sec)
```

If the server is restarted, the slave thread will be restarted too.

Checking whether a slave is running

We can check the running slave threads with a SHOW SLAVE STATUS query.
For example:

```
MariaDB [(none)]> SHOW SLAVE STATUS \G
*************************** 1. row ***************************
             Slave_IO_State: Connecting to master
    ...
          Slave_IO_Running: Connecting
         Slave_SQL_Running: Yes
    ...
                Last_Error:
    ...
2 rows in set (0.02 sec)
```

The output of this statement has many columns, so we truncated it. We left the
columns that are important to verify that a slave is running:

Column name	Description
Slave_IO_State	The current state of the I/O thread, as shown in SHOW PROCESSLIST.
Slave_IO_Running	Shows if the I/O thread is connected and working.
Slave_SQL_Running	The current state of the SQL thread, as shown in SHOW PROCESSLIST.
Last_Error	The last error encountered by the slave.

The Slave_IO_Running and Slave_SQL_Running columns should be set to Yes.
If either of them is not set to Yes, Slave_IO_State and Last_Error help us identify
the problem. For example, if a connection error occurs, we will see an error similar to
the following:

```
error connecting to master 'slave1@127.0.0.1:3310' - retry-time: 10
retries: 86400  message: Can't connect to MySQL server on '127.0.0.1'
(111 "Connection refused")
```

Reconfiguring an existing slave

Sometimes we want to reconfigure an existing slave. Probably we restored an old database into the master, or the filtering rules were not set correctly. But, whatever the reason is, we want a slave to forget the data it replicated until now and start again.

After the restart, the slave will need to replicate the master's binary log from the start. So, it must forget the current coordinates. The RESET SLAVE statement does the trick by deleting the current slave log files. This cannot be done while the slave is running, so it needs to be temporarily stopped.

Consider the following example:

```
MariaDB [(none)]> STOP SLAVE;
Query OK, 0 rows affected (0.17 sec)
MariaDB [(none)]> RESET SLAVE;
Query OK, 0 rows affected (0.00 sec)
MariaDB [(none)]> START SLAVE;
Query OK, 0 rows affected (0.18 sec)
```

Importing the data into a master

Sometimes, we want to replace an old master with a new one. Probably the older master was slow, or its hardware was damaged. But, whatever the reason is, we will need to load the old master's data into the new master's data.

We can choose to do this when the slaves are already running and connected to the master. In this case, we will use a dump of the data. In *Chapter 8, Backup and Disaster Recovery*, we discussed how to take this kind of backup using mysqldump and how to load the dump into a server. The dump will be automatically replicated by the slaves.

An alternative to using a logical backup is copying the files. In this case, the backup will not be automatically replicated, if the slaves are already running. We will need to copy the physical backup into the slave's data directory, too. In this way, they will be provided with the old master's data before starting to replicate the new master.

Importing the data into a slave from a master

A replication environment is not meant to be static. It is possible to add slaves at any time, to obtain more redundancy or to balance the workload across a higher number of MariaDB servers. In this case, we will need to load the current master data into the new slaves. Then, the slave can start to replicate the master.

It is possible to create a physical backup and copy it into the slave's data directories as explained in *Chapter 8, Backup and Disaster Recovery*. There is no difference between normal physical backups and backups used for replication.

It is also possible to use mysqldump. This tool has already been discussed, but it has some parameters that make the dump easier to restore into a slave. The dump can be taken from the master or from a slave. The latter option is useful to avoid overloading the master.

Dumping data from a master

When taking a backup from a master that must be restored into a slave, the --master-data option is particularly useful. It adds a CHANGE MASTER TO statement to the dump, so that slaves are automatically set up to replicate the master from the proper coordinates.

The --delete-master-logs option executes the PURGE BINARY LOGS statement on the master. This statement is used to delete the old binary log files and will be discussed later in this chapter.

Dumping data from a slave

If the master already has at least one slave, the dump can be taken from the slave to avoid the execution of the long locking queries on the master.

The main parameter that we will want to use is --dump-slave. It is very similar to --master-data, but they produce different CHANGE MASTER TO statements. If we use --master-data, mysqldump assumes that the statement will be used to replicate data from the server it is connecting to. Instead, --dump-slave assumes that this server is a slave, and the CHANGE MASTER TO statement will be used to replicate its server. This difference is very important.

Note that, while --dump-slave includes the replication coordinates in the dump, it does not include the master's hostname and port. Thus we may want to specify the --include-master-host-port option, which ensures the MASTER_HOST and MASTER_PORT clauses are included in the CHANGE MASTER TO statement. This option makes the configuration of a slave even easier, unless the dump is created on another slave, or the master's hostname or port is changed for some reason.

With `--apply-slave-statements` the dump will contain `STOP SLAVE` and `START SLAVE` before and after `CHANGE MASTER TO`. This is useful if the target slave is already running. If it is not running yet, the `START SLAVE` statement will make the replication start immediately. We do not want it to start immediately if we want to test the consistency of data before the slave starts its work.

Filtering binary log events

It is possible to avoid replicating some statements. This can be done on a master or on individual slaves.

The SET SQL_LOG_BIN statement

The `SET SQL_LOG_BIN` statement can be used to enable or disable the logging of subsequent statements into the binary log. It only affects the current session. Statements that are not written in the master's binary log cannot be replicated by any slave.

Consider the following example:

```
MariaDB [test]> SET SQL_LOG_BIN = 0;
Query OK, 0 rows affected (0.00 sec)
MariaDB [test]> /* this statement will not be logger or replicated */
    -> DROP TABLE orders;
Query OK, 0 rows affected (0.38 sec)
MariaDB [test]> SET SQL_LOG_BIN = 1;
Query OK, 0 rows affected (0.00 sec)
```

The @@skip_replication variable

The `@@skip_replication` session variable is similar to the `SET SQL_LOG_BIN` statements. However it does not inhibit the logging of statements; it just causes those statements to be flagged as `skip_replication` in the binary log. The slaves will receive such events. Their behavior depends on the value of the `@@replicate_events_marked_for_skip` variable:

- `REPLICATE`: This causes the events to be replicated: the flag is simply ignored. This is the default value.
- `FILTER_ON_SLAVE`: This causes the slaves to ignore such events. They will still receive them and log them, if the binary log is enabled. The flag is preserved on the slave's binary log.
- `FILTER_ON_MASTER`: With this the slave will not receive the events at all.

Filtering the replication of events on the slaves

The slaves have three dynamic variables that can be used to prevent some tables, or some complete databases, from being replicated. A comma-separated list of arguments can be provided to these variables. Before changing their values, it is necessary to stop the slave. Such variables are as follows:

- `@@replicate_skip_db`: This prevents the replication of the specified databases. This option does not affect multidatabase statements: to prevent them, `@@replicate_skip_table` must be used instead.

- `@@replicate_skip_table`: This prevents the replication of the specified tables. The names should be specified in the following form: `db_name.table_name`.

- `@@replicate_wild_skip_tables`: This is similar to `@@replicate_skip_table`, but the use of the `%` and `_` wildcard characters is allowed. These characters have the same meaning they have for the `LIKE` operator. For example, the following value prevents the replication of any table in any database whose name starts with "test": `test%.%`.

As an alternative, it is possible to disallow replication for all tables and databases, except for the specified subsets. This can be done using the following variables, which are the complement of the ones discussed earlier:

- `@@replicate_do_db`
- `@@replicate_do_table`
- `@@replicate_wild_do_tables`

Checksums of the binary log events

Since MariaDB 5.3, it has been possible to write each event's checksum into the binary log. This feature is not enabled by default, because it modifies the binary log format, adding an incompatibility. To write checksums, we can set the `@@binlog_checksum` variable to `1` (not `ON`). Enabling this option makes the replication more reliable, but we should avoid it when performance of the slaves is a problem.

It is possible to verify the checksums in several situations:

- The slave I/O thread verifies the checksums when it receives them from the master if `@@master_verify_checksum` is set to `1`. By default, it is `0`.

- The slave SQL thread verifies the checksums if `@@slave_sql_verify_checksum` is set to 1, which is the default value.

- The `mysqlbinlog` utility (discussed in *Chapter 8, Backup and Disaster Recovery*) verifies the checksums if it is invoked with the `--verify-binlog-checksum` option.

All the variables that affect the binary log events checksums are dynamic.

Configuring parallel replication

Usually, a database server processes requests from several clients at the same time. As far as these requests do not lock rows or tables to guarantee data integrity, they are processed simultaneously. In *Chapter 5, Users and Connections*, we discussed how simultaneous connections are handled. However, before MariaDB 10.0, slaves used only one thread to replicate all the events they received from the master. Because of this limitation, the write operations were much slower on the slaves, especially in environments where a master could execute many non-blocking writes. Parallel replication solves this issue by using multiple parallel threads to apply replication events.

As mentioned earlier, parallel replication is not used by default. To enable it, we must set the `@@slave_parallel_threads` server variable to a value higher than 0, on the master. This value is the number of parallel worker threads that will be used by all the slaves.

The following variables are only meaningful when used with parallel replication.

The `@@slave_parallel_max_queued` variable determines the amount of memory that the slaves must use to cache the next not-yet-executed relay log events. When at least the worker thread is free, the slaves examine this cache looking for events that can be executed in parallel.

The `@@slave_domain_parallel_threads` variable is useful when using parallel replication on a slave that replicates multiple masters. Imagine that a slave replicates three masters. Imagine that one of them (call it master1) executes a statement that takes several hours. This can happen with big tables. The slave will need to replicate this statement. Meanwhile, initially all connections will be able to allocate worker threads. But the worker threads associated to master1 will need to wait until the very long-running statement has been executed. When no more worker threads are free, the other connections will not be able to benefit from parallel replication anymore.

The purpose of `@@slave_domain_parallel_threads` is to prevent a single master connection from monopolizing the pool of threads. This value determines the maximum number of threads that can be allocated by the same master connection. If the value is not lower than `@@slave_parallel_threads`, it has no effect. But if it is lower than `@@slave_parallel_threads` divided by the number of master connections, some worker threads will never be used. The value should be left as high as possible to avoid preventing a master connection from allocating a thread when not necessary.

In real cases, finding the optimal value for `@@slave_parallel_threads` can be complex. It is highly dependent on the characteristics of the master's workloads. As a general rule, we can start with a value that is slightly lower than `@@slave_parallel_threads`, and then lower the value if a problem occurs because of long-running statements.

All these variables are dynamic, so changing the configuration of the parallel replication does not require the master to be restarted. However, the slaves should be stopped temporarily.

Delaying a slave

There are several reasons why we might want to have a delayed slave. For example, we may want to have a slave with a 30 minute delay to recover from errors. Alternatively, if we accidentally drop a table, we might have 30 minutes to recover it from the slave before the deletion is replicated. Or, we may have a slave with a delay of a day, week, or month. It would allow us to compare the most recent database with an older version, to find the recent structure or data modifications.

MariaDB does not natively support delayed replication. However, Percona Toolkit contains a tool that implements this feature on the client side: it is called `pt-slave-delay`. It is necessary to invoke the tool separately for each slave that needs to be delayed. This tool works by connecting to the slave and periodically checking how much the slave is lagging behind the master. When the delay is too low, `pt-slave-delay` stops the slave for a while. It is possible to only cause the delay for a given period of time, or permanently.

The following options are also very important:

- `delay`: This specifies the desired amount of delay. The `--interval` option determines the time interval between the checks.

- --run-time: This determines for how much time the tool will run; if not specified, it will never terminate spontaneously. By default, when the program terminates, the slave will be restarted, if it is not running. This applies even if the program is terminated by pressing *Ctrl + C*. To change this behavior, and stop the slave on exit if it is running, we can use the --continue option.

The time options can be specified with a number followed by a letter that represents the time unit. For example, 30m means 30 minutes.

An invocation example is as follows:

```
pt-slave-delay --delay 3h --interval 10m -uroot -proot
```

Multisource replication

All the procedures explained previously also apply to multisource replication. The difference is that, with multisource replication, each slave associates each master-slave connection to a unique ID. This allows the replication commands and the configuration variables to refer to a particular master.

For example, we generally do not want to start or stop all the I/O threads, but only one of them.

Thus, all replication-related SQL statements support a parameter that specifies which connection they refer to. For example:

- CHANGE MASTER 'connection_name' TO ...
- START SLAVE 'connection_name1' 'connection_name2'
- STOP SLAVE 'connection_name1' 'connection_name2'
- RESET SLAVE 'connection_name'

Also, it is possible to start or stop all the slave I/O threads using the following syntax:

- START ALL SLAVES
- STOP ALL SLAVES

When the connection name is not specified in a command, and the ALL keyword is not present, the default connection is used. Initially, it is an empty string. It can be changed or read with the `@@default_master_connection` server variable:

```
MariaDB [(none)]> SELECT @@default_master_connection;
+-----------------------------+
| @@default_master_connection |
+-----------------------------+
|                             |
+-----------------------------+
1 row in set (0.00 sec)
```

Also the variables used for filtering connections, by default, refer to the default connection. The following syntax can be used to specify a filter for a certain connection:

```
connection_name.variable_name
```

For example, to only replicate db via the connection `master1` and all databases via other connections, we can use:

```
SET GLOBAL master1.replicate_do_db = '';
```

Replication logs

The master's binary logs and the slave's replication logs keep growing while the masters perform their normal activities and the slaves replicate their work. They need to be rotated and old files need to be deleted, to avoid running out of disk space. This section explains how to do this.

Rotating the binary log

The current binary log filename is determined by the `--log-bin` startup option. If an extension is specified, it is ignored and only the basename is used. By default, the binary log is written into the `data` directory. If the filename is not set, the default value is the hostname followed by the `-bin` suffix.

The `max_binlog_size` server variable determines the maximum size of the current file, in bytes. When this size is reached, the binary log rotates: the current file is renamed and a new file with the same name is created. The archive files have names that follow this pattern: `<basename>.<prog_id>` where `basename` is identical to the current file's basename and `prog_id` is a sequence number consisting of six digits. The first number is `000001`. There is also an index file whose name follows this pattern: `<basename>.index`. The name of the index file can be changed with `--log-bin-index`. The index file is human-readable and contains a list of the existing archived files, plus the current one. It should not be deleted or manually edited.

The binary log rotation also happens on server restart, and when one of the following commands is executed:

* `FLUSH LOGS`
* `FLUSH BINARY LOGS`

It is important to keep a certain number of archived binary log files. They can still be useful for incremental backups, as explained in *Chapter 8*, *Backup and Disaster Recovery*. They are still useful for replication: remember that slaves do not immediately receive events when they are written into the logs. They could lag behind, and they can possibly need to read files that have been generated days or months ago.

To retrieve the list of existing binary log files, SHOW BINARY LOGS can be used:

```
MariaDB [(none)]> SHOW BINARY LOGS;
+----------------+-----------+
| Log_name       | File_size |
+----------------+-----------+
| binlog.000040  |      3402 |
| binlog.000041  |       384 |
| binlog.000042  |       342 |
| binlog.000043  |       390 |
| binlog.000044  |      6516 |
| binlog.000045  |       342 |
| binlog.000046  |       737 |
| binlog.000047  |       932 |
| binlog.000048  |       940 |
| binlog.000049  |      2891 |
| binlog.000050  |      2410 |
| binlog.000051  |       359 |
+----------------+-----------+
12 rows in set (0.00 sec)
```

The @@expire_logs_days server variable, if its value is not 0, causes the old binary log files to be automatically deleted when their age reaches the specified number of days. Setting this value is dangerous, unless we are absolutely sure that no slave still needs files that reached this age. But, when determining a safe value, we should consider that a slave could crash and stay down for a file, or serious network problems could arise. Such issues could perceptibly delay the replication.

The old files can also be deleted on demand, using SQL statements. This method is much safer, but requires more work. For this reason, it is generally done by a script that is triggered via a cron job.

The procedure to delete the binary logfiles that are no longer needed is as follows:

1. Execute SHOW SLAVE STATUS.

2. A row is returned for each slave. The Master_Log_File column indicates which binary logfile the slave is reading. A script can do this by ordering these values alphabetically.

3. Suppose that the oldest file in use is called binlog-000050.
   To delete older files, we will use the following statement:
   PURGE BINARY LOGS TO 'binlog.000050';.

The PURGE BINARY LOGS statement can also be used to delete the files that only contain statements older than a given datetime. For example:

```
PURGE BINARY LOGS BEFORE '2014-04-01 0:0:0';
```

When a running standalone server must become a replication master, we should take a backup of the current data, so that we can load it into the slaves. Then, the binary log can be completely deleted, because we do not need to replicate again the event that occurred until this point. To do this, we can use RESET MASTER. This statement completely deletes all the binary logfiles, empties the binary logfiles index, and recreates an empty current file whose sequence number is 000001.

Rotating the relay log

The relay log is written to files following the same rules as the binary log. By default, the relay logfiles have names following the pattern: <hostname>-relay-bin.<prog_id> where hostname is the name of the slave host, and prog_id is a sequence number that has the same format as the one used by the binary log. A different name can be specified with the --relay-log startup option. There is an index file that has the same purpose and format as the binary log index file. Its default name follows this pattern: <hostname>-relay-bin.index and can be changed with --relay-log-index. Both files are located in the data directory, if no path is explicitly specified.

When the current file reaches its maximum size, MariaDB creates a new relay logfile. The maximum size is determined by the `max_relay_log_size` server variable. If this variable is set to `0`, the maximum size is the value of `max_binlog_size`, which cannot be set to `0`.

A new relay log file is also created each time the slave I/O thread starts. The following statements can be used to force a new file creation:

- `FLUSH RELAY LOGS`
- `FLUSH LOGS`

When the slave SQL thread executed the last events in a relay logfile, the file is automatically deleted, unless it is the current file. There is no way or need to affect this mechanism.

The slave status logs

The master log information is stored by default in a file called `master.info`, in the `data` directory. Its name and path can be changed using the `--master-info-file` startup option. The relay log info is stored by default in a file called `relay-log.info`, which is in the `data` directory too. Its default name and path can be overridden by the `--relay-log-info-file` startup option.

These files should contain the information that is shown when a SHOW SLAVE STATUS statement is executed. However, while the slave threads are running, the information in the files is likely to be outdated, because the replication status data is stored in memory. The files should always be up-to-date when the slave is not running.

These files do not grow and no rotation or special maintenance operation is needed.

Checking the replication for errors

Calculating checksums is the best way to be sure that a server and a slave contain exactly the same data as the server. This check can be used in two situations:

- After loading data into a slave, to be sure that everything worked properly
- On running servers, on a regular basis, or when we suspect that a replication error happened

The second case is more complicated, because during the normal execution slaves can lag behind their masters. However, a tool explained next is able to perform this check automatically, by waiting until slaves reach a certain binary log event.

There are at least three methods to do this:

- Using the CHECKSUM TABLE statement
- Using the Percona pt-table-checksum tool
- Calculating a checksum of the physical files (only for physical backups)

Sometimes we only want to check a relatively small subset of data. If so, instead of checking the whole tables, we can write a query that returns that data and calculate the MD5 checksum of the result set.

The CHECKSUM TABLE statement

This statement returns the checksums for one or more tables. It has the following syntax:

```
CHECKSUM TABLE <table_list> [ QUICK | EXTENDED ]
```

The QUICK option only takes effect with MyISAM and Aria tables. These storage engines calculate a live checksum for the tables that have been created with the CHECKSUM or TABLE_CHECKSUM option set to 1. With the QUICK option, CHECKSUM TABLE returns the live value.

The EXTENDED option calculates a checksum of the table by reading each individual row. This can be very slow.

If no option is specified, QUICK takes effect.

Some storage engines do not support this statement. In this case, NULL is returned.

If the checksum is 0, the table is empty. Consider the following example:

```
MariaDB [test]> CHECKSUM TABLE customers, orders, products;
+-----------------+------------+
| Table           | Checksum   |
+-----------------+------------+
| test.customers  |          0 |
| test.orders     | 2720624778 |
| test.products   | 3036305396 |
+-----------------+------------+
3 rows in set (0.00 sec)
```

The pt-table-checksum tool

Similar to other tools that we have already discussed, `pt-table-checksum` is included in the Percona Toolkit suite. Its purpose is to report a reliable checksum and the number of rows in each table. It does this without slowing down the server too much, even with big databases.

The `pt-table-checksum` tool calculates a checksum for each table. Tables are never read with a long-running locking query. The `pt-table-checksum` tool uses relatively small queries to divide tables in smaller subsets. Based on the server's response times, `pt-table-checksum` composes queries that are not too heavy for its current workload. Moreover, it sets `@@innodb_lock_wait` to 1 second at session level, so that it disconnects when a table is locked by another session for a long time.

By default, `pt-table-checksum` also detects running slaves and connects to them to execute the checksums. The tool periodically executes a `SHOW PROCESSLIST` statement to monitor the connected slaves. If some of them lag behind the master or disconnect, `pt-table-checksum` waits until they recover. For this reason, this tool is probably the best way to periodically check the data integrity of the running servers.

After calculating the checksum for one table, the tool connects to the slaves and calculates the same checksum to verify that the tables are identical. Then, it prints out the checksum and the number of rows. It does not begin another table's checksum until this work is finished.

While `pt-table-checksum` has good fault tolerance, it could sometimes stop because of an error it cannot handle. In this case, it is possible to restart it with the `--resume` option specified, so that the work it already did is not lost.

Files checksum

Calculating file checksums is a good way to check that the copy of a physical backup worked properly, before starting a slave. Linux systems usually include the `md5sum` command, which reports the checksum of one or more files. For example:

```
root@this:/usr/local/mysql/data/open_fatture# md5sum
--binary fornitori.frm fornitori.ibd

4582a1f51dea7980cb739b1a055d3ba7 *fornitori.frm

de8ffec76f0303d0c129a536e015e14d *fornitori.ibd
```

The `--binary` option informs `md5sum` that the specified files contain binary data by default, or if the `--text` option is specified. It treats the file contents as texts. This is only useful with CONNECT and CSV tables, and logfiles.

Query checksum

In some cases, we can write a query that only returns the recently inserted rows, and perhaps the ones that are modified recently. We can use such queries to quickly check that no error occurred while replicating recent data. To do this, we can use again the md5sum Linux program.

Here is an example:

```
root@this:/usr/local/mysql# bin/mysql -uroot -proot
--execute="SELECT * FROM gest_pescara.orders WHERE o_time
> NOW() - INTERVAL 2 DAY;" | md5sum

a50786099fb580c0dcb564323103bee2  -
```

Troubleshooting

This section provides some hints to solve the most common replication errors.

A slave does not start

When we execute START SLAVE, we do not receive any error if the slave cannot connect to a master. By executing SHOW SLAVE STATUS we will know what the I/O thread is doing.

If the replication does not start, or if it crashes, we will need to find out the reason and solve the problem. The following list of question can be used to find out the most common trivial problems:

- Is the slave version equal to or minor than the master version?
- Is the binary log enabled on the master?
- Are the server IDs unique?
- Is a variable name mistyped in the configuration file? Can the file be used to successfully start a standalone server?
- Are the master's address, port, and login credentials correctly configured in the slave?
- Is an account for the slave configured in the server?
- Does the account have the REPLICATION SLAVE permission?
- Is there a firewall that blocks the slave connections?
- Are the replication filters correctly set?
- Is the slave's disk full?

When a slave starts, it should not stop replicating unless it receives a STOP SLAVE statement. However, if the slave threads are not running, the slave probably encountered a replication error. Another possibility is that we hit a MariaDB bug—this is unlikely, but it is always possible. Anyway, we should start our investigation from the slave's error log. Then, using the mysqlbinlog utility against the latest relay log file, we should try to find out which statement caused the slave threads to crash.

A slave lags behind

Executing a SHOW BINARY LOGS statement on a master shows which binary log files currently exist. If there are too many files, at least one slave is lagging behind. It is impossible here to define "too many": the DBA knows how much delay he/she can tolerate, or even desires, but this strictly depends on the workload on the master servers.

If we determine that we have too many binary logfiles, we will want to find out which slaves are lagging behind. To do this, we can examine the output of SHOW SLAVE STATUS. We should look at the filenames shown in the Master_Log_File and Relay_Log_File columns.

The Master_Log_File column shows which binary logfile is being read by each slave's I/O thread. If a filename is too old, the I/O thread is lagging behind. This is not a common situation. Probably, the network is too slow for our workload. There could be a network problem that is worth being investigated. Anyway, using connection compression should solve the problem. We should also wonder whether we chose the best binary log format, because this factor affects the quantity of information that is sent through the network.

The Relay_Log_File column shows which relay logfile is being processed by the SQL file. Having an SQL thread which lags behind is a quite common situation. Before MariaDB 10.0, this problem was much harder to solve. Having only one thread that executed the same workload that the master spreads through several threads is less than ideal. MariaDB 10.0 parallel replication should help greatly.

If enabling parallel replication, the most common problem consists of poor query optimization. We should examine the master's slow query log and find the problems.

Summary

In this chapter, we discussed how the replication works in MariaDB.

Implementation details about the replication threads and logs have been provided. We discussed how to rotate the binary log. While this rotation is needed even on the server that does not make use of the replication, the DBA should normally make sure that no file is deleted even if at least one slave still needs it.

We learned how to set up a master, a slave, and a slave who also acts as a master. We learned how to load the initial data into a slave and into a new master. We also learned how to verify if the replication is working properly and some hints were provided to identify and solve the most common replication troubles.

In the next chapter we will discuss table partitioning.

10
Table Partitioning

When a table becomes too large, queries on that table become slow.

One possible solution is table partitioning. This technique involves splitting a table into several physical files or tablespaces. Each file contains a fraction of the table data and thus becomes faster to read. Both read and write access to individual partitions will be much faster.

In this chapter, we will discuss:

- Partitioning types supported by MariaDB
- Subpartitioning
- How to split each partition into multiple files
- Maintenance of partitioned tables
- How the optimizer takes advantage of partitioning

Support for partitioning

All versions of MariaDB support version partitioning. However, there are two cases where partitioning is not available for a MariaDB installation:

- If MariaDB has been compiled without support to partitioning — while all official distributions have this support, partitioning is not compiled by default. If we compile the server from sources, we should specify the `-DWITH_PARTITION_STORAGE_ENGINE` compile option.
- If MariaDB has been started with the partitioning disabled — the option to do this is `--skip-partition`. In this case, we will simply need to restart MariaDB without this option. Disabling partitioning is generally not considered a useful optimization.

Checking whether the MariaDB installation supports partitioning is simple. Since partitioning is implemented as a plugin, we will just need to query the PLUGINS table in the information_schema database:

```
MariaDB [(none)]> SELECT * FROM information_schema.PLUGINS
WHERE PLUGIN_NAME = 'partition'\G
*************************** 1. row ***************************
          PLUGIN_NAME: partition
       PLUGIN_VERSION: 1.0
        PLUGIN_STATUS: ACTIVE
          PLUGIN_TYPE: STORAGE ENGINE
  PLUGIN_TYPE_VERSION: 100010.0
       PLUGIN_LIBRARY: NULL
PLUGIN_LIBRARY_VERSION: NULL
        PLUGIN_AUTHOR: Mikael Ronstrom, MySQL AB
   PLUGIN_DESCRIPTION: Partition Storage Engine Helper
       PLUGIN_LICENSE: GPL
          LOAD_OPTION: ON
      PLUGIN_MATURITY: Stable
  PLUGIN_AUTH_VERSION: 1.0
1 row in set (0.00 sec)
```

This example shows the metadata as they appear if partitioning is supported. If the server has been compiled without partitioning, no row will be retrieved by the preceding query. If the server is compiled with the support to partitioning but is started without the support, the PLUGIN_STATUS column will be set to DISABLED.

Partitioning is implemented at the storage engine level, thus not all engines support it. Engines that support partitioning include:

- InnoDB
- TokuDB
- MEMORY
- Aria
- MyISAM
- Archive
- BLACKHOLE

For BLACKHOLE, support for partitioning consists of preserving the partition's definition. When a partitioned table is converted to BLACKHOLE, and then converted back to InnoDB, the table will still be partitioned. This feature is not obvious, because the same procedure does not preserve foreign keys, and it is not allowed at all for tables that have virtual columns.

CONNECT and FederatedX cannot be partitioned, but they can be linked to the remote tables that are partitioned.

When trying to create a partitioned table with a storage engine that does not support partitioning, the following error is produced:

```
ERROR 1572 (HY000): Engine cannot be used in partitioned tables
```

Partitioning types and expressions

The partitioning is based on a value that is calculated for each row using a **partitioning expression**. The **partitioning type** is a method that is used to assign each row to a particular partition based on the partitioning expression. For example, the RANGE type assigns a range of values to each partition. When a row is inserted, its partitioning expression is calculated. The row will be written into the partition that matches the proper range.

Partitioning expressions

A partitioning expression is a SQL expression that returns a positive integer value or NULL. It is possible to use a temporal column in the partitioned expression as long as an integer value is returned. However, the return value cannot depend on the current timezone, so the TIMESTAMP and YEAR columns are not allowed. Some partitioning types can use expressions that return other data of different data types, such as DATE or CHAR; this will be discussed later.

The partitioning expressions must also return a deterministic nonconstant value. Stored functions and user-defined functions are not allowed, even if they are deterministic.

The / operator is not allowed because it can return a FLOAT value, even if both operands are INTEGER. The DIV and MOD operators (integer division and division's rest) are supported. Bit operators are not supported.

A partitioning expression should be able to operate as fast as possible. Ideally, it should include only one column and, if necessary, the function that is needed to obtain an integer value. In practice, more columns and calculations are sometimes necessary. However, note that the performance of the expression affects inserts, updates, and deletes.

The following temporal functions are optimized to be used in a partitioning expression:

- `YEAR()`
- `TO_DAYS()`
- `TO_SECONDS()`

Other functions, such as `MONTH()`, are not optimized for this purpose but can still be good candidates.

To achieve good performance with the `HASH` partitioning type, only one column should be used in the expression. A strict relationship should also exist between the column values and the expression return values: a change in a column value should cause a change in the return value that is directly proportional.

Some examples of fast partitioning expressions are as follows:

```
id
id MOD 8
YEAR(date)
ORD(name)
```

In the following sections, we will see how to use partitioning expressions.

Indexes and primary keys

With partitioned tables, the primary keys and the unique keys are subject to an important limitation. Each unique key, including the primary key, must include all columns that are necessary to calculate the partitioning expression.

In practice, this often means the following:

- The primary key must include columns of the partitioning expression
- Only a limited number of unique keys are allowed

For example, suppose that we want to create a table that contains data about all the employees of a company. The nonpartitioned table would look like the following code:

```
CREATE TABLE employee (
  id INTEGER UNSIGNED NOT NULL AUTO_INCREMENT,
  first_name VARCHAR(50) NOT NULL,
  last_name VARCHAR(50) NOT NULL,
  email VARCHAR(200) NOT NULL,
  vat_id VARCHAR(15),
  hire_date DATE NOT NULL,
  PRIMARY KEY (id),
  UNIQUE unq_email (email),
  UNIQUE unq_vat (vat_id),
  INDEX idx_hire (hire_date)
)
  ENGINE = InnoDB;
```

Then, we want to partition the table. For some reason, although this is not important now, we want the proper partition of each row to be determined by YEAR(hire_date). However, we will need to modify the table in two ways:

- First, we need a primary key that includes hire_date because that column is used by the partitioning expression. However, hire_date is not sufficient as a primary key because its values are not unique: multiple employees can be hired the same day. So, our primary key definition will become: PRIMARY KEY (id, hire_date). Note that this key is now longer than the previously defined primary key. Since all indexes in an InnoDB table include the primary key, all indexes will be longer.

- In this table, a unique index may or may not be useful for queries but it is useful as a constraint because it forces the email and vat_id values to be unique. However, in partitioned tables, all unique keys must contain all columns used by the partitioned expression. You can do this in three ways. We can add hire_date to the unique indexes, but they would not guarantee the uniqueness of those fields anymore. You can add the unique columns to the expression, but then this will become much slower and will slow down inserts and updates. The most common solution is simply avoiding unique indexes, which is what we will do in our case.

With the KEY partitioning type, the primary key is mandatory. It is, however, possible to partition a table without a primary key using any other partitioning type. However, a table without keys will probably be slow. Foreign keys are not allowed for partitioned tables. There are no restrictions for normal non-unique indexes.

Partition names

Some partitioning types require that some properties be specified for each partition. With other partitioning types, we can merely declare how many partitions we want for a table. In the first case, we must specify a name for each partition; in the latter case, MariaDB automatically assigns names.

Automatic partition names consist of a p followed by a partition progressive number, that starts from 0. Even if there are more than 10 partitions, there is no leading 0. Partition names are case insensitive and have a maximum length of 61 characters, which is slightly less than other objects' identifiers.

When we must specify partition names, it is a common practice to use the same criteria used for automatic names. However, this also allows us to assign meaningful names in some cases. For example, if a table has one partition that contains recent data and many partitions that contain historical data, the partition that contains the most recent data can be named current. This technique also allows us to explicitly name a partition in our queries.

Partitioning types

In this section, we will describe the partitioning types, discuss how they work, and show how to create tables using the desired type.

The RANGE and LIST basic types are quite similar and support the same administrative operations. There are also slightly different types called RANGE COLUMNS and LIST COLUMNS.

The HASH and KEY types are quite similar too, and there are slightly different types than the HASH and KEY types called LINEAR HASH and LINEAR KEY.

The RANGE type

The RANGE partitioning type assigns a different range of values to each partition. For each range, we only specify a higher bound. The first range starts with NULL, which is the lowest possible value. The other ranges start with the value that immediately follows the higher bound of the previous partition.

Consider the following example:

```
CREATE TABLE article (
    id INTEGER UNSIGNED NOT NULL AUTO_INCREMENT,
    date DATE NOT NULL,
    author VARCHAR(100),
    language TINYINT UNSIGNED,
    text TEXT,
    PRIMARY KEY (id, date)
)
    ENGINE = InnoDB
PARTITION BY RANGE (YEAR(date)) (
    PARTITION p0 VALUES LESS THAN (1990),
    PARTITION p1 VALUES LESS THAN (2000),
    PARTITION p3 VALUES LESS THAN (2010),
    PARTITION current VALUES LESS THAN (2020)
);
```

The last partition holds values that are less than `2020`. This will not be a problem for some years (the current year is 2014), but some day it may be problem. If we try to insert a row for which the partitioning expression returns an out-of-range value, we will get an error like the following:

```
ERROR 1292 (22007): Incorrect date value: '2020' for column
'date' at row 1
```

The error can be suppressed with the `IGNORE` clause, but the row will not be inserted.

However, the following syntax can be used to allow partition values that are too high to be stored in the previous partitions:

```
PARTITION p_name VALUES LESS THAN (MAXVALUE)
```

The parenthesis here are optional.

In the preceding example, we have a table that contains articles. The table is very large and we want to partition it to process common queries faster. Since the table contains very old articles, `RANGE` seems like a good partitioning type to use for the following reasons:

- The `YEAR(date)` type is an efficient partitioning expression.
- Common queries will only involve one partition.

- Some historical queries may involve only one partition or only a set of partitions.

- In future, we may want to delete very old data. In that case, we can probably do it in an easy and efficient way by dropping the oldest partition.

The LIST type

The LIST partitioning type is quite similar to RANGE though LIST assigns to each partition a list of values rather than a range. Each partition must be assigned at least one value. The order of partitions is not relevant for the LIST type. All possible values must be explicitly names; there is no way to put all unmentioned values into a partition, which is similar to what is done with MAXVALUE for the RANGE type. When trying to insert a value that is not assigned to a partition, we get an error shown as follows:

```
Error (Code 1526): Table has no partition for value 100
```

The following example shows how to create a LIST partitioned table:

```
CREATE TABLE article (
  id INTEGER UNSIGNED NOT NULL AUTO_INCREMENT,
  date DATE NOT NULL,
  author VARCHAR(100),
  language TINYINT UNSIGNED,
  text TEXT,
  PRIMARY KEY (id, language)
)
  ENGINE = InnoDB
PARTITION BY LIST (language) (
  PARTITION p0 VALUES IN (1),
  PARTITION p1 VALUES IN (2, 3),
  PARTITION p2 VALUES IN (4, 5, 6, 7, 8, 9, 10, 11),
  PARTITION px VALUES IN (NULL)
);
```

In this example, language acts a foreign key to a table that stores information about languages (probably just an incremental ID and their name). The reason why the foreign key has not been declared is that foreign keys are not supported for partitioned tables.

Here, the partitioning expression is a simple column name. This works because `language` is an integer column that only contains positive values. Of course, a CHAR column could be used too, for example, to store the language's ISO code; however, in that case, the expression should translate its string value into a number.

Despite the `language` column being an integer, the values cannot be sorted as per logic, thus splitting them into ranges would make no sense. There are several reasons why creating a LIST partitioned table based on the language can be a good choice:

- Common queries probably show articles in the selected languages, thus partitioning by language allows such queries to use only one partition.

- There can be a query that finds the languages in which a given article is available. This query is likely to be very fast, so we do not care if it accesses all partitions.

- If a high proportion of content is available in a language, that language can be stored in a dedicated partition. Other partitions can group several languages where a limited portion of content is available.

- Depending on our audience, it is possible that at least two partitions are frequently read. This is very unlikely to happen if we partition the articles by date, like we did in the previous example. Thus, partitioning by language allows us to split the most accessed partitions into different disks. This technique is described later in the *Partitions' physical files* section.

- If the content in a language grows sensibly, it is easy to move that language into a new partition.

The COLUMNS keyword

The RANGE and LIST partitioning types have two variations called RANGE COLUMNS and LIST COLUMNS. When they are used, there is no single partitioning expression: the values are assigned to partitions based on a list of columns. This list is sometimes called a **partitioned columns list** in the documentation and in technical articles. No functions, operators, or any kind of elaboration is allowed to transform the columns values. However, for COLUMNS partitioning types, more data types are allowed:

- All integer types (but only positive values are allowed)
- The DATE and DATETIME data types
- The VARCHAR , CHAR, VARBINARY, and BINARY data types

This is very important because as the use of functions is not allowed, there is no way to convert a noninteger value into an integer.

Note that the example used for the LIST type could be a LIST COLUMNS type too because it only included a column name.

The RANGE COLUMNS type is primarily useful when the range of values need to be based on multiple columns to obtain a good distribution of values. The following example shows the syntax to be used:

```
CREATE TABLE article (
  id INTEGER UNSIGNED NOT NULL AUTO_INCREMENT,
  date DATE NOT NULL,
  year CHAR(4) NOT NULL,
  author VARCHAR(100),
  language TINYINT UNSIGNED,
  text TEXT,
  PRIMARY KEY (id, language, year)
)
  ENGINE = InnoDB
PARTITION BY RANGE COLUMNS (language, year) (
  -- old english articles
  PARTITION p0 VALUES LESS THAN (1, '2010'),
  -- recent english articles
  PARTITION p1 VALUES LESS THAN (1, '2020'),
  -- old non-english articles
  PARTITION p2 VALUES LESS THAN (100, '2010'),
  -- recent non-english articles
  PARTITION p3 VALUES LESS THAN (MAXVALUE, MAXVALUE)
);
```

This partitioning strategy reflects a very common situation:

- We have abundant content in English and much less in other languages. Thus, the most reasonable division seems to be English or non-English.
- Within these groups, we want to separate recent content from the non-recent ones.

Note that we cannot use YEAR(date), so we choose to duplicate the year information into a string column. With all characters being digits, the order will not change, provided that all values consist of four characters.

A limitation is also worthy to be noted — we can only use the MAVALUE keyword for the last partition. It would seem reasonable, for example, to assign the values (1, MAXVALUE) to the second partition, but this would be a syntax error.

The LIST COLUMNS type is useful to match a list of values against a noninteger column. Let's go back to the example used for the LIST type. We store languages in the form of integer values, but maybe it's preferable to store a two-character ISO code. While this is not possible with the LIST type, LIST COLUMNS allows us to do this:

```
CREATE TABLE article (
  id INTEGER UNSIGNED NOT NULL AUTO_INCREMENT,
  date DATE NOT NULL,
  author VARCHAR(100),
  language TINYINT UNSIGNED,
  text TEXT,
  PRIMARY KEY (id, language)
)
  ENGINE = InnoDB
PARTITION BY LIST (language) (
  PARTITION p0 VALUES IN ('en'),
  PARTITION p1 VALUES IN ('fr', 'de'),
  PARTITION p2 VALUES IN ('es', 'it', 'ir', 'is', 'nl', 'ru', 'ro', 'sr'),
  PARTITION px VALUES IN (NULL)
);
```

The HASH and KEY types

The HASH and KEY partitioning types are similar. Their purpose is to provide a more uniform row distribution among partitions. Each different value returned by the partitioning expression has equal probabilities to be assigned to each partition. A group of contiguous values will be assigned to different partitions. However, if the distribution of unique values has very high peaks (that is, a limited set of values occur very often), it is possible that some partitions will sensibly contain more data than others. The KEY and HASH types work better if the distribution of unique values is uniform.

With HASH and KEY, the target partition for new rows is determined automatically by the server. It uses the following formula:

```
target_partition = expression_result MOD number__of_partitions
```

In the previous syntax, MOD is the modulus operator that returns the rest of a division.

The choice between HASH and KEY depends on the partitioning function that we want to use. The difference between these types is similar to the difference between LIST and LIST COLUMNS, which makes it easier to remember.

- The HASH type accepts any partitioning function that returns a positive integer or NULL.

- The KEY type accepts a single column of any of the types allowed for LIST COLUMNS. No calculations are allowed on that column.

With the KEY type, a hash of the return value is calculated. The hash uses the PASSWORD() function, which uses a variation of an SHA algorithm.

Usually, the following syntax is used to create a table partitioned by HASH:

```
CREATE TABLE article (
    id INTEGER UNSIGNED NOT NULL AUTO_INCREMENT,
    date DATE NOT NULL,
    author VARCHAR(100),
    language TINYINT UNSIGNED,
    text TEXT,
    PRIMARY KEY (id, date)
)
    ENGINE = InnoDB
PARTITION BY HASH(YEAR(date))
PARTITIONS 8;
```

In fact, most of the time we only want to determine the partitioning expression and the number of partitions. In this case, we have chosen YEAR(date) as the partitioning expression so that all articles published in the same year will be in the same partition. This will allow most queries to access only one partition.

The following syntax is also allowed:

```
...
PARTITION BY HASH(MONTH(date)) (
    PARTITION p0,
    PARTITION p1
);
```

This allows us to specify a name for each partition. A path for each partition's files can also be specified, as explained later in this chapter in the *Partitions' physical files* section.

To create a table partitioned by KEY, use the following code:

```
CREATE TABLE article (
    id INTEGER UNSIGNED NOT NULL AUTO_INCREMENT,
    date DATE NOT NULL,
    author VARCHAR(100),
    language TINYINT UNSIGNED,
    text TEXT,
    PRIMARY KEY (id, date)
)
    ENGINE = InnoDB
PARTITION BY KEY(id)
PARTITIONS 8;
```

In this example, we partitioned the table with an AUTO_INCREMENT key, which will provide a distribution of the most uniform values.

Again, we can specify a name for each partition, like we did in the HASH example.

Otherwise, we can use an even more concise syntax. Since id is the primary key, it need not be explicitly named for KEY partitioning:

```
...
PARTITION BY KEY()
PARTITIONS 8;
```

The LINEAR keyword

The LINEAR HASH and LINEAR KEY partitioning types are identical to HASH and KEY, except that a much more complicated algorithm is used to select new rows to target partitions. The linear formula is less efficient for normal database operations, such as row reads and writes. However, it makes some administering operations much faster. If the performance of partition creation, drop, split, and merge are a problem, using the LINEAR keyword can be a solution.

Splitting into subpartitions

Main partitions can be split into multiple subpartitions. Only one subpartitioning level is supported, which means that subpartitions cannot be further split. Each partition must have the same number of subpartitions.

A table with subpartitions can only be partitioned by RANGE or LIST and subpartitioned by HASH or KEY. The COLUMNS and LINEAR keywords are allowed. Using any other combination of types produces the following error:

```
ERROR 1500 (HY000): It is only possible to mix RANGE/LIST partitioning
with HASH/KEY partitioning for subpartitioning
```

The syntax to create a subpartitioned table is as follows:

```
CREATE TABLE article (
  id INTEGER UNSIGNED NOT NULL AUTO_INCREMENT,
  date DATE NOT NULL,
  author VARCHAR(100),
  language TINYINT UNSIGNED,
  text TEXT,
  PRIMARY KEY (id, date)
)
  ENGINE = InnoDB
PARTITION BY RANGE COLUMNS (date)
SUBPARTITION BY LINEAR HASH (id) (
  PARTITION p0 VALUES LESS THAN ('2000-01-01') (
    SUBPARTITION s0,
    SUBPARTITION s1
  ),
  PARTITION p1 VALUES LESS THAN ('2020-01-01') (
    SUBPARTITION s2,
    SUBPARTITION s3
  )
);
```

Note that each subpartition must have a unique name within the table. Each partition can be stored in a different path, as explained in the *Partitions' physical files* section.

A concise syntax can also be used, if we do not need to specify names or paths for subpartitions:

```
...
PARTITION BY RANGE COLUMNS (date)
SUBPARTITION BY LINEAR KEY (id)
SUBPARTITIONS 2 (
  PARTITION p0 VALUES LESS THAN ('2000-01-01'),
  PARTITION p1 VALUES LESS THAN ('2020-01-01')
);
```

 Note that, in this case, the subpartitioning expression must be explicitly specified. The primary key is used by default for KEY partitions but not for subpartitions.

Administering partitioned tables

Partitions support the same maintenance operations that are supported for regular tables, such as repairing and defragmenting, plus other specific operations. MariaDB provides a set of SQL extensions that allow us to perform all necessary maintenance tasks. It also provides some system tables that store metadata about the partitions. This section covers these topics.

Obtaining information about partitions

MariaDB provides several ways to obtain information about partitions.

The output of SHOW TABLE STATUS and the Create_options column contains the partitioned string for partitioned tables.

The easiest way to get human-readable information about partitions' definitions is running SHOW CREATE TABLE.

The PARTITIONS table in the INFORMATION_SCHEMA database contains information about the partitions. Subpartitioned tables have a row for each subpartition; other tables have a row for each partition. Some columns are identical to the columns in the TABLES table. The most relevant columns are:

- PARTITION_METHOD: This column describes the partitioning type. This value is repeated for each partition in the same table.

- PARTITION_EXPRESSION: This column describes the partitioning expression. This value is repeated for each partition in the same table.

- PARTITION_NAME: This column describes the name of the partition.

- PARTITION_ORDINAL_POSITION: This column describes the position of the subpartition, starting from 1.

- SUBPARTITION_METHOD, SUBPARTITION_EXPRESSION, SUBPARTITION_NAME, and SUBPARTITION_ORDINAL_POSITION: These columns are the same as the previous columns, but they refer to subpartitions, not partitions.

Consider the following query as an example:

```
MariaDB [information_schema]> SELECT
    -> CONCAT(PARTITION_NAME, '.', SUBPARTITION_NAME) AS
SUBPARTITION_NAME,
    -> SUBPARTITION_ORDINAL_POSITION
    -> FROM information_schema.PARTITIONS
    -> WHERE TABLE_SCHEMA = 'test' AND TABLE_NAME = 'article';
+------------------+------------------------------+
| SUBPARTITION_NAME | SUBPARTITION_ORDINAL_POSITION |
+------------------+------------------------------+
| p0.p0sp0         |                            1 |
| p0.p0sp1         |                            2 |
| p1.p1sp0         |                            1 |
| p1.p1sp1         |                            2 |
+------------------+------------------------------+
4 rows in set (0.00 sec)
```

If an InnoDB-partitioned table has been created with the @@innodb_file_per_table variable ON, each partition or subpartition is written into a different tablespace. This means that its partitions or subpartitions are visible in the INNODB_SYS_TABLESPACES table in the information_schema database.

The only difference for partitioned tables' tablespaces is the name format, shown as follows:

```
<db>/<table>#P#<part_name>
<db>/<table>#P#<part_name>#SP#<part_name><subpart_name>
```

Consider the following query as an example:

```
MariaDB [information_schema]> SELECT *
    -> FROM information_schema.INNODB_SYS_TABLESPACES
    -> WHERE NAME LIKE 'test/article#P#p1#%' \G
*************************** 1. row ***************************
        SPACE: 748
         NAME: test/article#P#p1#SP#p1sp0
         FLAG: 0
  FILE_FORMAT: Antelope
   ROW_FORMAT: Compact or Redundant
    PAGE_SIZE: 16384
ZIP_PAGE_SIZE: 0
*************************** 2. row ***************************
        SPACE: 749
         NAME: test/article#P#p1#SP#p1sp1
         FLAG: 0
  FILE_FORMAT: Antelope
   ROW_FORMAT: Compact or Redundant
    PAGE_SIZE: 16384
ZIP_PAGE_SIZE: 0
2 rows in set (0.00 sec)
```

Changing partitions' definitions

MariaDB supports several ALTER TABLE commands that allow us to create, drop, or modify partitions. The RANGE and LIST partitioning types allow a richer set of commands, with a series of caveats that the DBA should be aware of. The HASH and KEY types support a more limited set of commands. For this reason, the statements for the different partitioning types will be discussed in two different subsections.

Modifying RANGE and LIST partitions

For the examples in this section, we will use the `article` table partitioned in this way:

```
CREATE TABLE article (
  id INTEGER UNSIGNED NOT NULL AUTO_INCREMENT,
  date DATE NOT NULL,
  author VARCHAR(100),
  language TINYINT UNSIGNED,
  text TEXT,
  PRIMARY KEY (id, date)
)
  ENGINE = InnoDB
PARTITION BY RANGE (YEAR(date)) (
  PARTITION p0 VALUES LESS THAN (1990),
  PARTITION p1 VALUES LESS THAN (2000),
  PARTITION p3 VALUES LESS THAN (2010),
  PARTITION p4 VALUES LESS THAN (2020)
);
```

With RANGE and LIST partitioning types, four operations are supported to modify the partitions:

- Dropping a partition
- Adding a new partition
- Reorganizing one or more partitions
- Removing all partitions

Dropping an existing RANGE or LIST partition deletes all the records contained in that partition. For example, if we want to drop the partition p0, all articles published before 1990 will be lost. The following is the syntax to do this:

```
ALTER TABLE article DROP PARTITION p0;
```

New partitions can be added with a simple statement. However, there is a limitation in this operation: the new partition can only contain values that are not stored in any other partition. With the RANGE type, this means that the new partition can only be added to the end. Of course, this can only be done if the last partition does not catch all VALUES LESS THAN MAXVALUE to avoid ranges intersection. Here is an example:

```
ALTER TABLE article ADD PARTITION (
  PARTITION p5 VALUES LESS THAN (2030)
);
```

The DROP PARTITION and ADD PARTITION clauses support the IF EXISTS and IF NOT EXISTS options. With this option, a note (instead of an error) will be produced if you try to drop a partition that does not exist, or add an existing partition. These options exist for many MariaDB statements and make installation or update scripts more robust and easy to write. The following example shows what happens when trying to drop a nonexisting partition:

```
MariaDB [test]> ALTER TABLE article DROP PARTITION p0;
ERROR 1507 (HY000): Error in list of partitions to DROP
MariaDB [test]> ALTER TABLE article DROP PARTITION IF EXISTS p0;
Query OK, 0 rows affected, 1 warning (0.00 sec)
Records: 0  Duplicates: 0  Warnings: 1
Note (Code 1507): Error in list of partitions to DROP
```

The REORGANIZE command allows us to split partitions or rename them. It replaces one or more partition with one or more new partitions defined in the command. Its stronger limitation is that it cannot modify the partitions' ranges, except for the last one, whose range can be extended. This makes complex merge and split operations impossible, such as splitting two partitions into three or merging two partitions into one.

In the following example, p1 is split again into the two original partitions:

```
ALTER TABLE article REORGANIZE PARTITION p1 INTO (
  PARTITION p0 VALUES LESS THAN (1990),
  PARTITION p1 VALUES LESS THAN (2000)
);
```

If we want to merge them again, we can use REORGANIZE to avoid data loss:

```
ALTER TABLE article REORGANIZE PARTITION p0, p1 INTO (
  PARTITION p1 VALUES LESS THAN (2000)
);
```

Let's rename p4 into the current one:

```
ALTER TABLE article REORGANIZE PARTITION p4 INTO (
  PARTITION current VALUES LESS THAN (2020)
);
```

To remove a table partitioning without losing its data, use the following:

```
ALTER TABLE article REMOVE PARTITIONING;
```

Normally, it is not desirable to remove a table partitioning. However, this can be done to bring the table to an intermediate state which allows us to change its partitioning type or its partitioning expression, or to perform a complex reorganization that cannot be accomplished using REORGANIZE PARTITION.

Modifying HASH and KEY partitions

In this section, we will use the article table partitioned by HASH:

```
CREATE TABLE article (
  id INTEGER UNSIGNED NOT NULL AUTO_INCREMENT,
  date DATE NOT NULL,
  author VARCHAR(100),
  language TINYINT UNSIGNED,
  text TEXT,
  PRIMARY KEY (id, date)
)
  ENGINE = InnoDB
PARTITION BY HASH(YEAR(date))
PARTITIONS 8;
```

The following operations are allowed for tables partitioned by HASH or KEY:

- Add partitions
- Merge existing partitions
- Changing partition properties
- Remove partitioning

In the *Modifying RANGE and LIST partitions* section, we already discussed how and why we can remove partitioning and this topic will not be repeated.

Adding a partition is simple. The syntax is the same that we used for a partitioned table of the RANGE type. Given the nature of HASH and KEY partitioning types, they do not impose any restrictions to the creation of new partitions. In the following example, we will add two partitions:

```
ALTER TABLE article ADD PARTITION PARTITIONS 2;
```

The extended syntax is also allowed:

```
ALTER TABLE article ADD PARTITION (
    PARTITION p8,
    PARTITION p9
);
```

This syntax can be used to specify nondefault names or paths for the new partitions. See the *Partitions' physical files* section for details on how to distribute partitions over multiple disks.

The HASH and KEY types do not support the DROP operation: because of their nature, it is never desirable to destroy a partition and all its data. However, it is possible to use COALESCE to merge one or more partitions to others. The data will not be lost; instead, they will be copied to other partitions. This operation is relatively fast. The following example shows how to eliminate two partitions from the article table:

```
ALTER TABLE article COALESCE PARTITION 2;
```

Note that the value after COALESCE PARTITION is the number of the partition that will disappear, not the number of partitions that we want to remain after the statement execution.

For these partitioning types, the REORGANIZE command can only be used to rename a partition or change its options. The following example shows how to rename a partition:

```
ALTER TABLE article REORGANIZE PARTITION p0 INTO (
    PARTITION p000
);
```

Copying data between a partition and a table

The techniques described here work with all partitioning types though they are hardly useful with partitioned tables of the HASH and KEY types. The reason is that, when using these types, logical sets of rows are distributed over all the partitions.

However, the RANGE and LIST types allow us to divide data into groups that are assigned to a particular partition based on one or more values. Usually, the partitioning expression is simple, also for performance reasons. This allows a human being to easily find out which partition, or group of partitions, stores a set of rows.

MariaDB 10.0 supports an ALTER TABLE clause that allows us to exchange the data stored in a partition with the data stored in a nonpartitioned table.

It is important to remember that the copy is bidirectional. If we only want to copy a table's contents into a partition, we may want to TRUNCATE the partition first. If we want to copy the partition's contents into a table, we will probably need to TRUNCATE the table. In both cases, the original container of the data will be emptied.

Now, suppose we have the article table defined with the following RANGE partitions:

```
CREATE TABLE article (
  id INTEGER UNSIGNED NOT NULL AUTO_INCREMENT,
  date DATE NOT NULL,
  author VARCHAR(100),
  language TINYINT UNSIGNED,
  text TEXT,
  PRIMARY KEY (id, date)
)
  ENGINE = InnoDB
PARTITION BY RANGE (YEAR(date)) (
  PARTITION p0 VALUES LESS THAN (1990),
  PARTITION p1 VALUES LESS THAN (2000),
  PARTITION p3 VALUES LESS THAN (2010),
  PARTITION current VALUES LESS THAN (2020)
);
```

In the following example, we want to move the rows from the current partition to a new table called recent_article. To do this, we need to create the new table whose definition is identical to the definition of this article, except that recent_article must not be partitioned. The easiest way to do this is to copy the table structure and then remove the partitioning from the new table. Then, we can exchange the data, which is shown as follows:

```
MariaDB [test]> CREATE TABLE recent_article LIKE article;
Query OK, 0 rows affected (1.79 sec)
MariaDB [test]> ALTER TABLE recent_article REMOVE PARTITIONING;
Query OK, 0 rows affected (1.51 sec)
Records: 0  Duplicates: 0  Warnings: 0
MariaDB [test]> ALTER TABLE article
    -> EXCHANGE PARTITION current
    -> WITH TABLE recent_article;
Query OK, 0 rows affected (0.44 sec)
```

If we don't want to empty the original row's container, or the version of our MariaDB server is older than 10.0, we can use the well-known SELECT ... INSERT or CREATE TABLE ... SELECT statements. If we want to use it to exchange data on an old MariaDB version, we will need to create a temporary table.

When copying data from a partition on MariaDB 10.0, we can use a particular SELECT extension that only returns data from the specified partitions. This extension will be explained later in this chapter, in the *Query optimizations* section. However, it is intuitive enough to show its use in data copying in this section. The following example shows how to copy the content of the current partition into the recent_article table, without deleting the original rows:

```
MariaDB [test]> CREATE OR REPLACE TABLE recent_article
    -> SELECT * FROM article PARTITION (current);
Query OK, 0 rows affected (0.59 sec)
Records: 0  Duplicates: 0  Warnings: 0
```

Maintenance operations statements

The SQL statements that are used to perform maintenance operations on a normal table also work with partitioned tables. Some ALTER TABLE clauses can be used to perform the same operations on one or more partitions, not necessarily the entire table.

The following table shows the maintenance operations and the corresponding ALTER TABLE clauses:

Table statement	ALTER TABLE clause
ALTER TABLE ... FORCE	REBUILD PARTITION list
OPTIMIZE TABLE	OPTIMIZE PARTITION list
ANALYZE TABLE	ANALYZE PARTITION list
CHECK TABLE	CHECK PARTITION list
REPAIR TABLE	REPAIR PARTITION list
TRUNCATE [TABLE]	TRUNCATE PARTITION list

The list clause is a list of one or more partitions that must be involved in the operation. The ALL keyword can be used to execute the operation on all partitions.

For example, if the `article` table has three partitions called p0, p1, and p2, the following statements are equivalent:

- The `ANALYZE TABLE` article
- The `ALTER TABLE` article with `ANALYZE PARTITION p0, p1, p2;`
- The `ALTER TABLE` article with `ANALYZE PARTITION ALL;`

The following statement will analyze only one partition:

```
ALTER TABLE article ANALYZE PARTITION p0;
```

None of these operations can be executed on individual subpartitions.

For `CHECKSUM TABLE`, there is no corresponding `ALTER TABLE` clause. However, the statement works on partitioned tables.

Partitions' physical files

If `@@innodb_file_per_table` is set to `OFF` when the table is partitioned, all partitions are stored in the InnoDB system tablespace, but in different areas. If this variable is set to `1`, each partition is stored in a different file.

Storage engines that store data and indexes in separate files, such as Aria and MyISAM, create a `data` file and an `index` file for each partition.

The extension of partition `data` or `index` files is the same that is used for unpartitioned tables. The basename of the files is the name of the table, plus `#P#`, plus the name of the partition. So, the name pattern is as follows:

```
<table_name>#P#<partition_name>.<extension>
```

Like all tables, partitioned tables have a `.frm` file that contains the table definition. They also have a file with partitions' definitions, which has a `.par` extension.

For example, let's suppose we have an InnoDB table called `employee`, with two partitions called p0 and p1. We will have the following files:

```
employee.frm
employee.par
employee#P#p0.ibd
employee#P#p1.ibd
```

If it is an Aria table, we will have the following files:

```
employee.frm
employee.par
employee#P#p0.MAD
employee#P#p0.MAI
employee#P#p1.MAD
employee#P#p1.MAI
```

For subpartitioned tables, each subpartition has a separate file. The basename of these files is the name of the table, plus the partition suffix, plus a subpartition suffix. For example, let the previous InnoDB `employee` table have two subpartitions per partition, called `s0`, `s1`, `s2`, and `s3`. We will see the following files:

```
employee.frm
employee.par
employee#P#p0#SP#s0.ibd
employee#P#p0#SP#s1.ibd
employee#P#p1#SP#s2.ibd
employee#P#p1#SP#s3.ibd
```

When setting the value of `@@table_open_cache` (explained in *Chapter 6, Caches*), we must remember that each partition will require a separate file handle.

By default, partitions' files are stored in the database path in the `data` directory. It is possible to specify a path for each partition's `data` file and `index` file. By doing so, we can distribute the partitions through several disks, reducing the overhead of disks input and output. This feature is very useful, and it generally is the main reason why we may want to use partitioning. The syntax to do this is the following:

```
CREATE TABLE employee (
  id INTEGER UNSIGNED NOT NULL AUTO_INCREMENT PRIMARY KEY
)
ENGINE = InnoDB
PARTITION BY RANGE (id) (
    PARTITION p0 VALUES LESS THAN (10000)
  DATA DIRECTORY '/disk_x',
    PARTITION p1 VALUES LESS THAN MAXVALUE
);
```

In this example, a `database` directory will be created on `disk_x` if it does not exist, and it will contain the `data` file for partition `p0`. Even if all partitions are stored on nonstandard paths, the `data` directory will still contain the `.par` file.

 Specifying `DATA DIRECTORY` and `INDEX DIRECTORY` at table level has no effect if the table is partitioned. However, they are silently ignored and no warning is issued.

Query optimizations

If the partitioning expression and the partition type have been carefully selected, most queries will only involve one partition or a set of partitions.

In many cases, the optimizer will find out which partitions are not relevant for the current query. This optimization is called **partition pruning**.

Also, the user can use a SQL clause to specify the list of partitions that must be used. This is called **partition selecting**.

 However, in MariaDB, queries are never parallelized. Even if the optimizer knows that two partitions must be read, and those partitions are on different disks, the same thread will read them sequentially. In particular, one can expect full table scans and full index scans on partitioned tables to run much faster because of parallelization, but this is not the case.

Partition pruning

In MariaDB, partition pruning is possible with `RANGE` and `LIST` partitioning, but not with `RANGE COLUMNS` or `LIST COLUMNS`. When a statement references the columns used by the partitioning expression, the optimizer is usually able to determine whether one or more partitions can be excluded by the query plan. Often, it can exclude all partitions but one. In some cases, it can even detect an `Impossible WHERE` and avoid executing the query at all.

The optimizer examines the `WHERE` clause in the following statements to determine whether partition pruning can be applied:

- `SELECT`
- `INSERT ... SELECT`
- `REPLACE ... SELECT`

- DELETE
- UPDATE

For the INSERT statements, the optimizer examines the inserted values. For the REPLACE statements, both the WHERE clause and the new values are examined.

When the optimizer analyzes a WHERE clause, it can use the following operators for pruning:

- =
- !=
- <
- >
- <=
- >=
- BETWEEN
- IN

If a partition only contains rows for which the partitioning expression returns NULL values, IS NULL and IS NOT NULL can also be used for pruning.

To obtain a statement execution plan, the EXPLAIN command can be used. We discussed this in *Chapter 3, Optimizing Queries*. Now that we are dealing with partition, we need to use an EXPLAIN extension: the PARTITIONS option. It adds the partitions' columns to the output of EXPLAIN. This column contains a list of the partitions that will be used to execute the statement. This extension has been specifically added to check whether and how partition pruning is applied. We will use it in the following examples.

For the following examples, we will use the article table, with a RANGE partitioning based on the column ID:

```
CREATE TABLE article (
  id INTEGER UNSIGNED NOT NULL AUTO_INCREMENT,
  date DATE NOT NULL,
  author VARCHAR(100),
  language TINYINT UNSIGNED,
  text TEXT,
  PRIMARY KEY (id, date)
)
  ENGINE = InnoDB
```

```
PARTITION BY RANGE (id) (
  PARTITION p0 VALUES LESS THAN (5000),
  PARTITION p1 VALUES LESS THAN (10000),
  PARTITION p2 VALUES LESS THAN (15000),
  PARTITION p3 VALUES LESS THAN (20000)
);
```

Queries that contain a WHERE condition based on the ID column are very likely to take advantage of partition pruning. Consider the following example:

```
MariaDB [test]> EXPLAIN PARTITIONS
    -> SELECT *  FROM article WHERE id > 5000 \G
*************************** 1. row ***************************
           id: 1
  select_type: SIMPLE
        table: article
   partitions: p1,p2,p3
...
1 row in set (0.00 sec)
```

Only the relevant columns are shown here. Since the first partition only contains VALUES LESS THAN (5000), the optimizer understands that it cannot contain any relevant row. Thus, p0 is not accessed, which is shown as follows:

```
MariaDB [test]> EXPLAIN PARTITIONS
    -> SELECT *  FROM article WHERE id BETWEEN 8000 AND 13000 \G
*************************** 1. row ***************************
           id: 1
  select_type: SIMPLE
        table: article
   partitions: p1,p2
...
1 row in set (0.00 sec)
```

This technique works perfectly with a range of values that are spread over multiple partitions, as shown in this example where p0 and p4 are not accessed:

```
MariaDB [test]> EXPLAIN PARTITIONS
    -> SELECT *  FROM article WHERE id = 11000 \G
*************************** 1. row ***************************
```

```
            id: 1
   select_type: SIMPLE
         table: article
    partitions: p2
...
1 row in set (0.00 sec)
```

Queries that retrieve a single row, or at least search for a single value, should always be able to only access one partition. For common cases, this is the best case, shown as follows:

```
MariaDB [test]> EXPLAIN PARTITIONS
    -> SELECT * FROM article WHERE id = 9999999 \G
*************************** 1. row ***************************
            id: 1
   select_type: SIMPLE
         table: NULL
    partitions: NULL
...
         Extra: Impossible WHERE noticed after reading const tables
1 row in set (0.00 sec)
```

In this case, no partition can contain the value we are looking for. As clearly stated in the Extra column, an impossible WHERE was detected after examining the partitions' definitions. Thus, the query is not executed at all, which is shown as follows:

```
MariaDB [test]> EXPLAIN PARTITIONS
    -> SELECT *  FROM article WHERE id = 18000 OR id < 10000 \G
*************************** 1. row ***************************
            id: 1
   select_type: SIMPLE
         table: article
    partitions: p0,p1,p3
...
1 row in set (0.00 sec)
```

This example merely shows that partition pruning also works when more value ranges are queried, even if different operators are used.

We will try some queries on `LIST` partitioned tables too, just to demonstrate that partition pruning works with this partitioning type. The table definition we will use is the following:

```
CREATE TABLE article (
  id INTEGER UNSIGNED NOT NULL AUTO_INCREMENT,
  date DATE NOT NULL,
  author VARCHAR(100),
  language TINYINT UNSIGNED,
  text TEXT,
  PRIMARY KEY (id, language)
)
  ENGINE = InnoDB
PARTITION BY LIST (language) (
  PARTITION pn VALUES IN (NULL),
  PARTITION p0 VALUES IN (1),
  PARTITION p1 VALUES IN (2,3),
  PARTITION p2 VALUES IN (4,5,6,7),
  PARTITION p3 VALUES IN (8,9,10,11)
);
```

Now, let's try some queries, shown as follows:

```
MariaDB [test]> EXPLAIN PARTITIONS
    -> SELECT *  FROM article WHERE language = 1 \G
*************************** 1. row ***************************
          id: 1
  select_type: SIMPLE
        table: article
   partitions: p0

...

1 row in set (0.00 sec)
```

Only the first query contains the value `1`, and the optimizer prunes other partitions away:

```
MariaDB [test]> EXPLAIN PARTITIONS
    -> SELECT *  FROM article WHERE language IN (1, 10) \G
*************************** 1. row ***************************
```

```
          id: 1
  select_type: SIMPLE
        table: article
   partitions: p0,p3
...
1 row in set (0.00 sec)
```

This time we queried the table for noncontiguous values that cannot be stored on contiguous partitions, shown as follows:

```
MariaDB [test]> EXPLAIN PARTITIONS
    -> SELECT *  FROM article WHERE language BETWEEN 2 AND 5 \G
*************************** 1. row ***************************
          id: 1
  select_type: SIMPLE
        table: article
   partitions: p1,p2
...
1 row in set (0.00 sec)
```

Looking for a range of values across multiple partitions also works as expected.

Partition selection

With partition pruning, the optimizer automatically determines which partitions must be accessed to execute a statement. MariaDB 10.0 also provides a way for the user to explicitly declare which partitions must be involved in the query: the PARTITION clause.

This clause can be specified after any table name, in any of the following SQL statements:

```
SELECT, including JOIN and UNION queries;
CREATE TABLE ... SELECT;
INSERT ... SELECT;
INSERT;
UPDATE;
DELETE;
REPLACE;
LOAD DATA INFILE;
LOAD XML INFILE;
```

The syntax of the `PARTITION` clause is the following:

```
<table_name> PARTITION (<partition_list>)
```

The `partition_list` variable is a list of one or more partitions, separated by a comma. Subpartitions can also be included in the list, concatenating their name with their main partition's name.

For example, if we have a tab table, the following statement returns all rows from the partition `p0`, and the `s3` subpartition in the partition `p1`:

```
SELECT * FROM tab PARTITION (p0, p1s3);
```

If any of the specified partitions or subpartitions do not exist, the whole statement fails with an error similar to the following:

```
ERROR 1735 (HY000): Unknown partition <partition_name> in table
<table_name>
```

By contrast, existing partitions can be named more than once in any order, and the subpartitions can be named even if their main partition is included in the list.

Since partition pruning is automatic and it was implemented in MariaDB even before partition selection, this feature can seem useless at first glance. However, it can be useful in several ways. For example:

- It works with any partitioning expression.
- It works with all partitioning types.
- It allows us to specify subpartitions that cannot be automatically pruned.
- It can be used in rare situations where the optimizer does not apply an optimal partition pruning, perhaps because of a bug.
- For complex queries, it can slightly speed up the optimizer.
- It can be less verbose than the corresponding `WHERE` clause.
- Statements that destroy or modify existing data, such as `DELETE` and `UPDATE`, can cause a data loss if the `WHERE` clause is not correct. An additional `PARTITION` clause can reduce the risks when similar damages occur.
- Similarly, a `PARTITION` clause can be added to statements that add a huge amount of data to prevent the writing of incorrect values. This technique causes the whole bulk insertion to fail if at least one row does not fit one of the specified partitions. The `IGNORE` clause does not affect this behavior.
- It allows us to quickly query one partition or subpartition at a time to analyze the overall data distribution.

Summary

In this chapter, we learned how to use partitioning to optimize very big tables.

We learned which partitioning types are supported by MariaDB and how to write a good partitioning expression. We examined a sample table and learned how we can benefit from different partitioning strategies. We discussed subpartitioning. We learned the SQL statements that can be used to maintain partitions. Finally, we discussed how the optimizer excludes the irrelevant partitions from a statement execution, and how the use can force the exclusive use of some partitions.

In the next chapter, we will discuss how to distribute data across multiple servers.

11
Data Sharding

In this chapter, we will discuss three important forms of data sharding provided by MariaDB:

- Balancing the I/O over multiple storage devices
- Implementing a simple cluster using `FEDERATEDX` or `CONNECT`
- The `SPIDER` storage engine

Distributing files between multiple disks

The bottleneck of a database server is usually the I/O. Reading or modifying data that is not stored in the memory implies accessing a storage device. Of course, buying fast disks will speed up the I/O operations, and using SSD devices could be further optimization. However, any existing storage device is just too slow to satisfy a high number of accesses per second. The main way to diminish this problem is to properly configure the caches, as described in *Chapter 6, Caches*. However, the set of data that is often accessed might be too large for the RAM to contain it entirely. Also, the logs probably need to be written frequently. A good configuration can mitigate this problem, but database reliability always requires data to be written to disks.

Also, the capacity of the storage devices is limited. A big database cannot be entirely contained in one device. This section describes how to distribute physical files over multiple storage devices.

Determining the path of table files

When a table is created, its files are placed in the `data` directory of the server by default. Its path is determined by the `@@datadir` server variable, which is not dynamic and thus, can only be set in the options files or via the `--datadir` startup option.

It is possible to specify different paths for a table's `data` and `index` files using the `DATA DIRECTORY` and `INDEX DIRECTORY` table options. Specifying only `DATA DIRECTORY` does not affect the path of the `index` file.

If a specified path does not exist, an error is produced and the table is not created.

For storage engines that do not use a separate file for indexes, such as InnoDB, specifying `INDEX DIRECTORY` generates a warning shown as follows:

```
Warning (Code 1030): Got error 140 "Wrong create options" from storage
engine InnoDB
```

Consider the following example:

```
CREATE TABLE chars (
  ch CHAR(1)
)
  ENGINE = MyISAM,
  DATA DIRECTORY = '/tmp',
  INDEX DIRECTORY = '/tmp';
```

The `DATA DIRECTORY` and `INDEX DIRECTORY` table options can only be specified on table creation. If we try to change them with an `ALTER TABLE` statement, we obtain a warning:

```
MariaDB [test]> ALTER TABLE chars DATA DIRECTORY = '/any/other/path';
Query OK, 0 rows affected, 1 warning (0.13 sec)
Records: 0  Duplicates: 0  Warnings: 1
Warning (Code 1618): <DATA DIRECTORY> option ignored
```

For partitioned tables, the `DATA DIRECTORY` and `INDEX DIRECTORY` options can be set for individual partitions. This technique has been discussed in *Chapter 10, Table Partitioning*.

InnoDB can have a separate `data` directory. It can be specified in the `@@innodb_data_home_dir` variable, in the configuration file. By default, the `data` directory of MariaDB is also used by InnoDB.

As explained in *Chapter 7, InnoDB Compressed Tables*, InnoDB has a file-per-table mode. It is enabled if the `@@innodb_file_per_table` variable is set to `ON`, which is the default value in MariaDB 10.0 but not in older versions. If the file-per-table mode is `ON`, any table can be created with the `DATA DIRECTORY` option. If it is `OFF`, all tables are created in the system tablespace, and thus this option does not make sense. The system tablespace is stored in the `data` directory of InnoDB. Storing the system tablespace on a rotating disk and the separate tablespaces on SSD devices is good practice.

By default, the `data` directory also contains the server logs. These logs have been discussed in *Chapter 2*, *Debugging* and *Chapter 3*, *Optimizing Queries*, while *Chapter 8*, *Backup and Disaster Recovery* summarizes the logs that exist and how to change their path.

InnoDB logfiles

InnoDB keeps two special logs to implement transactions:

- The undo log
- The redo log

The undo log is used to rollback transactions if they fail, or in case they remain incomplete. The changes to data are always made to the data itself (in the cache or on the disk), not on separate copies. Thus, in case a transaction rolls back, the data that it modified must return to its previous state. The undo log contains a copy of the original data and the information that is necessary to restore it.

As explained in *Chapter 6*, *Caches*, all modifications are usually written to the buffer pool. Pages that are modified in-memory are called **dirty** pages. At some point, they need to be flushed to the disk in order to make the changes persistent. However, before they are flushed, a disaster might occur, for example, a MariaDB crash, a system crash, or a power failure. InnoDB must protect the data from similar accidents. To do so, it temporarily writes the modifications into the redo log on the disk. If a disaster occurs, when MariaDB is restarted, InnoDB will replay all the transactions that are recorded in the redo log.

These logs must be written regularly on a storage device. Also, long-running transactions lead to large transaction logs. For these reasons, it is sometimes a good idea to store them on separate devices.

Both these logs cause many nonsequential writes, thus they perform better when stored on SSD devices.

Configuring the undo log

By default, the undo log is written into the system tablespace, in the InnoDB `data` directory. To store it in a different path, perhaps on a different storage device, the following variables must be set:

- `@@innodb_undo_directory`: This variable determines where the undo log files are created.

- `@@innodb_undo_tablespaces`: This variable represents the number of tablespaces (files) in which the undo log is written. If its value is `0`, the default, the undo log is written in the system tablespace. In all other cases, the undo log files are written in the path specified with `@@innodb_undo_directory`. The maximum value is `126`.

Both the preceding variables are not dynamic, and must be set in the configuration files or via the `--innodb_undo_directory` and `--innodb_undo_tablespaces` startup options.

For performance reasons, we may also want to set `@@innodb_undo_logs`, which is a dynamic variable. If the `performance_schema` table regularly shows a mutex on the undo log, increasing the number of segments per log file is probably a good idea. The maximum value is `128`.

 Be aware that the number of undo log files never decreases while the server is running. This value should not be increased, unless we are sure that it is necessary to reduce the mutex contention. Testing new values on the development server before using them in production is good practice.

Configuring the redo log

The storage of redo log files is affected by the following variables:

- `@@innodb_log_group_log_dir`: This is the path where the files are stored
- `@@innodb_log_files_in_group`: This is the number of redo log files
- `@@innodb_log_file_size`: This is the size of each individual file

These variables are not dynamic.

The redo log files have names starting with `ib_logfile` followed by a progressive number, starting from `0`. InnoDB starts populating the first file until it reaches its maximum size. When the last file reaches the size limit, InnoDB reuses the first file. The total maximum size of all files has a limit, which is close to 512 GB. Setting the limit to 500 GB is safe.

By default, two redo log files are stored in the MariaDB `data` directory. They are called `ib_logfile0` and `ib_logfile1`. Each of them has a 48 MB size limit.

While moving the redo log files to a separate device can reduce the I/O on the main disk, it is not recommended to change the number of log files.

Note that large values for `@@innodb_log_file_size`, in MariaDB versions older than 5.5, caused InnoDB recovery to take a long time. This is no longer an issue on the modern versions of MariaDB.

The FEDERATEDX and CONNECT storage engines

The FEDERATEDX and CONNECT storage engines allow us to use a remote table as if it were located in the local server. Local FEDERATEDX and CONNECT tables act as a proxy between the client and the remote server. When the client sends a SQL statement to the tables, the tables send it to the remote server; when the remote server returns some results, the tables send the result to the client.

This is not the most advanced solution to share data between multiple servers. The SPIDER storage engine has more features and optimizations, as explained in the next section. However, FEDERATEDX and CONNECT may have some advantages.

MariaDB Knowledge Base explains that the initial version of FEDERATEDX has been developed for Cisco. Its devices did not have much storage space, so they needed a MySQL storage engine to access remote data. This engine at the time was called FEDERATED, and was included in MySQL 5.0. More features were added in MySQL 5.1 to make it more usable for the majority of users. Since MariaDB developers thought that Oracle did not invest enough resources to maintain FEDERATED, they created a fork called FEDERATEDX, which is included in MariaDB. The author of this fork is the original developer of FEDERATED. The fork is fully compatible, but it contains more bug fixes and features. The most notable features are transactions (when the underlying table supports them) and the support for the ODBC protocol, to connect to database systems other than MariaDB or MySQL.

The CONNECT storage engine has already been mentioned in several chapters of this book. It basically allows the user to access a wide variety of external data sources as if they were MariaDB tables. This includes non-relational data sources, such as the text files written in several formats; CSV, XML, HTML and INI are just some examples, and the files can also be compressed with gzip. Even more exotic data sources are also supported; for example, on Windows, even directories and MAC network addresses can be read as tables. One of the supported data sources is a connection to a remote database server. Specific MariaDB/MySQL protocols are supported, as well as the generic ODBC standard. The CONNECT storage engine was then included in MariaDB 10.0.

While both FEDERATEDX and CONNECT are able to transparently use a remote MariaDB or MySQL table or view, their different histories determine different features and optimizations.

Some common features of FEDERATEDX and CONNECT are as follows:

- When creating the local table, the columns' definition can be omitted. In this case, the remote table's definition will be used.

- It is possible to exclude some remote columns from the local table.

- The local table cannot have additional columns. An exception is that CONNECT supports virtual columns.

- No indexes are created locally; this is impossible by design, since modifying the remote table does not require accessing the local table.

Creating a FEDERATEDX table

For backward compatibility, the FEDERATEDX storage engine must be referred to as FEDERATED in MariaDB. It is a built-in plugin, so it need not be installed and cannot be uninstalled.

Let's see how to create the FEDERATEDX table with some examples. First, we need to create the underlying table on a server, which we will call **remote**. We can use any storage engine. Consider the following example:

```
remote> CREATE TABLE db1.user (
    -> id INTEGER UNSIGNED NOT NULL AUTO_INCREMENT,
    -> username VARCHAR(50),
    -> password VARCHAR(50),
    -> PRIMARY KEY (id)
    -> )
    -> ENGINE = InnoDB;
Query OK, 0 rows affected (0.47 sec)
```

Then, we will create FEDERATEDX on another server. We will do this on a server called local, shown as follows:

```
local> CREATE TABLE test.user_fed
    -> ENGINE = FEDERATED
    -> CONNECTION = 'mysql://user1:pwd@remote_server/db1/user';
Query OK, 0 rows affected (0.20 sec)
```

We did not provide the structure of the table, so it will be identical to the structure of the remote table. The CONNECTION table option specifies the information necessary to connect to the remote table. The string passed to this option is called a **connection string** and it contains the following information:

- The protocol to use: `mysql://`
- A username: `user1`
- A password: `pwd`
- The IP address or hostname of the remote server: `remote_server`
- The database that contains the table: `db1`
- The name of the remote table: `user`

If not specified, the database name and table name are the same as the ones used for the FEDERATEDX table.

 With very old versions of the FEDERATED storage engine, the COMMENT table option was used instead of CONNECTION to store the connection data. It was sort of a trick implemented to work around issues with the storage engine's architecture. As a side effect, the user could not associate a comment to the FEDERATED tables. In modern versions of both FEDERATEDX and FEDERATED, the CONNECTION option must be used.

Defining a link to a remote server

The syntax shown previously to create a FEDERATEDX table is convenient when we want to access only one table on a remote server. However, if a remote server contains several tables that we want to access, we do not want to repeat the same long connection string for each table.

A good solution is to define a link to a remote server or, more specifically, a remote database. This can be done using the CREATE SERVER statement. A link created in this way can be used with all the storage engines that allow access to tables from remote servers:

- The FEDERATED and FEDERATEDX storage engines
- The CONNECT storage engine
- The SPIDER storage engine

Here's an example of CREATE SERVER usage:

```
CREATE SERVER srv1
  FOREIGN DATA WRAPPER `mysql`
  OPTIONS (
    USER 'root',
    PASSWORD 'root',
    HOST '127.0.0.1',
    DATABASE 'remote_server'
  );
```

Note that there is no way to specify a table name.

We can now create a new table using this link:

```
CREATE TABLE test.t
  ENGINE = FEDERATED
  CONNECTION 'srv1/user';
```

The connection string, in this case, is the link name followed by the table name. If the table name is omitted, the remote table name is assumed to be equal to the new table name.

Links are stored in the tables present on the servers, in the mysql system database. Like all tables in the mysql database, servers should not be directly modified, but queried to examine the existing links, shown as follows:

```
MariaDB [test]> SELECT * FROM mysql.servers WHERE Server_name = 'srv1' \G
*************************** 1. row ***************************
Server_name: srv1
       Host: remote_server
         Db: db1
   Username: root
   Password: root
       Port: 0
     Socket:
    Wrapper: mysql
      Owner:
1 row in set (0.00 sec)
```

Note that the only supported Wrapper is mysql, and the Owner property is currently not supported.

The following statement can be used to drop a link:

```
DROP SERVER IF EXISTS srv1;
```

The existing links cannot be edited, but they can be dropped and recreated. Note that dropping or recreating them has no effect on the existing tables. To update a table definition, it is necessary to drop and recreate it.

Creating a MYSQL CONNECT table

The CONNECT storage engine supports several table types. Each of them allows us to use a different type of data source. The data sources that allow us to communicate the remote DBMSs are MYSQL and ODBC. The MYSQL type works for both MariaDB and MySQL servers, using the native protocol. The ODBC type works for any DBMS that supports the ODBC standard. In this chapter, we will only discuss the MYSQL type.

The syntax used to create a FEDERATEDX table can also be used to create a MYSQL CONNECT table, except that no indexes can be defined:

```
CREATE TABLE test.user (
  id INTEGER UNSIGNED NOT NULL,
  username VARCHAR(50),
  password VARCHAR(50)
)
  ENGINE = CONNECT
  TABLE_TYPE = MYSQL
  CONNECTION = 'mysql://user1:pwd@remote_server/db1/user';
```

Similar to FEDERATEDX, CONNECT requires the connection string to be specified in the CONNECTION option, not in COMMENT.

A server name can be specified instead of a complete connection string:

```
CREATE TABLE test.user (
  id INTEGER UNSIGNED NOT NULL,
  username VARCHAR(50),
  password VARCHAR(50)
)
  ENGINE = CONNECT
  TABLE_TYPE = MYSQL
  CONNECTION = 'srv1';
```

The CONNECT storage engine also supports the DBNAME and TABNAME table options, which specify a remote database name and a remote table name. They can be combined with a connection string, shown as follows:

```
CREATE TABLE test.user (
  id INTEGER UNSIGNED NOT NULL,
  username VARCHAR(50),
  password VARCHAR(50)
)
  ENGINE = CONNECT
  TABLE_TYPE = MYSQL
  DBNAME = 'test'
  TABNAME = 'user'
  CONNECTION = 'mysql://user1:pwd@remote_server/';
```

If a database name and table name are provided in the connection string and via the DBNAME and TABNAME options, the values specified in the connection string will be used.

A view name can be specified instead of a table name, using any of the preceding syntaxes. It is also possible to specify a query, which will be used as an unnamed view:

```
CREATE TABLE test.user (
  id INTEGER UNSIGNED NOT NULL,
  username VARCHAR(50),
  password VARCHAR(50)
)
  ENGINE = CONNECT
  TABLE_TYPE = MYSQL
  SRCDEF = 'SELECT * FROM db1.user WHERE id > 1000000'
  CONNECTION = 'mysql://user1:pwd@remote_server/';
```

Sending SQL statements to a remote server

The CONNECT storage engine allows us to send arbitrary SQL statements to a remote server. This is mainly useful for sending administrative commands or creating new tables remotely without directly accessing a remote MariaDB server.

To be able to directly send statements to a remote server, a special CONNECT table must be created. Here is an example:

```
CREATE TABLE srv1_sql (
  statement VARCHAR(128) NOT NULL FLAG = 0,
  number INTEGER NOT NULL FLAG = 1,
  message VARCHAR(255) FLAG = 2,
  warnings INTEGER NOT NULL FLAG = 3
)
  ENGINE = CONNECT,
  TABLE_TYPE = MYSQL,
  CONNECTION 'srv1',
  OPTION_LIST = 'Execsrc=1,Maxerr=10';
```

The table and column names are not relevant and can be defined arbitrarily. We used the name of a defined server followed by the _sql suffix. This seems quite logical, if we decide to define special CONNECT tables to send statements to all the remote servers. This can be useful even if we decide to use FEDERATEDX or SPIDER to access the remote tables. However, we must be cautious while setting the permissions for these special tables. Usually, they should only be accessible by root, or other users who have the SUPER privilege.

The OPTION_LIST table option is what makes CONNECT aware of the purpose of this special table. The key option is Execsrs. The Maxerr option can be used to set the maximum number of errors and warnings that can be received from the remote server, in response to each statement we send.

Each column in the table has a special meaning. While their meanings are made clearer for us if we use descriptive names, the purpose of the columns is defined using FLAG, a column option specific to CONNECT. For example, renaming the message column will not alter its purpose, as long as the FLAG option remains unchanged. The following table shows the meanings of the various FLAG values:

FLAG value	Column meaning
0	Statement to be executed
1	Number of rows affected by a write statement, or returned by a query
2	An informative message
3	Number of errors and warnings

The default value for the FLAG option is 0, so FLAG=0 can always be omitted in the CREATE TABLE statement.

The following example shows how to execute a statement remotely using the previously created table:

```
MariaDB [test]> SELECT * FROM srv1_sql WHERE statement = '
    '> CREATE OR REPLACE TABLE db1.new_table (id INT) ENGINE = InnoDB
    '> ';
+-------------------------------------------------------------------------+-----
---+---------------+----------+
| statement                                                               |
number | message       | warnings |
+-------------------------------------------------------------------------+-----
---+---------------+----------+
|
CREATE OR REPLACE TABLE db1.new_table (id INT) ENGINE = InnoDB
   |        0 | Affected rows |         0 |
+-------------------------------------------------------------------------+-----
---+---------------+----------+
1 row in set (0.85 sec)
```

The executed statement has been sent via the WHERE condition and then returned in the statement column. We know that the statement succeeded because the warnings value is 0. The message and number columns tell us that the number of rows affected by CREATE TABLE is 0; this is normal, because CREATE TABLE always returns this value.

Just to verify that the CREATE TABLE statement succeeded on the remote server, we will now create a CONNECT table that is linked to it:

```
MariaDB [test]> CREATE TABLE new_table (
    -> id INT
    -> )
    -> ENGINE = CONNECT,
    -> TABLE_TYPE = MYSQL,
    -> CONNECTION 'srv1/new_table';
Query OK, 0 rows affected (0.13 sec)
MariaDB [test]> SELECT COUNT(*) FROM new_table;
+----------+
```

```
| COUNT(*) |
+----------+
|        0 |
+----------+
1 row in set (0.00 sec)
```

It is also possible to send more than one statement to the remote server using a single SELECT statement against the CONNECT table. This can be done using the IN operator. In this case, a row will be returned for each executed statement:

```
MariaDB [test]> SELECT * FROM srv1_sql WHERE statement IN (
    -> 'SET @@global.innodb_file_per_table = 1',
    -> 'SET @@global.innodb_strict_mode = 1'
    -> );
+-------------------------------------+--------+----------------+------
----+
| statement                           | number | message        |
warnings |
+-------------------------------------+--------+----------------+------
----+
| SET @@global.innodb_file_per_table = 1 |     0 | Affected rows  |
0 |
| SET @@global.innodb_strict_mode = 1    |     0 | Affected rows  |
0 |
+-------------------------------------+--------+----------------+------
----+
2 rows in set (0.00 sec)
```

By default, only fatal errors are returned, and they are contained in the message (FLAG=2) column:

```
MariaDB [test]> SELECT * FROM srv1_sql WHERE statement =
'SET @@global.performance_schema = 1' \G
*************************** 1. row ***************************
statement:
SET @@global.performance_schema = 1

  number: 1238
 message: Remote: Variable 'performance_schema' is a read only variable
warnings: 0
1 row in set (0.23 sec)
```

In most situations, this is enough, but there are cases in which we prefer to assess each warning in order to debug messages. To do this, there are three special commands that we can send to the special table as if they were normal SQL statements. The CONNECT storage engine will parse those commands and it will not send them to the remote server. Examples of such commands are:

- Note
- Warning
- Error

They tell CONNECT to show notes, warnings, and errors in the result set of the current SELECT statement. For example:

```
MariaDB [test]> SELECT * FROM srv1_sql WHERE statement IN (
    -> 'Note','Warning', 'Error',
    -> 'DROP TABLE IF EXISTS t1',
    -> 'Note','Warning', 'Error',
    -> 'CREATE TABLE t1 (c INT) ENGINE = MySAM'
    -> );
+-------------------------------------------+--------+-------------------------------------------+
| statement                                 | number | message                                   |
| warnings                                  |        |                                           |
+-------------------------------------------+--------+-------------------------------------------+
| DROP TABLE IF EXISTS t1                    |      0 | Affected rows                             |
|        1 |                                                                                    |
| Note                                      |   1051 | Unknown table 'db1.                       |
| t1'                                       |      0 |                                           |
| CREATE TABLE t1 (c INT) ENGINE = MySAM    |      0 | Affected rows                             |
|        2 |                                                                                    |
| Warning                                   |   1286 | Unknown storage                           |
| engine 'MySAM'                            |      0 |                                           |
| Warning                                   |   1266 | Using storage engine                      |
| InnoDB for table 't1'                     |      0 |                                           |
+-------------------------------------------+--------+-------------------------------------------+
5 rows in set (0.42 sec)
```

In the preceding example, the first Note informs us that the table we tried to DROP does not exist. More importantly, the last two warnings tell us that we mistyped MyISAM, and thus, the InnoDB storage engine has been used instead.

This technique does not provide a direct way to retrieve a result set from a remote server. However, this can be done with an easy procedure:

1. Send a CREATE TABLE ... SELECT statement to the remote server
2. Create a CONNECT table that points to the new remote table
3. Query the local table

Note that the local table must be recreated every time the remote table changes, unless its columns remain the same.

The following example shows how to retrieve the remote server version:

```
MariaDB [test]> SELECT * FROM srv1_sql WHERE statement = '
    '> CREATE OR REPLACE TABLE a.output AS SELECT version(),
@@global.version_comment
    '> ';
+---------------------------------------------------------------------
----------+--------+----------------+----------+
| statement
| number | message        | warnings |
+---------------------------------------------------------------------
----------+--------+----------------+----------+
|
CREATE OR REPLACE TABLE a.output AS SELECT version(),
@@global.version_comment
|      1 | Affected rows  |        0 |
+---------------------------------------------------------------------
----------+--------+----------------+----------+
1 row in set (0.75 sec)


MariaDB [test]> CREATE OR REPLACE TABLE output
    ->       ENGINE = CONNECT,
    ->       TABLE_TYPE = MYSQL,
    ->       CONNECTION 'srv1/output';
Query OK, 0 rows affected (0.09 sec)


MariaDB [test]> SELECT * FROM output;
+--------------------+-------------------------+
| version()          | @@global.version_comment |
+--------------------+-------------------------+
| 10.0.11-MariaDB-log | MariaDB Server          |
+--------------------+-------------------------+
1 row in set (0.25 sec)
```

Merging multiple CONNECT MYSQL tables

The TBL table is another useful table type. It represents a collection of identical (or very similar) CONNECT tables. Such a collection can be queried as if it were a single table. Used with the MYSQL table type, TBL allows us to implement a simple form of data sharding over several servers. It is possible to define a local set of CONNECT MYSQL tables, which are linked to several remote tables spread on multiple servers. A table of type TBL can then be built on such MYSQL tables. Queries against the TBL table will be sent to the MYSQL tables, and data will be retrieved from all the relevant remote servers.

Note that the TBL table type has an important limitation: it is read-only. Data in the underlying tables cannot be modified through TBL, which makes it unusable in many situations. However, it can still be an option when we want to shard read-only data through several MariaDB servers.

The syntax to create a TBL table is as follows:

```
CREATE TABLE <table_name>
   ENGINE = CONNECT,
   TABLE_TYPE = TBL,
   TABLE_LIST = '<table_list>';
```

The <table_list> variable is a comma-separated list of CONNECT table names. Each name can optionally be specified as database_name.table_name. If the database name is omitted, the table is assumed to be located in the same database as the TBL table.

While a TBL table, technically, can only be built on CONNECT tables, it can still be indirectly linked to tables that use different storage engines, such as InnoDB or MyISAM. This is done by creating MYSQL tables that point to such tables and build a TBL table on them. The result will be slower than a direct access because a connection to the local server will be used. However, it should still be faster than connecting a remote server. This technique is useful if we want to distribute data over multiple servers, including the local server.

The CONNECT engine can solve an important performance issue that cannot be solved easily using other storage engines, such as FEDERATEDX or SPIDER. Imagine that we work for a company that has several physical stores. Each store has its own database, which contains, among other data, the stocked products, product categories, and recent transactions. Assume that we are asked to write a query, which returns the average quantity of phones sold last week in all the stores. To do this, we need to perform JOIN between three tables: product_category, product, and transaction.

However, this JOIN must be executed separately for each store; comparing the transactions of one store with the products of another store may or may not lead to wrong results, depending on how the system is designed, but it would require a huge amount of network traffic and would be way too slow. To execute the JOIN query on a store basis, we can create a MYSQL CONNECT table for each store; this table will be based on that query, using the SRCDEF option as shown in the following code. Such tables, when queried, will return the associations between categories, products, and transactions for each store. Then, we can build a TBL table on top of these MYSQL tables, and perform a query that returns the desired average. Only the relevant rows will be sent from the databases in the stores to the local MariaDB server.

A special syntax can be used to achieve the same result without defining a new CONNECT table for each remote server. The SRCDEF option can be specified directly in the TBL table definition, and a list of remote servers can be provided in the TABLE_LIST option:

```
CREATE TABLE <table_name>
  ENGINE = CONNECT,
  TABLE_TYPE = TBL,
  SRCDEF = '<query>',
  TABLE_LIST = '<server_list>';
```

The SPIDER storage engine

Like the FEDERATEDX storage engine and the CONNECT MYSQL table type, SPIDER allows remote access to tables as if they were on the local server. However, the SPIDER storage engine has been specifically designed for data sharding. Its main function is to access data from a multitude of servers by querying a single local table.

Data sharding is implemented in SPIDER using table partitioning. If a SPIDER table is partitioned, each partition can be linked to a different remote table. The SPIDER storage engine is suitable with the RANGE and LIST partitioning methods, including RANGE COLUMNS and LIST COLUMNS.

The SPIDER storage engine supports both regular SQL transactions and XA transactions, if the remote tables support them too.

The SPIDER storage engine has been originally designed for MySQL. The version distributed along with MariaDB is slightly modified to take advantage of the MariaDB-specific features.

The original author of SPIDER is Kentoku Shiba. The project's official site is http://www.spiderformysql.com/.

Explaining the working of the SPIDER storage engine

The SPIDER storage engine is essentially a storage engine that communicates with the local server's optimizer on one side and the remote server on the other side. When the optimizer chooses an execution plan for a query, which involves SPIDER tables, SPIDER translates this plan into calls to one or more remote servers, acting like a MariaDB client.

When SPIDER is asked to insert data into more than one remote server, it internally uses a transaction with a two-phase commit. The problem with a single-phase commit is that it guarantees data integrity only if it involves one server. When all the modifications have been requested, the commit makes them effective. However, imagine that the modifications involve two servers. We send the commands to both servers, and we get no error. Then, we issue a commit on server 1 and it succeeds. Finally, we send the commit to server 2. If this commit fails, we have created an inconsistency. In fact, the changes we requested are already effective on server 1 and they cannot be undone anymore. For this reason, a single-phase commit is not suitable to execute a transaction between multiple servers.

The two-phase commit transaction model is the same as the model used for the XA transactions. XA commands can be sent to SPIDER by the user because they are fully supported. However, even if a normal transaction is used, SPIDER uses a two-phase commit to make the changes effective across multiple servers. With this technique, when a server receives a commit, it does not immediately apply the changes. It knows that the transaction is finished, but it waits for a second commit. If any of the remote servers returns an error or is not reachable, SPIDER rolls back the transaction on each involved server, avoiding data corruption. Only if the first commit succeeds on all the remote servers, SPIDER sends a second commit to each server. The second commit makes data effective.

When a query involves multiple SPIDER partitions, or multiple unpartitioned SPIDER tables, they are broken into multiple threads. A separate thread is used for each remote server that needs to be accessed by the query. Keeping this in mind, the DBA can augment the parallelization of queries by adding more partitions that point to a remote server.

Query results are buffered by SPIDER until they can be sent to the clients. The incomplete result sets can be stored on the remote servers or on the local server.

The SPIDER storage engine maintains in-memory statistics on remote tables and indexes. These statistics are updated at regular intervals of time. Like other storage engines, SPIDER communicates these values to the optimizer so that it can use them to choose good query plans.

Installing the SPIDER storage engine

The SPIDER storage engine is compiled in official MariaDB distributions, but it is not enabled by default. Before we start using it, the following steps are necessary:

1. Installing the plugin
2. Executing install_spider.sql

Like all plugins, the SPIDER storage engine can be installed while the server is running, with the SQL INSTALL statement.

The exact location of the install_spider.sql file depends on the MariaDB distribution and the operating system we are using. It is generally located in the share subdirectory. This file creates the system tables used by SPIDER, in the mysql database.

The following example shows a successful installation of SPIDER:

```
MariaDB [(none)]> INSTALL SONAME 'ha_spider';
Query OK, 0 rows affected (0.07 sec)
MariaDB [(none)]> SOURCE /usr/local/mariadb/share/install_spider.sql;
```

Then, we can check that the SPIDER system tables have been installed:

```
MariaDB [(none)]> SHOW TABLES FROM mysql LIKE '%spider%';
+----------------------------+
| Tables_in_mysql (%spider%) |
+----------------------------+
| spider_link_failed_log     |
| spider_link_mon_servers    |
| spider_tables              |
| spider_xa                  |
| spider_xa_failed_log       |
| spider_xa_member           |
+----------------------------+
6 rows in set (0.01 sec)
```

Creating a SPIDER table

The SPIDER storage engine supports a special syntax to specify where the remote tables are located. This syntax is different from the syntaxes used for FEDERATEDX and CONNECT, and it must be used in the COMMENT table option.

The following example shows how to create a simple, unpartitioned SPIDER table, which connects to a remote table. We will use the user table, which we already used for some FEDERATEDX and CONNECT examples:

```
CREATE TABLE test.user (
  id INTEGER UNSIGNED NOT NULL,
  username VARCHAR(50),
  password VARCHAR(50)
)
  ENGINE = SPIDER,
  COMMENT = 'user "user1", password "pwd" host "remote_server",
port "3306", database "db1", table "user"';
```

If table is not specified, it will be the same as the local table name. If database is not specified, it will be the same database as the one that contains the local table.

We can also provide a defined server name, shown as follows:

```
CREATE TABLE test.user (
  id INTEGER UNSIGNED NOT NULL,
  username VARCHAR(50),
  password VARCHAR(50)
)
  ENGINE = SPIDER,
  COMMENT = 'srv1';
```

The SPIDER storage engine can automatically discover the structure of the remote table and create an identical local table. Thus, we can simply write:

```
CREATE TABLE test.user
  ENGINE = SPIDER,
  COMMENT = 'server "srv1"';
```

The SPIDER storage engine tables are really useful when they are partitioned. Each partition can point to a different remote table. The following example shows how to create a SPIDER partitioned table:

```
CREATE TABLE test.user (
  id INTEGER UNSIGNED NOT NULL,
  username VARCHAR(50),
  password VARCHAR(50)
)
```

```
ENGINE = SPIDER
PARTITION BY RANGE (id)
(
  PARTITION p0 VALUES LESS THAN (1000000)
    COMMENT = 'server "srv1"',
  PARTITION p1 VALUES LESS THAN (2000000)
    COMMENT = 'server "srv2"',
  PARTITION p2 VALUES LESS THAN (3000000)
    COMMENT = 'server "srv3"'
);
```

The following table options can be used to create a `SPIDER` table, or partition, which connects to a remote server using SSL:

Option name	Description
SSL_CA	This is the name or path of the authority certificate
SSL_CAPATH	This is the path of the authority certificate's directory
SSL_CERT	This is the name or path of the certificate
SSL_CIPHER	This is a comma-separated list of the encryption algorithms that can be used
SSL_KEY	This is the path of the public key
SSL_VERIFY_SERVER_CERT	If set to 1, the remote server's certificate will be verified

For further details about SSL connections in MariaDB, see *Chapter 5*, *Users and Connections*.

Logging of queries and errors

Statements sent by the users to a `SPIDER` table can be logged into the general query log, similar to all the other statements. And, of course, if a command generated by `SPIDER` returns an error, the remote server can record this error in the error log. This behavior depends on the `@@general_log` and `@@log_error` server variables, as explained in *Chapter 3*, *Optimizing Queries*.

However, when a `SPIDER` table queries a remote table, the remote server does not log the command by default. It is possible to log such commands by setting the `@@spider_general_log` server variable to `ON` in the remote servers. The `SPIDER` commands will be written in the general query log.

When a command generated by SPIDER returns an error on the remote server, the error can also be logged into the local servers by setting the @@spider_log_result_errors server variable to ON.

Executing arbitrary statements on remote servers

Some **User Defined Functions (UDFs)** provide an easy way to execute arbitrary SQL statements against remote servers. Such UDFs are automatically installed with SPIDER.

Unlike MYSQL CONNECT tables with a SRCDEF clause, these functions can return a result set.

Note that these functions can be invoked to remotely execute SQL statements in any situation. In fact, while they are designed to assist the management of a cluster based on SPIDER, they work even if SPIDER is not used at all.

Explaining the spider_direct_sql() function

The spider_direct_sql() function allows us to execute arbitrary SQL statements against a remote MariaDB or MySQL server. The results of the query are copied into a temporary table that needs to be explicitly created before calling this function. Note that the table needs to be temporary.

Consider the following example:

```
MariaDB [test]> CREATE TEMPORARY TABLE output (
    -> v VARCHAR(255)
    -> ) ENGINE = InnoDB;
Query OK, 0 rows affected (0.21 sec)
MariaDB [test]> SELECT spider_direct_sql(
    -> 'SELECT VERSION() AS v',
    -> 'output',
    -> 'user "user1", password "pwd", host "remote_server", port "3306"'
    -> ) AS v;
```

```
+---+
| v |
+---+
| 1 |
+---+
1 row in set (0.06 sec)
MariaDB [test]> SELECT * FROM output;
+--------------------+
| v                  |
+--------------------+
| 10.0.11-MariaDB-log |
+--------------------+
1 row in set (0.01 sec)
```

Let's examine the `spider_direct_sql()` call. It has three parameters:

- The SQL command that we want to execute on a remote server.
- The name of the temporary table that will store the result set. Note that the table has been previously created. The function does not automatically create it.
- A string that contains the information necessary to access the remote server. The syntax is the same that is used to create SPIDER tables. It is also possible to specify a defined server name.

Explaining the spider_bg_direct_sql() function

When `spider_direct_sql()` is called, the current connection stays on hold until the remote query execution is completed and its result set is stored into the specified temporary table. However, sometimes we need to execute a long-running statement, and we do not want the current connection to wait until it is completed. In these cases, we can use the `spider_bg_direct_sql()` function. As the name suggests, it executes the query in the background.

The syntax of `spider_bg_direct_sql()` is identical to the syntax of `spider_direct_sql()`.

Summary

In this chapter, we discussed how to spread some files over multiple disks to obtain better performance when the I/O operations are the system's bottleneck. Both table files and logs can be moved to different storage devices. Particularly, moving some InnoDB tables and logs out of the system tablespace can be very beneficial.

We also discussed how to distribute data over multiple servers to balance the workload. MariaDB is distributed with three storage engines that provide these functionalities:

- FEDERATEDX
- CONNECT
- SPIDER

The FEDERATEDX storage engine is designed to access a single remote table. The CONNECT storage engine is used to access external data in a wide variety of formats, and among other data sources, it supports remote servers. The SPIDER storage engine is specifically designed to implement clusters of tables using MariaDB storage engine's API. In all these cases, the communication between the local server and remote servers is transparent for the user, who can query a FEDERATEDX, CONNECT, or SPIDER table just like any other table.

In the next chapter, we will discuss how to implement a cluster of MariaDB databases using Galera.

12
MariaDB Galera Cluster

In this chapter, we will discuss MariaDB Galera Cluster. This technology consists of a cluster of MariaDB nodes, which implement a high-performance and high-availability solution for data redundancy. The following topics will be discussed:

- An overview of MariaDB Galera Cluster
- Installing nodes
- Starting nodes and configuring the cluster
- Dealing with the split brain problem using Galera Arbitrator
- Diagnosing and solving performance problems
- Optimally distributing the workload between nodes using Galera Load Balancer

MariaDB Galera Cluster key concepts

Galera Cluster, or simply Galera, is a cluster implementation for MariaDB and MySQL. The project site is `http://galeracluster.com/`. MariaDB Galera Cluster is an official MariaDB distribution that contains the Galera technology. It follows the same major version numbers as the underlying MariaDB version. The first version was 5.5. Another distribution, Percona XtraDB Cluster, is based on Percona Server.

MariaDB Galera Cluster can be installed and updated from the MariaDB official repositories, or the Linux generic binaries can be downloaded from the MariaDB site. Some documentation about MariaDB Galera Cluster is included in *MariaDB Knowledge Base*. When we are searching for information that is not documented in the knowledge base, we can search the documentation of Galera Cluster for MySQL: `http://galeracluster.com/documentation-webpages/`.

This section provides general information about the technology used by Galera.

An overview of Galera Cluster

Galera Cluster propagates data over a cluster of servers using a synchronous multisource replication. All nodes in a cluster accept statements from the users, acting like a standalone MariaDB server. They reply to the user's queries and apply the requested data changes locally. Then, they propagate them to other nodes.

Nodes of Galera Cluster mostly behave like a normal MariaDB server, but they have several minor limitations. The users should be aware of what they can or cannot do with a MariaDB server, when it is part of Galera Cluster. The main limitation is that Galera only runs on Linux. Only the InnoDB storage engine is fully supported in Galera. An experimental support to MyISAM has been implemented, but its use is not recommended. A complete list of limitations can be found later in this chapter, in the *Listing the limitations of Galera Cluster* section.

There is no lower or upper limit to the number of nodes within a cluster. However, the cluster is guaranteed to be crash-safe only if there are at least three nodes.

Galera does not use loose consistency models such as the eventual consistency that is used by most MySQL products. Instead, it provides a high consistency level that is generally required for a DBMS. Even if the users can send SQL statements to any server, the writes are always applied in a given order. There is no sensible lag between nodes. On slow networks, a delay will be noticed, but it should only involve the commits. A query sent at a given time will always return the same result set, no matter which node it was addressed to. This is guaranteed thanks to synchronous replication.

Because of its nature, Galera can be used for several purposes. It can be used for load balancing, since all the nodes are constantly up to date. If nodes are geographically very distant, clients can even interact with the nearest node, reducing the latency. Galera also allows using one or more nodes as a backup that is always up to date, avoiding the loss of recent data that usually happens when restoring a normal backup. Or, it can simply be used as a traditional replication system, with all the clients querying only one master and considering other nodes as passive slaves.

> Note that in Galera, each node uses multiple slave threads. While MariaDB 10.0 supports multithreaded replication, this characteristic is particularly interesting for Version 5.5.

Galera Cluster suits cloud computing well. The reason is a feature called **automatic node provisioning**, which makes scaling very easy.

Synchronous replication

All other MariaDB and MySQL replication solutions, including the built-in replication, are asynchronous. Asynchronous replication guarantees that all write operations that occur on a master are propagated to all its slaves. However, there is no guarantee about when it will happen. In fact, it is not uncommon on a busy environment that some slaves lag behind their master with a delay of hours, or even several days.

The characteristic of synchronous replication is that masters and slaves are synchronized. Transactions are processed at the same time and no delay should occur, in theory. As mentioned previously, synchronous replication has two important consequences: no data is lost after a master crash, and transactions are committed in the same order by all nodes.

However, implementing synchronous replication is a challenging quest for developers. Traditionally, this is done using distributed locks or two-phase commits. For example, SPIDER uses two-phase commits, as explained in *Chapter 11, Data Sharding*. Both these methods are much slower than asynchronous replication. Galera uses a different model, which is based on a transaction certification. A node, when it receives a SQL statement, executes it and propagates the write sets to the other nodes without waiting for a commit. The transaction is processed in parallel. Each node applies the writes without making them effective. If the modifications succeed, the node certificates the write set. When the first node receives a commit and all the nodes certify the write set, it makes the write sets effective and propagates the commit. Transactions are reordered before they are propagated. This diminishes the probabilities that they fail in some node (and thus in the whole cluster) because of a conflict. Statements that implicitly cause a commit are isolated from other write sets. This new model is the result of recent academic works on group communications and reordering technique. The following document describes the process in depth: http://infoscience.epfl.ch/record/32566/files/EPFL_TH2090.pdf.

While this is the model used by Galera, each node internally uses the traditional transactions provided by InnoDB. These mechanisms are executed autonomously by each server. For this reason, the replication implemented by Galera is sometimes called **virtually synchronous replication**.

Synchronous replication is made possible by wsrep, an API to implement this feature in MySQL and MariaDB. The wsrep API is a free acronym for the Write Set Replication API. Galera can be thought of as an implementation of this API, and as a plugin for MariaDB and MySQL. For this reason, it is sometimes called a wsrep provider. Other providers, independent from Galera, may come in the future.

The description of `wsrep` in the Launchpad project page says:

> *"wsrep API defines a set of application callbacks and replication library calls necessary to implement synchronous writeset replication of transactional databases and similar applications. It aims to abstract and isolate replication implementation from application details. Although the main target of this interface is a certification-based multi-master replication, it is equally suitable for both asynchronous and synchronous master/slave replication."*

The repository of the wsrep project can be found at the following address: `https://launchpad.net/wsrep`.

Setting up a cluster

This section discusses how to set up a cluster. However, let's first discuss the requirements of a cluster.

Requirements

As mentioned earlier, all cluster nodes must run on Linux systems.

There are no particular hardware requirements; in fact, if a server can smoothly run a standalone MariaDB server, it can also run on a Galera node. During normal operations, the additional amount of memory used for a Galera replication is minimal and wouldn't make much of a difference. The only exception is that the copying of the entire database from one node to another consumes a lot of memory. This happens when a new node joins the cluster, or when a disconnected node rejoins the cluster. However, when choosing the hardware of individual nodes, we should keep in mind that the cluster will be as slow as its slowest node.

The connection between nodes must be fast enough for the workload we are going to run. If possible, MariaDB Galera Cluster should run on a subnetwork that does not contain any other hosts. Since Galera replication implies constant communication between all the nodes, having non-related network traffic on the same network will reduce the performance. Also, preventing external hosts from directly connecting to the cluster nodes is an important security enhancement.

Of course, nodes that accept connections from the clients will need more memory to perform the queries. We might also want to use a load balancer to optimally distribute the queries over multiple nodes. This technique is described later in this chapter.

Installation

MariaDB Galera Cluster is included in the official MariaDB repositories. Generic Linux binaries can also be downloaded from the MariaDB site. The DEB and YUM packages are available for the officially supported Linux distributions: Debian, Ubuntu, Fedora, Red Hat, and CentOS. It is also possible to compile MariaDB Galera Cluster from sources, if necessary.

The packages that need to be installed are:

- `mariadb-galera-server`: The MariaDB Galera Cluster itself
- `galera`: The `wsrep` provider

Some dependencies will probably be installed. If the `mariadb-server` package is installed, it will be automatically removed.

MariaDB Galera Cluster nodes communicate using non-standard ports. By default, the ports it uses are:

- `4567`
- `4568`
- `4444`
- `3306` (standard port)

If **SELinux** or **AppArmor** is installed, by default they will block all the communication on non-standard ports, preventing the cluster from working. In this case, we will need to add proper SELinux or AppArmor policies, or disable them all. Note that SELinux heavily affects the performance of database servers, so disabling it could be a good idea. SELinux is generally enabled, by default, on distributions derived from Red Hat. AppArmor is enabled by default on Ubuntu.

To disable SELinux, run the following command:

```
setenforce 0
```

To disable AppArmor, run the following commands:

```
cd /etc/apparmor.d/disable/
ln -s /etc/apparmor.d/usr.sbin.mysqld
service apparmor restart
```

In both cases, we must be a root user.

If iptables, or similar firewall software, is installed, it will probably need to be configured to allow access on non-standard ports.

At this point, we are ready to start our first MariaDB Galera Cluster!

Starting the nodes

Starting a MariaDB Galera Cluster node means to start a MariaDB server so that we can call the `mysqld` binary or the `mysqld_safe` script.

Before starting a node for the first time, we should prepare the configuration file. The following example shows a minimal configuration:

```
wsrep_provider=/usr/lib/galera/libgalera_smm.so
default_storage_engine=InnoDB
binlog_format=ROW
innodb_autoinc_lock_mode=2
innodb_doublewrite=0
innodb_support_xa=0
query_cache_size=0
```

Here's an explanation of the options we set:

- The `wsrep_provider` option is the most important. It tells Galera where the `wsrep` library is located. Its path depends on your system.
- Since storage engines other than InnoDB should not be used, it is important to set `default_storage_engine` correctly.
- The `binlog_format` variable is set to the only allowed value, `ROW`.
- The `innodb_autoinc_lock_mode` variable must be set to `2`.
- The InnoDB doublewrite buffer and XA transactions are not supported in Galera.
- The query cache is not supported.

When starting the first node, we must specify the `--wsrep-new-cluster` option. So we can start the cluster this way:

```
mysqld --wsrep-new-cluster
```

If this node crashes, it must not be restarted using the previous command because it will not reconnect to the existing cluster. For this reason, we should not use `mysqld_safe` to start a cluster. Instead, the node must be added to the cluster again as if it was a new node.

After a node is started, some permission needs to be set. Each node in the cluster must allow any other node to connect as root to create a copy of the databases when needed. This mechanism is called node provisioning, and will be described in the *Node provisioning* section in this chapter. So, we will execute statements like this on each node:

```
GRANT ALL ON *.* TO 'root'@'node_hostname';
```

The `node_hostname` variable must be replaced with the new node's name or IP address.

Every node in the cluster is identified by a unique URL. To add a new node to the cluster, we need to specify the URL of at least one cluster node that is currently running. While one node is normally sufficient, a more robust practice is providing the addresses of multiple nodes, possibly all. Consider the following example:

```
mysqld_safe --wsrep_cluster_address=gcomm://214.140.10.5
```

No other information is needed. The specified node will communicate the URLs of the other existing nodes to the new node. Then, the new node will inform the existing nodes about its presence.

After a node has been set up, we might want to check that it is working. Galera provides some status variables for diagnostic purposes. All Galera-related status variables have names starting with `wsrep_`, shown as follows:

```
MariaDB [(none)]> SHOW STATUS LIKE 'wsrep%';
+------------------------------+----------------------+
| Variable_name                | Value                |
+------------------------------+----------------------+
| wsrep_cluster_conf_id        | 18446744073709551615 |
| wsrep_cluster_size           | 0                    |
| wsrep_cluster_state_uuid     |                      |
| wsrep_cluster_status         | Disconnected         |
| wsrep_connected              | OFF                  |
| wsrep_local_bf_aborts        | 0                    |
| wsrep_local_index            | 18446744073709551615 |
| wsrep_provider_name          |                      |
| wsrep_provider_vendor        |                      |
| wsrep_provider_version       |                      |
| wsrep_ready                  | ON                   |
+------------------------------+----------------------+
11 rows in set (0.04 sec)
```

Note that this query has been executed on a node that has been started but is not connected to the cluster.

The variables we want to check, in this case, are the following:

- `wsrep_ready`: This states whether the node is connected to the cluster and waiting to receive replication events. The `ON` value is the value that we want to see. The only other value is `OFF`.

- `wsrep_connected`: This states whether the node is connected to a wsrep provider.

- `wsrep_cluster_status`: This states whether the node is connected to the cluster. If no other nodes are connected, the value is `Disconnected`. Otherwise, we will see `Primary` or `Non Primary`.

- `wsrep_cluster_size`: This states the number of nodes in the cluster.

Before the new node can start replicating the events it receives from other nodes, the current data must be copied into the new server. This operation is called node provisioning or state transfer, and it is described in the *Node provisioning* section later in this chapter.

Determining a node URL

As explained previously, to start a new node or restart a node after a crash, the URL of another node must be specified. Thus, the DBA needs to know how to determine a node's URL.

The formal syntax of a Galera URL is as follows:

```
<schema>://<address><:port>[?option=value[&option=value …]]
```

Two schemas are supported:

- `gcomm`: This is the schema used for fully working Galera Cluster. It must always be used in production.

- `dummy`: This is the schema used to test the Galera configuration. If it is used, the data is not replicated.

The address is an IP address or a hostname, optionally followed by a port number. The default port is `4567`, for example, `214.140.10.5:9999`.

It is possible to list multiple addresses separated by a comma, for example, `214.140.10.5,214.140.10.6`. It is possible to use multicast addresses, such as IPv4 or IPv6 addresses whose last part is `1` to identify all the hosts in the subnet.

A set of options can be specified, separated by semicolons. These options are the same that are contained in `wsrep_provider_options`, which will be described later. For these settings to be applied after a node restart, they must be specified in a configuration file, not in the URL.

Some examples of URLs are as follows:

- gcomm://server_name
- gcomm://214.140.10.5,214.140.10.6
- gcomm://server_name:9999,214.140.10.5,214.140.10.6

Node provisioning

Node provisioning, or state transfer, consists of copying a full backup of the data from one node to another. The backup is often referred to as **snapshot** or **state**, to highlight that it is a consistent version of the data in a precise point in time. The node that sends its state is called the **donor**, and the node that receives it is called the **joiner**, because this operation occurs when a node joins the cluster. This may happen because a new machine has been added or because an existing node has crashed and, after restart, needs to receive the latest data changes.

There are two main node provisioning methods:

- **State Snapshot Transfer (SST)** consists of transmitting a full snapshot
- **Incremental State Transfer (IST)** consists of transmitting the modifications

In practice, these methods consist of using a full backup or an incremental backup.

State Snapshot Transfer

This node provisioning method is used when a new node joins the cluster because it contains no data. There are two ways to execute an SST:

- `mysqldump`: This method uses the `mysqldump` tool to generate the SQL statements needed to recreate the database on another node. This method is slower because it usually requires a huge amount of network traffic. The donor is made read-only via a global lock for the whole duration of the state transfer. Also, this method requires that the joiner node is already running. The use of `mysqldump` is necessary if the nodes use different MariaDB versions, or a different data directories layout.

- `rsync`, `rsync_wan`, and `xtrabackup`: These tools are used to copy the data files from the donor to the joiner. This method is much faster. The files can be copied using `rsync`, which only copies the files that have been modified; the `rsync_wan` method uses `rsync` with the delta transfer algorithm, which should be used to copy data through a **Wide Area Network (WAN)** or a slow network, but is slower in any other situation. Percona XtraBackup makes a copy of tables without locking the server. The `rsync` method and XtraBackup have been discussed in *Chapter 8, Backup and Disaster Recovery*. The `rsync` method is faster than XtraBackup but it is a blocking method. These methods require that the settings that affect the way files are stored, such as `@@innodb_file_per_table` or `@@innodb_file_format`, have the same values on both the nodes. Note that if one of these methods is used, the joiner node must not be initialized before the transfer.

To choose the method to be used for SST, the `wsrep_sst_method` option can be set in the joiner's configuration file. Consider the following example:

```
wsrep_sst_method=xtrabackup
```

> The SST method supports a scriptable interface. This feature allows us to write scripts, which customizes the data transfer operations, adapting them to our specific use case. This is a very powerful characteristic but it is beyond the purpose of this chapter. The Galera documentation contains more detailed information about this topic.

Incremental State Transfer

All write sets committed by a node are written to a special cache called Galera Cache (**GCache**). Its purpose is to speed up the data I/O operations. When a node crashes and is restarted, it is possible that the write sets performed by other nodes are completely stored in the GCache of at least one node. In this case, the Incremental State Transfer method is used to bring the new node up to date. This method has two important advantages. Data provisioning is much faster than SST because only the recently modified data is sent to the joiner. There is no need to lock the donor, which can continue to replicate the events it receives during the state transfer.

The split brain problem

Clusters of any type must be prepared to solve a problem called split brain. To understand what this problem is and a possible real case, imagine that a cluster of database servers is spread over two data centers. Also, imagine that one of the data centers loses its Internet connection. The cluster is now split into two partitions. However, its node still works and local clients are able to connect to it and send queries. If the cluster is not prepared to deal with a situation like this, both the data centers will probably continue to modify the same set of data. When the Internet connection of the disconnected data center is repaired, there will be many conflicts in the database. A cluster may still be able to automatically solve these conflicts; this is called an optimistic approach to the split brain problem. If the cluster cannot handle the conflicts, we can say that a disaster has happened.

Galera adopts a pessimistic approach to split brain. The technique it uses is called weighted quorum and it is a variation of the quorum-consensus algorithm described in the book *Distributed Systems: Concepts and Design* by *George Coulouris*, *Jean Dollimore*, *Tim Kindberg*, and *Gordon Blair*, *Pearson Publication*. Let's see how it works.

All the nodes in a cluster keep a count of the cluster size, which is the number of nodes in the cluster. This count is constantly updated. If a new node is added, the cluster size is increased. If a node gracefully shuts down, it communicates to the other nodes that it is leaving the cluster. However, if a node crashes or a permanent network failure occurs, it cannot communicate anything; it simply becomes unreachable.

If a node is unreachable for a given amount of time, other nodes assume that it is not reachable anymore. The timeout is 5 seconds by default, but it can be customized via the `evs.suspect_timeout` option, in the `wsrep_provider_options` server variable, which will be discussed later in this chapter.

When some nodes detect that another node is not reachable, the quorum algorithm is used. If more than half of the nodes in the cluster are still reachable, the current partition of the cluster is still a primary cluster. This is the default situation even before any crash occurs. This means that the current partition can continue to perform all its normal operations.

If only half or less than half of the original number of nodes is reachable, the current partition becomes a non-primary cluster. The nodes will still be able to accept connections and run the queries sent by the clients, but their databases are made read-only. As mentioned earlier, we can check whether the current cluster partition is primary cluster or not by querying the `@@wsrep_cluster_status` status variable.

If a cluster only has two nodes and the connection between them is lost, no partition will be bigger than the other one. The same problem occurs if one node crashes. In both cases, none of the resulting partitions will be primary, so none of the nodes will be able to write data. This explains why all Galera Cluster should consist of at least three nodes.

This algorithm guarantees that if a cluster is split into two or more partitions, only one of them will be primary. In no situation, more than one partition can modify data.

However, we already mentioned that Galera uses a variation of the quorum algorithm called weighted quorum. This means that nodes can be assigned different weights. When a node is unreachable, Galera does not really count the size of the current partition; instead, it calculates the weight of the partition, which is the sum of all the individual node's weights. By default, each node's weight is 1; thus, the weight of a partition is identical to its size.

A different weight can be assigned using the `pc.weight` option. The allowed range is from 0 to 255. If the weight of a node is 0, the node does not affect the result of the quorum formula. If the weight of a group of nodes is increased, and those nodes lose their Internet connection, the group will probably become the primary cluster. This makes sense, for example, if a data center has less database servers than the others, but it is vital that it keeps modifying its data.

Even if the weight of the nodes is explicitly set, it is always guaranteed that no more than one partition can become a primary cluster.

The weighted quorum formula used by Galera is much more complex than what it seems like from this description. The algorithm has been simplified here for the sake of clarity.

The weighted quorum algorithm can be disabled by enabling the `pc.ignore_quorum` option in the `wsrep_provider_options` server variable. See the *Setting the wsrep parameters* section in this chapter for details about how to do this. However, note that if the `pc.ignore_quorum` option is enabled, a split brain problem can occur. In this case, we need to know how to solve conflicts without the help of Galera; for example, in some cases it could be acceptable to overwrite the changes performed by a partition.

The Galera arbitrator

An arbitrator is a special type of node designed to help solve the split brain problem.

It communicates with the rest of the cluster as if it was a normal node, but it does not replicate any data. Its only purpose is incrementing the size of the partition it can communicate to, possibly making it become a primary cluster.

For example, suppose we only have two nodes. As explained previously, if one of them crashes or if the connection between them is lost, the resulting partitions will be non-primary. However, if we have an arbitrator, the node that did not crash or lose its connection will be able to communicate with the arbitrator. Technically, the nodes will form a cluster of two nodes, which will be the primary cluster.

A more complex example is when two data centers form Galera Cluster and each data center contains the same number of nodes. This example, while involving a higher number of servers, is almost identical to the previous one; if the connection between the data centers is lost, none of them will be able to become a primary cluster. The problem can be solved without adding any new node. We can set up an arbitrator, which is not located in any of the two data centers. If one of them loses its Internet connection, the other one will still communicate with the arbitrator and become a primary cluster.

To start an arbitrator, we need to call the **Galera Arbitrator Daemon (garbd)** binary. Its system variables and the `wsrep` parameters are the same as the options of regular nodes. The exception here is that the `wsrep` parameters in the `repl` group are missing in the arbitrator because they do not make sense for a node that does not replicate anything.

To use a configuration file with `garbd`, we can start it this way:

```
garbd --cfg /path/to/garb.cnf --daemon
```

To stop an arbitrator, we can kill the `garbd` process. This is safe, since the arbitrator does not write any data.

Configuring the cluster

MariaDB Galera Cluster nodes can be configured by setting generic MariaDB system variables and Galera-specific variables. The most important variable is `wsrep_provider_options`; it can be used to set many `wsrep` parameters, separated by a semicolon. This variable is dynamic.

The most important variables and parameters are explained in this section. A complete list of options and parameters can be found in the *MariaDB Knowledge Base*.

Explaining the important Galera system variables

All Galera-specific variables have a `'wsrep_'` suffix. To list them, we can use the following query:

```
SHOW VARIABLES LIKE 'wsrep%';
```

A discussion follows about the most important Galera system variables. They have been split into groups to make the discussion clearer.

Generic cluster settings

The following list shows us what the generic cluster settings stand for:

- `wsrep_provider`: This is the path of the `wsrep` library.
- `wsrep_cluster_address`: This is the address of one or more cluster nodes. As explained earlier, setting this value is necessary to add a node to a cluster. This variable is not dynamic.
- `wsrep_cluster_name`: This is the name of the cluster. Nodes refuse to connect to other nodes if they do not belong to the same cluster. This variable is dynamic and can be used to split a cluster.
- `wsrep_node_address`: This can be used to explicitly set the address of the current node. This variable is not dynamic.
- `wsrep_node_name`: This sets the node name. By default, the hostname is used.
- `wsrep_on`: This determines whether the node replicates data. It can be used to temporarily pause a node.

Performance and reliability

The following list shows the settings that can be used to tune performance and reliability:

- `wsrep_data_home_dir`: This sets the `data` directory for the current node.

- `wsrep_slave_threads`: This determines the number of concurrent threads used for replication. This may or may not speed up most operations; it is especially useful to speed up the synchronization of nodes. The minimum recommended value is 4 multiplied by the number of CPU cores, but the optimal value can sometimes be much higher. This variable is not dynamic, so it could be necessary to restart a node several times to test its performance with several values. Note that if this value is higher than 1, `innodb_locks_unsafe_for_binlog` must be set to 1.

- `wsrep_causal_reads`: If this variable is set to `OFF`, it causes faster nodes to apply a write set and start the execution of new statements without waiting for slower nodes. This behavior is the default value, but it causes small inconsistencies for a short period of time. Setting this variable to `ON` prevents these inconsistencies, but increases the latency. Its default value is `OFF`.

- `wsrep_max_ws_size setd`: This determines the maximum size of write sets, expressed in bytes. This variable is not dynamic.

- `wsrep_max_ws_rows`: This sets the maximum number of rows in a single write set. This variable is not dynamic.

- `wsrep_retry_autocommit`: This helps dealing with frequent conflicts within the cluster. It sets the maximum number of retries when a transaction fails because of such conflicts. This variable is not dynamic.

- `wsrep_load_data_splitting`: This splits long running `LOAD DATA INFILE` statements into multiple transactions, making them faster but less reliable.

Settings affecting the behavior of State Snapshot Transfer

The following settings affect the behavior of the SST:

- `wsrep_sst_donor`: This is a comma-separated list of the nodes that can be used as donors. The nodes' names must be used here instead of their addresses.

- `wsrep_sst_donor_rejects_queries`: This determines whether the current node refuses to act as a donor for other nodes. By default, this value is `OFF`, which means that it can act as a donor.

- `wsrep_sst_method`: This determines the SST to be used, as explained in the *State Snapshot Transfer* section.

- `wsrep_sst_auth`: This is only relevant for SST methods that imply a connection to a running server, such as `xtrabackup` or `mysqldump`. This variable contains the username and password to be used for authentication, separated by a colon, for example, `root:my_password`.

Dealing with Galera limitations

The following settings are useful when dealing with Galera Cluster limitations:

- `wsrep_replicate_myisam`: This determines whether experimental MyISAM replication will be used. Its default value is OFF, which means that the MyISAM tables will simply be ignored.

- `wsrep_convert_LOCK_to_trx`: This can sometimes help the transition of applications from MyISAM to InnoDB. If it is set to ON, the LOCK TABLES and UNLOCK TABLES statements are silently converted into START TRANSACTION and COMMIT. Its default value is OFF. If we enable this feature, we should be sure to check whether our applications work correctly.

- `wsrep_certify_nonPK`: This instructs Galera to automatically add primary keys for tables that do not have one. This solves several replication problems. It is ON by default.

Setting the wsrep parameters

Many `wsrep` settings can be specified using the `wsrep_provider_options` variable. The settings must be separated with a semicolon, as seen in the following syntax:

```
SET  wsrep_provider_options = 'option=value;option=value';
```

Similar to server variables, the `wsrep` options can be dynamic or not. If an option is not dynamic, the node must be restarted in order to change its value.

Almost all the option names have a prefix, which approximately indicates the component the option refers to. The pattern is as follows:

```
group_name.option_name
```

Most of these parameters require a deep knowledge of wsrep. Only the most important ones are explained here. The complete list can be found in the *MariaDB Knowledge Base*.

- `base_host`: This is the node's IP address or hostname.
- `base_port`: This is the port used for replication.
- `evs.inactive_timeout`: This determines the amount of time a node can be unreachable before the weighted quorum algorithm is used to handle the problem.
- `evs.user_send_window`: This determines the number of packets that can be replicated together. If the network is slow, this value should be increased. This option is dynamic.

- `gcache.dir`: This sets a path for the GCache files. This allows writing the GCache files on a different storage device to optimize the performance. This is not dynamic.

- `gcache.mem_size`: This is the maximum size of the GCache. This is not dynamic.

- `gcache.page_size`: This is the size of the GCache pages. This is not dynamic.

- `gcs.fc_master_slave`: This can be set to ON if only one node in the cluster can be used as a master, which means that all the clients only connect to that node. This allows some `wsrep` optimizations. This is not dynamic.

- `gcs.max_throttle`: This determines how much the node provisioning can be accelerated, slowing down normal replication. The lower this value, the more the state transfer will be throttled. With a value of 0, the replication will completely stop until the state transfer is completed. Remember that in Galera, slowing down the replication for one node means to slow down the replication for all the nodes.

- `pc.ignore_quorum`: This disables the weighted quorum algorithm. Setting this value to 1 implies that we know how to handle conflicts if a split brain problem occurs.

Monitoring and troubleshooting

Galera provides a set of status variables, which can be used to monitor the status of each node. Like Galera server variables, each status variable starts with the `'wsrep_'` prefix. This allows visualizing all the variables easily with the following query:

```
SHOW STATUS LIKE 'wsrep%';
```

There are at least two ways to automate the monitoring of MariaDB Galera Cluster:

- Using a plugin called **Galera Cluster Nagios**. It is developed and maintained by FromDual, and can be downloaded from their site: `http://www.fromdual.com/`. This plugin is not covered by this book. The FromDual's website provides the needed documentation.

- Using Galera automatic notifications.

Notification scripts

The `wsrep_notify_cmd` server variable can be set to a shell command or script, which will be automatically called when the node changes its status. Some parameters will be added to the invocation to provide the notification script with all the information it may need. The script can then use this information to perform any desired action, such as logging an event on a file, logging an event in a MariaDB table, or sending a mail to inform the database administrator that a major problem has occurred.

The notification script will be invoked with the following syntax:

```
<command> --status <new_status> --uuid <state_UUID> --primary [yes|no]
--members <members_list> --index <node_index>
```

Here's an explanation of the parameters:

- `command`: This is the command specified in the `wsrep_notify_cmd` variable
- `new_status`: This is the current status of the node
- `state_UUID`: This is a **Universally Unique Identifier (UUID)** associated with the last state change
- `--primary`: This argument indicates whether the node is a member of a primary cluster
- `members_list`: This is a comma-separated list of the nodes connected to the node's cluster partition

The following example is not very useful but it shows how to write a notification script, which does something useful. The following code is a bash script. It simply sends an e-mail to the DBA if `Node1` becomes part of a non-primary node. The code is as follows:

```
#!/bin/sh -eu
while [ $# -gt 0 ]
do
  case $1 in
  --primary)
    [ "$2" != "yes" ]
    echo "Node1 is not in a primary cluster anymore!"> $EMAILMESSAGE
    /bin/mail -s "Galera Problem" "some.valid@mail.com" < $EMAILMESSAGE
    shift
    ;;
  esac
  shift
done
```

To instruct Galera to call this script, we can use a statement similar to the following:

```
SET @@global.wsrep_notify_cmd = '/path/to/notify.sh';
```

Checking the status variables

There are several checks that can be performed periodically to verify the integrity of a cluster. These checks fall into four categories:

- **Cluster health**: We want to know whether the cluster is partitioned and, if it is, we want to know whether all the nodes are running
- **Individual node health**: For each node, we want to check whether it is running and, if it is not, we need to find out the reason
- **Replication health**: Even if all the nodes are running, we want to check that the replication lag is acceptable
- **Network performance**: The speed of the network communication

The health of a cluster

A status variable that we may want to periodically check is `wsrep_cluster_size`. If this value is lower than the expected one, at least one node has crashed or the cluster has been split into multiple partitions. Checking this variable on one node is sufficient. However, if we detect that the size of the cluster is too low, we will want to check other nodes to verify what happened.

In this case, we can check the `wsrep_cluster_state_uuid` and `wsrep_cluster_conf_id` variables in each node. These values are UUIDs, which in normal conditions are identical for all nodes. If two nodes have different values for `wsrep_cluster_state_uuid`, they are not connected to the same cluster. If those values are identical, but the value of `wsrep_cluster_conf` differs, the cluster has been partitioned.

If the cluster is partitioned, we may want to connect to a node for each partition to check which of them is the primary node. To do this, we can query the `wsrep_cluster_status` status variable. Checking this variable for each node in the cluster is another way to find out whether the cluster is partitioned; if at least one node does not belong to the primary cluster, more than one partition exists.

Individual node health

If the cluster's size is small, we may want to check each node to find out whether it is running or not.

The best way to check whether a node is properly running is to query the `wsrep_ready` status variable. If the node is in good health, its value must be true. If not, we must try to find out what is going wrong.

The `wsrep_connected` status variable indicates whether the `wsrep` library is running and connected to MariaDB. This probably means that `wsrep` could not be loaded because of a configuration error. In this case, we will check the correctness of variables like `wsrep_cluster_address`.

If the value of `wsrep_connected` is `true`, we can check the value of `wsrep_local_state_comment`. If it is `'Joining'`, `'Waiting for SST'`, or `'Joined'`, the node is still connected to the cluster. With big databases and slow connections, the `'Waiting for SST'` phase can take a lot of time.

The health of a replication

In synchronous replication, a cluster is not faster than the slower node. This happens because all nodes, after performing a transaction, have to wait until all the other nodes have performed the same transaction. For this reason, it is important to periodically check the `wsrep_flow_control_paused` status variable in Galera. This value is in the range between `0` and `1` and represents the fraction of time that the node spent waiting until the other nodes completed a transaction. If the value is not very close to `0`, we have a latency problem.

In this case, we will need to identify the slow nodes. To do this, we will check two status variables:

* `wsrep_flow_control_sent`
* `wsrep_local_recv_queue_avg`

Slower nodes have higher values.

If a node is slow, we should try to increase the number of parallel threads used for replication. Do not forget to check common MariaDB performance problems such as bad usage of the buffer pool.

Network performance

If none of the nodes is sensibly slower than the others and we are still not happy with the performance, the bottleneck is probably the network speed. To verify this, we can check the `wsrep_local_send_queue_avg` status variable. A slow network leads to a high number of queued messages. The trivial but vital ping tool can confirm poor network performance. Or `iftop` can show us data about the network traffic, confirming whether the bandwidth is saturated.

There are many possible reasons for a slow network and this topic cannot be covered by a book about MariaDB. Some general tips are as follows:

- Galera needs a dedicated subnetwork. Other communications slow down the replication.

- Check the configuration of the systems including the firewall software settings.

- If the cause is hard to find, the network's physical layer should be considered. Sometimes we might find out that a long cable is rolled, or that it is close to a magnetic source. Electro Magnetic Interference is likely to slow down a network or make it unreliable.

Load balancing

An optimization that can be applied to any computer cluster consists of balancing the requests among the nodes, so that all of them have approximately the same amount of work. The clients connect to a load balancer, which acts like a proxy trying to equally redirect the communication. Several load balancers exist, both open source and proprietary ones. Most of them are generic balancers, designed to work with any communication. So, they can be used for web servers, file servers, or in general, any type of servers. Not all load balancers perform well with database servers.

In this book, we will focus on a load balancer that has been specifically designed for Galera Cluster: **Galera Load Balancer**.

Listing the limitations of Galera Cluster

MariaDB Galera Cluster has several limitations by design. The developers and the DBA should be aware that some of the features provided by standalone MariaDB servers are not available for the Galera nodes.

First, as we mentioned earlier, Linux is the only operating system supported by Galera.

Galera is designed to be used with the InnoDB storage engine. An experimental support for MyISAM is available but disabled by default. To enable it, the `wsrep_replicate_myisam` server variable must be set to 1. The Galera team discourages its use in production environments. No other storage engines can be used with Galera.

The binary log must be enabled and its format must be ROW. Statement-based or mixed replication isn't supported.

Statements that acquire explicit locks, such as SELECT ... FOR UPDATE, SELECT ... LOCK IN SHARE MODE, LOCK TABLES, or FLUSH TABLES ... FOR EXPORT are not supported. This makes the use of MyISAM even less desirable. The SERIALIZABLE isolation level, which turns all plain queries into locking queries, is not supported either. The reason being that read operations and locks are not propagated over the cluster. So the locks are only acquired on one node, causing potential conflicts. There is an exception: if all the clients connect to the same node, the locks are safe.

Galera is designed to replicate tables that have a primary key. Various problems may occur with tables that don't have an explicit primary key, for example, DELETE will not be supported, XA transactions will not be supported, the InnoDB double write buffer will be disabled, and the query cache will not be supported.

Statements that explicitly modify a table in the mysql database are not supported. The general query log and error log, if enabled, cannot be written into system tables.

Galera Load Balancer

Galera Load Balancer (GLB) is a third-party tool produced by FromDual. Downloads and official documentation is available on their site: http://www.fromdual.com/. Similar to Galera, GLB only runs on Linux.

It consists of a daemon called glbd.

There is no client to manage GLB. To send administrative commands to GLB, for example to add or drop nodes, the generic nc tool can be used. The nc tool can communicate with a TCP daemon and print the reply on the screen, which is basically all we need to manage GLB. Here's the general syntax to send a command to glbd from the command line:

```
echo "<command>" | nc -q 1 <host_address> <port>
```

The host_address variable is the hostname or IP address, which glbd is running on, probably 127.0.0.1. The port variable is the port which glbd is listening to. There is no standard port; we have to specify it when we start the daemon.

The syntax to start glbd is as follows:

```
glbd [OPTIONS] <port> <node_list>
```

The port variable can be a complete address if the machine has multiple network interfaces: address:port.

The `node_list` variable is a space-separated list of Galera nodes. Each node can be specified as `address:port:weight`. The weight is an important concept for `glbd`, but it is only used if the daemon was started with the `--top` or `--single` option, or if the used policy (described next) takes the node's weight into account. With the `--top` option, the nodes with a higher weight will always be used if at least one of them is running. This option has no effect if all the running nodes have the same weight. With the `--single` option, only one node with the highest weight is used until it crashes. The node's weight is a useful feature if some servers run on machines with low resources, and should only be used for replication, unless the other nodes crash.

The standard informative options are supported in `glbd`. The `--help` and `--version` options can be used, respectively, to print a help message or the version number and exit the program. The `--verbose` option can be used to print more information on the screen.

Some of the most important options are:

- The `--daemon` option runs `glbd` as a daemon.
- The `--control <port>` option specifies which port will be used to accept administrative commands via `nc`.
- The `--discovery` option enables the autodiscovery of new nodes when they are added to the cluster. The list of nodes is obtained from running known nodes.
- The `--top` and `--single` options instruct `glbd` to take the node's weight into account, as explained previously.
- The `--max_con <number>` option sets the maximum number of accepted connections to avoid overloading the cluster. Even if this option is not specified, a limit is imposed by the operating system.
- The `--threads <number>` option specifies the number of threads to be used. By default, only one thread is used.
- Normally, `glbd` merges small packets of data into bigger packets to optimize the network usage. The `--nodelay` option disables this mechanism.

Unless the `--single` option is used, we usually want to determine the policy that `glbd` will use to choose the destination of each SQL statement. The policy can be chosen by specifying the corresponding option. The following are the supported policies:

- The least connected is the default policy, which is used when no other policy is specified. It redirects each connection to the node that has received few connections until now. The node's weight is also kept into account, so heavy nodes will receive more connections than the lighter nodes.

- In the --round option, glbd uses a circular list of nodes. When a connection request is received, it is redirected to the current node, and the cursor advances or goes back to the first node in the list.

- In the --random option, each connection is redirected to a random node.

- In the --source option, each client is assigned to a different server. All connection requests from the same client will always be redirected to the same node, unless the node crashes.

Here are a couple of examples of the glbd invocations:

```
glbd --daemon --control 8765 --threads 4 3306 host1:4567:1 host2:4567:1
host3:4567:1
```

In this example, the daemon will listen to the 3306 port (the standard MariaDB and MySQL port) for client connections, and the 8765 port for administrative commands. We have three hosts with the same weight and the standard policy is used. The glbd variable will use four concurrent threads:

```
glbd --daemon --single 3306 host1:4567:3 host2:4567:2 host3:4567:1
```

In this example, glbd runs on the standard MariaDB port but does not listen to any port for the administrative commands, so it will not be possible to modify the list of nodes at runtime. There are three nodes with different heights, but only host1 will be used. If host1 crashes, host2 will be used, and if that node crashes too, glbd will use host3.

In the following example, we will use nc to add a new host:

```
echo "host4:4567:1" | nc -q 1 127.0.0.1 8765
```

The daemon is supposed to run on the local machine and listen to the 8765 port for administrative commands. The added node is node4. Its weight is 1.

The following example shows how to eliminate a host from the list:

```
echo "host2:4567:-1" | nc -q 1 127.0.0.1 8765
```

In the preceding example, we are setting host2 with a negative weight (-1). Negative weights are used to drop servers from the list, so host2 will not be used anymore.

We can also use `nc` to get some usage statistics from the daemon, as shown in the following example:

```
echo "getinfo" | nc -q 1 127.0.0.1 8765
Router:

--------------------------------------------------------

    Address       : weight   usage   conns
191.52.7.1:4567 :  1.000    0.000     0
191.52.7.2:4567 :  1.000    0.000     0
191.52.7.3:4567 :  1.000    0.000     0

--------------------------------------------------------

Destinations: 3, total connections: 0
```

Summary

In this chapter, we discussed how to set up and manage a cluster of MariaDB servers.

We discussed how to install, configure, and start individual nodes by connecting them together. We learned how to use a Galera arbitrator to deal with situations where one group of nodes loses the connection to the rest of the cluster.

We discussed how to monitor the cluster and find out the causes of performance problems.

Despite MariaDB Galera Cluster nodes being very similar to normal MariaDB servers, we learned the most important limitations of a cluster. For example, now we know that we must avoid using the query cache or XA transactions with Galera.

Finally, we learned about Galera Load Balancer, which can be used to distribute the workload among the nodes.

In this book, we covered several advanced topics concerning MariaDB optimization, administration, and setup. Now we should master the necessary knowledge to solve all the common problems that can arise during a server activity, as well as implement a backup plan and set up a replication environment or cluster. Of course, the knowledge is not enough; the reader needs to put the theory into practice and accumulate experience. This can be the hardest part, but with the help of this book and online documentation, we should be able to find the information we need from time to time.

Index

L

M

repairing 226
REPAIR TABLE statement 228, 229
tables, repairing with myisamchk and
    aria_chk tools 230-232
non-repeatable reads 96
not found conditions 34
notification script
--primary parameter 340
command parameter 340
members_list parameter 340
new_status parameter 340
state_UUID parameter 340

O

one thread per connection 126
On Line Transaction Processing (OLTP) 126
OpenQuery 21
OpenSSL 120
OPTIMIZE TABLE command 49
OQGRAPH storage engine 21
outliers 73
output, EXPLAIN command
analyzing 82
Extra column 82
filtered column 82
id column 82
index access methods 85, 86
internal temporary files 84
internal temporary tables 84
JOIN clause index optimizations 86, 87
key column 82
key_len column 82
partitions column 82
possible_key column 82
ref column 82
rows column 82
select_type column 82
simple SELECT statements 82
subqueries optimization 87, 88
table column 82
type column 82
UNION queries 85
overflow pages 172
overlow pages 142

P

page cache 158
page cleaner 145
pager program 14
pam plugin 123
parallel replication 238
partial backups. *See* **incremental backups**
partitioned columns list 273
partitioned tables
administering 279
data, copying between partition
    and table 285-287
HASH and KEY partitions,
    modifying 284, 285
information, obtaining 279-281
maintenance operations statements 287
partitions definition, changing 281
RANGE and LIST partitions,
    modifying 282, 283
partitioning expression
about 267, 268
MONTH() function 268
TO_DAYS() function 268
TO_SECONDS() function 268
YEAR() function 268
partitioning types
about 267, 270
COLUMNS keyword 273, 274
HASH 275
KEY 276
LINEAR keyword 278
LIST 272, 273
RANGE 270, 271
partition_list variable 296
partition pruning 290-295
partition selecting 290
partition selection 295, 296
partitions physical files 288, 289
PARTITIONS table
columns 280
PASSWORD() function 116, 276
Percona Toolkit project
pt-query-digest command 71

Thank you for buying
Mastering MariaDB

About Packt Publishing

Packt, pronounced 'packed', published its first book "*Mastering phpMyAdmin for Effective MySQL Management*" in April 2004 and subsequently continued to specialize in publishing highly focused books on specific technologies and solutions.

Our books and publications share the experiences of your fellow IT professionals in adapting and customizing today's systems, applications, and frameworks. Our solution based books give you the knowledge and power to customize the software and technologies you're using to get the job done. Packt books are more specific and less general than the IT books you have seen in the past. Our unique business model allows us to bring you more focused information, giving you more of what you need to know, and less of what you don't.

Packt is a modern, yet unique publishing company, which focuses on producing quality, cutting-edge books for communities of developers, administrators, and newbies alike. For more information, please visit our website: www.packtpub.com.

About Packt Open Source

In 2010, Packt launched two new brands, Packt Open Source and Packt Enterprise, in order to continue its focus on specialization. This book is part of the Packt Open Source brand, home to books published on software built around Open Source licenses, and offering information to anybody from advanced developers to budding web designers. The Open Source brand also runs Packt's Open Source Royalty Scheme, by which Packt gives a royalty to each Open Source project about whose software a book is sold.

Writing for Packt

We welcome all inquiries from people who are interested in authoring. Book proposals should be sent to author@packtpub.com. If your book idea is still at an early stage and you would like to discuss it first before writing a formal book proposal, contact us; one of our commissioning editors will get in touch with you.

We're not just looking for published authors; if you have strong technical skills but no writing experience, our experienced editors can help you develop a writing career, or simply get some additional reward for your expertise.

Getting Started with MariaDB

ISBN: 978-1-78216-809-6   Paperback: 100 pages

Learn how to use MariaDB to store your data easily and hassle-free

1. A step-by-step guide to installing and configuring MariaDB.

2. Includes real-world examples that help you learn how to store and maintain data on MariaDB.

3. Written by someone who has been involved with the project since its inception.

MariaDB Cookbook

ISBN: 978-1-78328-439-9   Paperback: 282 pages

Over 95 recipes to unlock the power of MariaDB

1. Enable performance-enhancing optimizations.

2. Connect to different databases and file formats.

3. Filled with clear step-by-step instructions that can be run on a live database.

Please check **www.PacktPub.com** for information on our titles

Pentaho Analytics for MongoDB

ISBN: 978-1-78216-835-5   Paperback: 146 pages

Combine Pentaho Analytics and MongoDB to create powerful analysis and reporting solutions

1. This is a step-by-step guide that will have you quickly creating eye-catching data visualizations.

2. Includes a sample MongoDB database of web clickstream events for learning how to model and query MongoDB data.

3. Full of tips, images, and exercises that cover the Pentaho development lifecycle.

Getting Started with LevelDB

ISBN: 978-1-78328-101-5   Paperback: 130 pages

Store and retrieve key-value based data quickly on iOS and OS X using LevelDB

1. Understand how a sorted key-value store such as LevelDB can support any app.

2. Learn to use LevelDB from simple C++ code on iOS and OS/X.

3. Use LevelDB as a support for any OS/X, iPhone, or iPad app through a series of practical examples.